GW01279297

EUROPEAN EQUITY INVESTOR

For those investors wanting to look outside their national frontiers for new investments, this book will provide key insights into how the European equity investment landscape is evolving. It is a highly readable tour around Europe which provides a valuable detailed historical perspective on, and essential data about, the structure of the major national stock markets; how they developed, the regulatory environment, the challenges that each bourse faces and brief descriptions of Europe's leading companies.

The authors forcibly show us that although great advances have been made towards promoting a 'European equity culture', the development of a more sophisticated integrated European capital market will be constrained by its regulatory environment as much as by investor funds. As such, this book should be read not only by potential investors in Europe, but also by all those interested in the broader political process required to shape the next stage of developing Europe's financial landscape.

Ian Harnett, Managing Director, Head of European Equity Strategy, UBS Warburg

An indispensable reference guide for any serious investor.
Lee Hodgkinson, Director of Business Development, Virt-X

EUROPEAN EQUITY INVESTOR

Markets, Companies, Culture

HUW JONES AND JONATHAN ELEY

REUTERS

Published by **Pearson Education**
London ■ New York ■ New Delhi ■ Toronto ■ Sydney ■ Tokyo ■ Singapore
Hong Kong ■ Cape Town ■ Madrid ■ Paris ■ Amsterdam ■ Munich ■ Milan ■ Stockholm

PEARSON EDUCATION LIMITED

Head Office:
Edinburgh Gate
Harlow CM20 2JE
Tel: +44 (0)1279 623623
Fax: +44 (0)1279 431059

London Office:
128 Long Acre
London WC2E 9AN
Tel: +44 (0)20 7447 2000
Fax: +44 (0)20 7447 2170
Website: www.financialminds.com

First published in Great Britain in 2002
© Huw Jones and Jonathan Eley 2002

The right of Huw Jones and Jonathan Eley to be identified as Authors
of this Work has been asserted by them in accordance
with the Copyright, Designs and Patents Act 1988.

ISBN 1 903 68430 7

British Library Cataloguing in Publication Data
A CIP catalogue record for this book can be obtained from the British Library

All rights reserved; no part of this publication may be reproduced, stored
in a retrieval system, or transmitted in any form or by any means, electronic,
mechanical, photocopying, recording, or otherwise without either the prior
written permission of the Publishers or a licence permitting restricted copying
in the United Kingdom issued by the Copyright Licensing Agency Ltd,
90 Tottenham Court Road, London W1P 0LP. This book may not be lent,
resold, hired out or otherwise disposed of by way of trade in any form
of binding or cover other than that in which it is published, without the
prior consent of the Publishers.

10 9 8 7 6 5 4 3 2 1

Typeset by Pantek Arts Ltd, Maidstone, Kent
Printed and bound in Great Britain by Bookcraft Ltd, Midsomer Norton

The Publishers' policy is to use paper manufactured from sustainable forests

ABOUT THE AUTHORS

Huw Jones has written about markets for seven years as a correspondent for Reuters. He covered Wall Street during the bull market in the 1990s, and the development of a pan-European stock market after the launch of the euro in 1999. Educated at Manchester University and the Paris Institute of Political Studies, he worked on local newspapers and journals before joining Reuters in New York in 1995. He lives in London.

Jonathan Eley first wrote about equities as a reporter and editor with the AFX News group in the Far East, where he covered the Asian Crisis and its aftermath before moving back to the UK. For the past two years, he has written for the leading investment magazine *Investors Chronicle*. He studied modern languages at Aston University, and wrote for trade journals in the UK and US before moving into equity market reporting. He lives in London with his wife and daughter.

CONTENTS

Foreword / **xi**

Acknowledgements / **xv**

CHAPTER 1 ■ **Introduction** / **1**

Pension problem / **3**

Lagging behind Uncle Sam / **5**

European equities / **7**

CHAPTER 2 ■ **United Kingdom** / **9**

From bonds to equities / **10**

Us and them / **11**

Loadsamoney! / **12**

The London Stock Exchange – waking up at last / **15**

The small-cap alternative / **18**

The Takeover Panel / **19**

Company culture: how do they do it in the US? / **22**

Top listings in the UK / **26**

CHAPTER 3 ■ **Germany** / **29**

Shareholder capitalism takes root / **30**

The drivers of change / **32**

Frankfurt consolidates its position / **35**

The Neuer Markt – Europe's Wild West / **37**

Minding your own business / **40**

Hostile takeovers? *Nein danke!* / **44**

Top listings in Germany / **48**

CHAPTER 4 ■ France / 53

American style / **55**

Move over bond / **56**

Corporate goverance – *je vous ai compris?* / **61**

Manning the barricades: shareholder activism / **63**

Euronext – a tale of four cities / **65**

Top listings in France / **68**

CHAPTER 5 ■ Benelux / 73

The Netherlands – punching above its weight / **73**

Top listings in the Netherlands / **82**

Belgium – left behind in the equity rush / **84**

Top listings in Belgium / **92**

Luxembourg – the independent minnow / **93**

CHAPTER 6 ■ Switzerland / 97

The markets / **99**

The virt-x project / **101**

Regulation / **103**

We know best / **103**

Top listings in Switzerland / **111**

CHAPTER 7 ■ Scandinavia / 115

The markets / **118**

The Norex alliance / **122**

Helsinki – the odd man out / **124**

State-owned companies that work / **126**

Top listings in Scandinavia / **129**

CHAPTER 8 ■ Italy, Spain and Portugal / 139

Italy – *Salòtto buono* still in business / **139**

Top listings in Italy / **149**

Spain – the Latin American connection / **151**

Top listings in Spain / **159**

Portugal – in Spain's shadow / **161**

Top listings in Portugal / **164**

CHAPTER 9 ■ Pan-European investing / 167

Improving corporate governance – shareholders unite! / **168**

Out of court / **171**

Pan-European stock indices – the battle of the benchmarks / **172**

Superbourse – a slow train coming? / **174**

Modest progress towards a pan-European holy grail / **177**

Floating / **179**

Regulation – watchdogs bark to Brussels tune / **182**

Logging on – the online share revolution pauses / **185**

CHAPTER 10 ■ Conclusion – a steep learning curve / 191

Evolution not revolution / **194**

Banks speak with forked tongues / **195**

Harmonizing corporate governance / **196**

Shareholders man the barricades / **198**

Bibliography / 203

Glossary of terms / 205

FOREWORD
by Reto Francioni, Chairman of the Swiss Exchange

Look back at capital markets around the globe over the past 25 to 50 years and we see a rapid, even exponential, increase in equity values. But with that has come a new phenomenon: strong increases in volatility.

Since the autumn of 2000, we have found ourselves in something of a crisis. Stock exchanges are experiencing a dramatic pullback. It has affected everyone who observes and follows stock markets – and especially those who have invested either directly or indirectly in equities. The negative consequences of this downturn are becoming clearer every day. Investors become uncertain and their trust in the capital markets starts to weaken fundamentally. Even the viability of well-positioned companies becomes threatened by the deepening scepticism.

The degree of uncertainty has grown greater still in the aftermath of the attacks on the World Trade Center. The tendency to think – and trade – in the short term has intensified. And that affects business: the option of raising funds at the lowest possible cost on the capital markets is closed off. The acquisition currency for financing growth – through mergers and acquisitions – is devalued, if it is even available at all. The value of staff share options ceases to rise, which can have a major effect on the corporate culture, especially of young and dynamic companies. Taken together, these factors are having fundamental implications and we need to think hard about how we should deal with this new dimension of uncertainty.

Although this is a global phenomenon, there are some specifically European aspects of secondary markets and areas where the European corporate and regulatory landscape remains heterogenous – something the chapters of this book discuss in detail. In many countries, the trading of shares and other securities has a long tradition; in others, such as Germany, there was and is a lot of catching up to do.

For all their different traditions, one thing all capital markets have in common is that punters are nowhere near adequately prepared for a crisis. And every crisis has its own story – an element of surprise and things that were unforeseeable, or even unimaginable.

Yet despite the body blows of the past few months, the long-term development of capital markets will not be halted. After all the causes and effects of the economic downturn have been dissected, after the end of the 'new economy' has been lamented, after its stock-option millionaires have been obliged to look for new employers, one thing will be certain: the march of the capital markets will continue, and at a faster pace. This will be reinforced by political and social trends, such as the changing relationship between state and personal pension provision.

Greater involvement with financial transactions and decisions of all kinds will lead to greater understanding, and that is something that will affect all of society. What has hitherto been referred to as 'equity culture' has generally meant little more than the sale and purchase of equities. We need more than that. We need capital market integration across whole societies, because capital market integration leads to mature capital markets. And that requires, above all, transparency, so that market participants can conduct their business with confidence.

It is this process of integration and maturing that we are experiencing right now. The exaggeration and the naivety, the euphoria and the tendency to become starry eyed at stock markets and the riches they can create, seen most vividly at the start of 2000, are things of the past. There is growing recognition that this way of looking at things is obscuring factual discussion. A period in which we lost hold of reality has been followed by a period in which we seem to have lost all sense of normality.

Back to the fundamentals: the internationalization of equity and capital markets remains intact, not least because of globalization. Worldwide flows of capital, including over the internet, have been reality for a long time.

And new technology has also made its presence felt in exchange-based trading – something that has far-reaching consequences for the promotion and consolidation of a pan-European capital market of maturity.

The single European market of the future needs a single European system of regulation for exchange-based trading of company shares, and for this reason we must forge ahead with the integration and meshing together of the different European trading and settlement areas. Not only would such growing European market integrity save enormous costs, it would also encourage a greater awareness and understanding of the markets. But that's not the same as calling for a monopolization of capital markets. The individual marketplaces should, of course, continue to trade in healthy competition with each other. To have federal elements does not contradict the ideal of greater European integration.

At the same time, we need pan-European rules for trading and for admission, for initial public offerings and for clearing and settlement. The development of capital markets, which runs at different speeds and intensities in different countries, must not be held back by fear of such new thoughts. We have to shed our national approach and develop a pan-European perspective within which time zones cease to exist. Only in that way can we steer developments in capital markets in the right direction from the start. We have to think about the way the customer sees things - namely that there are sectors that are ripe for pan-European consolidation, such as the bigger European blue chips, and other sectors that are only really viable on national markets. They include many of the medium and smaller stocks with less liquidity.

One of the most important prerequisites for the regulation of stock exchanges and capital markets is that punishment for wrongdoers is significantly expanded from the levels that prevail today. And the new awareness of the importance of transparency must not just be encouraged, it must be required. Here, Europe has the chance – if not the responsibility – to be in the vanguard of the development of capital markets, rather than simply following that development.

If in the future we succeed in shifting our gaze from national problems on to pan-European solutions, and establish that pan-European capital market integration, then the winner will be that European market, which will gain immeasurably in stability and strength.

ACKNOWLEDGEMENTS

This book could not have been written without the help of the equity strategists, fund managers, stock exchanges, public relations companies, consultants and shareholder rights groups quoted in the text. Others equally expert in their fields chose to share their knowledge off-the-record, but their insights were equally useful.

Thanks to Reto Francioni, Marc Vienot, John Parry, Euroshareholders Association, Paul Arlman, Eric de Keuleneer, Giuliano Gregorio, Joao Paulo Peixoto, Karel Lanoo, Marco Becht, Antonio Salvi, Peter Paul de Vries, Arnaud de Bresson, Jelle Mensonides.

Staff at many brokers and banks were also generous with their time and patience, including UBS Warburg, ABN Amro Rothschild, Schroder Salomon Smith Barney, Goldman Sachs, Lehman Brothers, Morgan Stanley, HSBC, JP Morgan Chase, BNP Paribas, Societe Generale, and consultancy Deminor. Others that gave their help included Christopher Chandiramani, Lars-Erik Fosgårdth at Aktiespararna, Claus Silfverberg at the Danish Shareholders Association, Poul Erik Skanning-Jorgenson at Norex, Rüdiger von Rosen and Franz-Josef Leven at Deutsche Aktien Institut, Petra Krüll at DSW, Brian Winterflood of Winterflood Securities, Chris Dillow at *Investors Chronicle*.

The authors also thank Izabel Grindal, Alexander Smith and others at Reuters for their encouragement in this project. Our gratitude also goes to Martin Drewe at Pearson Education for expert guidance, and to Corrie Parsonson and Paul Scruton at Reuters Graphics for their excellent handling of the charts in this book. Thanks also go to the Reuters photographers whose pictures have been used.

1

INTRODUCTION

Philosopher: And what kind of business is this about which I have often heard people talk but which I neither understand nor have ever made efforts to comprehend?

Shareholder: I really must say that you are an ignorant person, friend Greybeard, if you know nothing of this enigmatic business which is at once the fairest and most deceitful in Europe. I will fulfil your wish to be informed about the origin of this business, and you will see that the stocks do not exist merely for fools but also for intelligent people.

Joseph de la Vega, *Confusion de Confusiones*, 1688

JOSEPH DE LA VEGA was a Portuguese author who wrote in Spanish about life on the Amsterdam stock exchange, the world's first bourse, set up at the start of the seventeenth century. It was trading in shares of the world's first listed firm, the United East India Company. De la Vega blamed speculators for wild rides in share prices, just as many commentators like to do today. In 1841 another landmark in the history of stock markets, *The Extraordinary Popular Delusions and the Madness of Crowds* by Charles Mackay, argued that mass hysteria lay behind seismic stock market events like Tulipmania or the South Sea Bubble.

De la Vega and Mackay would no doubt have blamed speculators and mass hysteria for creating the technology stocks bubble that burst so spectacularly between 2000 and 2001. The pricking of that bubble slammed the brakes on Europe's fledgling equity culture as global share markets grappled with finding more sustainable levels after their long bull run into the record books. It was the first time that Europe's new breed of small investors had experienced a bear market or a major shock to the global financial system, such as the terror attacks on the World Trade Center in New York and on the Pentagon in Washington, or the scandal surrounding the US energy giant Enron whose collapse in December 2001 was the biggest corporate failure in American history.

The failure of many internet stocks, massive corporate debt, lack of independent analysis served up by some banks and brokers, and moves by Britain's Boots company and others to shift their pension fund into bonds from equities have questioned the long-term future for stocks. 'I don't think the equity culture is dead, but people who feel the 1990s were the norm are going to be disappointed because it was too good to be true,' says Paul Marsh of the London Business School and co-author of a study on long-term investment returns. 'Equities are likely to do better than bonds, but just not quite as well as in the past which has been phenomenally good,' Marsh said. So Europe's appetite for equities can only grow over coming years, because the euro single currency has made the region's national market boundaries irrelevant. Cross-border trading opens up a wider range of shares to investors, allowing them to buy shares based on industry sectors like telecommunications or pharmaceuticals, and gain access to types of shares that may be poorly represented in their home market.

This book explains why stocks are becoming more important for Europe's future financial security, and how investors now, and to an increasing extent in the future, have little choice but to take part in this trend.

PENSION PROBLEM

The pensioners bomb is ticking away in Europe, where a quarter of the population in the five largest EU countries will be over 65 by 2030. Governments provide about 80 per cent of retirement benefits in Europe at present, in pay-as-you-go programmes funded by taxes on workers. But this is becoming unsustainable as there will be too few workers to tax in order to support the growing number of retired people. The UK and the Netherlands introduced pension reforms long ago and are relatively well placed, but Italy, France, Spain and Germany have serious pension provision problems, and the solution is expected to involve forcing individuals to save for their own retirement.

A study by Deloitte Research and Goldman Sachs in early 2002, forecast that bank deposits will lose their traditional leading role and more than halve from 35 percent of total savings in Europe to just 17 percent by 2010, while other types of investments like pensions, bonds and equities will increase. The shift from public to private pensions will result in a market worth €4 trillion by 2010, rising to €11 trillion by 2030.

The market for long-term savings in Europe will be worth €26 trillion by 2010, up from €12 trillion in 1999, with a core component of this going into private pensions, indicating there will be a strong, sustained pool of cash going into stocks and bonds in the region. The Deloitte/Goldman study forecast that direct investments in equities will rise to 17 percent of total European savings by 2010, up from 11 percent in 1999. Investment funds, pensions and life insurance – all products that hold stocks as well as bonds – will also increase over the next few years.

Clearly, Europe's equity market is set to grow, even if not all the new money goes into stocks. The portion of equities in a typical US or UK portfolio has been 60 to 70 percent or more during the bull run, the rest in bonds and cash. But as much as half of continental European pension funds have traditionally been made up of bonds, with a much smaller amount in equities, though experts expect the equities portion to rise to about 50 percent over coming years.

Whether directly by investing in individual shares or mutual funds, or indirectly through company pension schemes, Europeans will have to become more familiar with the world of stocks. Investment bank Morgan Stanley reckons that demand for European equities in the decade to 2010 will top $10 trillion (*see* Table 1.1). The driver will be money going into mutual funds as more people save. At the end of 1996, just under a third of money held in European mutual funds was in the form of stocks. The percentage rose to about 50 percent by late 2000 (*see* Fig. 1.1), with bonds the biggest losers. In the US, equities account for 60 percent of mutual fund assets.

(US$ billion)	2000	2001	2005	2010	Total (US$ billion) 2001–10
New flows					
Mutual funds	220	204	248	317	2.6
Pension funds	87	131	201	289	2.1
Insurance funds	77	86	135	153	1.2
Households	70	60	92	132	0.9
Sub-total	454	481	676	890	6.8
Recycled flows					
Cash acquisitions	295	204	149	190	1.6
Dividend	29	33	53	95	0.6
Buybacks	33	46	118	213	1.3
Sub-total	357	284	320	499	3.5
International flows					
Net	0	(4)	(20)	(40)	(0.2)
Gross demand	811	761	977	1,349	10.1
Less total supply	(264)	(219)	(487)	(878)	(5.4)
Net demand	547	542	489	471	4.7

Source: Morgan Stanley

Table 1.1 Annual demand for European equity by investment vehicle (2000–10)

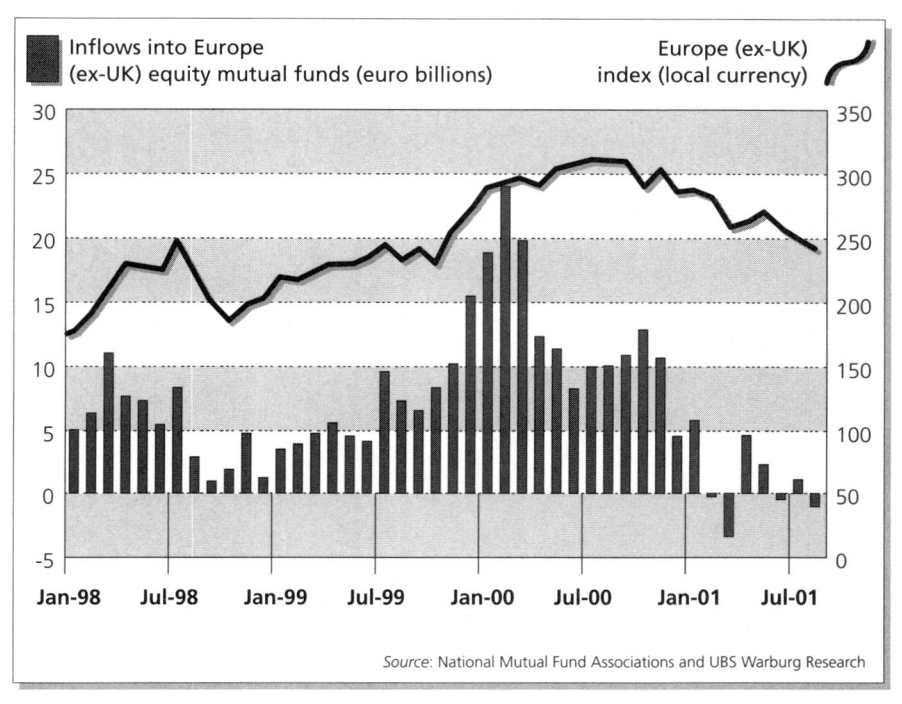

Figure 1.1 European equity mutual funds

LAGGING BEHIND UNCLE SAM

Europe still has to catch up with the US when comparing its stock market capitalization, or total value of companies listed, to gross domestic product (GDP). At the start of 2001 Europe had a total market capitalization of $8.6 trillion or 98 percent of GDP, compared with $13.6 trillion or 148 percent of GDP (*see* Fig. 1.2). And with national markets increasingly unable to offer a one-stop venue for buying the necessary range of shares, investors need to know about stock markets, companies and equity culture beyond their own national border.

A number of other factors will increasingly whet Europeans' appetite for shares:

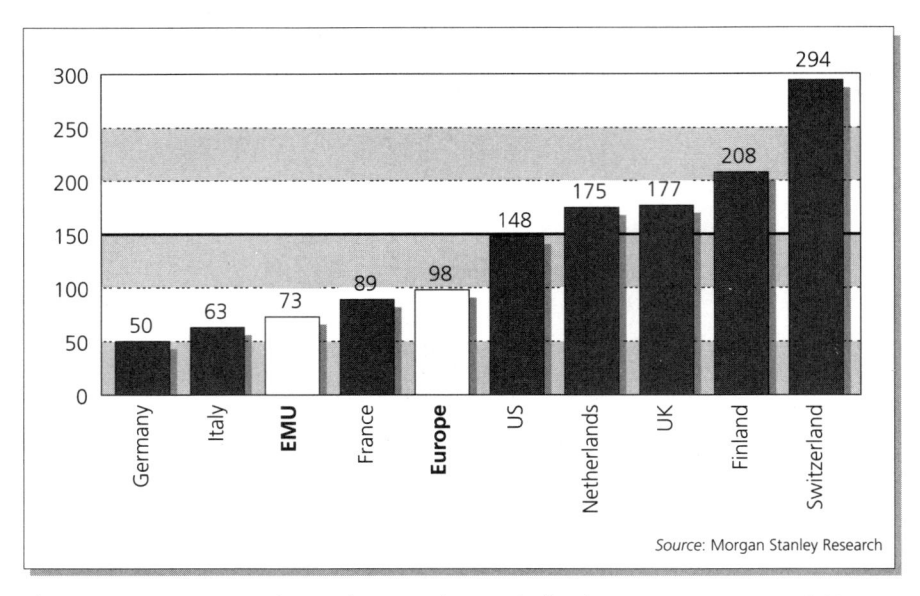

Figure 1.2 Europe's equity markets: market capitalization as a percentage of GDP (January 2001)

Germany 50; Italy 63; EMU 73; France 89; Europe 98; US 148; Netherlands 175; UK 177; Finland 208; Switzerland 294.

Source: Morgan Stanley Research

- As companies operate in a European and global market, weak participants will become takeover targets. This merger and acquisition (M&A) activity fuels interest in shares.
- More companies, especially in continental Europe, are turning to the stock market to raise cash for expansion rather than taking the traditional route of borrowing money from banks.
- Improvements in corporate governance, or how listed companies manage themselves and relate to their shareholders and the public, will give investors more confidence about investing in shares. Companies now have to pay attention to so-called shareholder value if they want people to buy their stock.
- Pan-European regulation will eventually make it easier for investors from many countries to take part in any initial public offering in the region.

> **Companies now have to pay attention to so-called shareholder value if they want people to buy their stock**

- Laws have been changed to make it easier for companies to buy back some of their shares, a measure which is supportive and gives investors in the company a boost.
- Buying and selling shares listed and traded outside the domestic stock market is getting easier and cheaper, especially with Europe's new breed of online brokers. Trading shares across borders in Europe costs seven to ten times higher than trading in a home market because of taxes and multiple clearing and settlement organizations, but cross-border trading is set to become cheaper in future as the industry streamlines.

EUROPEAN EQUITIES

The following chapters on national markets examine each country's equity culture, how it came about, and what factors are shaping its future. The chapters also look at the pitfalls of investing in some countries, examining issues such as regulatory and corporate governance standards. The reader will also be guided through the stock markets in each country, how the bourse works, what the key share indices are, and which organizations handle clearing and settlement – the crucial post-trade functions that ensure investors get shares in return for their money.

The UK, Germany, France and Switzerland are Europe's biggest stock markets and a chapter is devoted to each one. Italy and Spain, two of Europe's key medium-sized markets are examined in one chapter, including a section on Portugal. Belgium and the Netherlands, two contrasting but neighbouring markets, are treated in one chapter, while another chapter looks at Scandinavia, dominated by the two mobile-phone giants Nokia and Ericsson. The chapters also advise investors about where they can go for help when trades go wrong. Finally, no stock market could exist without the companies themselves. Each national chapter gives an overview of the leading companies, describing what they do and the role they have in the country or sector.

A chapter on pan-European investing looks at how the building blocks of a truly single, regional market in shares is coming together. The issues considered are the improvement of corporate governance, better regulation, the use of pan-European share indices, the consolidation among stock exchanges and post-trading service providers, and cross-border online trading. The concluding chapter looks ahead to likely trends in Europe's stock market.

Europe's stock market is evolving rapidly, so to help the reader keep abreast of developments website addresses are included of all the key market participants such as exchanges, shareholder groups and companies.

Just as Joseph de la Vega aimed to throw light on the different players in Amsterdam's early equity history, we hope to show the reader that stocks do indeed exist not merely for fools but for intelligent people too. We hope that after reading this book investors can navigate the equity market and make more informed choices about where they put their money.

2

UNITED KINGDOM

The gentleman capitalist is about as rare these days as the gentleman farmer. The gifted amateur has given way to the dynamic investment banker. The day starts at 7am, not 9am, 70 percent of analysts work over 60 hours per week and designer water has replaced the boozy lunch.
Philip Augar, *The Death of Gentlemanly Capitalism*

EUROPE'S BIGGEST AND MOST DEVELOPED stock exchange is perhaps the best place to begin any overview of European equity investing. Although not the oldest – that accolade rests with Amsterdam – London is without doubt the one stock exchange in Europe with truly global scale and influence. Despite the best efforts of Frankfurt, Paris and Zürich, London remains by far and away the continent's most significant financial centre. The City of London's economy towers over almost every aspect of life in the capital and its immediate hinterland – soaring house prices and catastrophically overcrowded public transport are the direct consequences of London's success in attracting international capital. Similarly, the practice of buying and selling shares is possibly more engrained in the British population than in any other populous European country. The waves of privatization in the 1980s and 1990s created millions of small shareholders, while deregulation of the financial markets has made share dealing cheaper and easier than ever. In the UK more than anywhere else in Europe, the cult of equity has taken root. So firmly, in fact, that many Europeans refer to the 'Anglo-Saxon' model of shareholder capitalism, by which they mean that practised in the UK and the US.

FROM BONDS TO EQUITIES

It wasn't always so. The London Stock Exchange, founded in a coffee shop some 200 years ago, was for decades not really an equity market at all. The main class of securities traded was fixed income – either in the shape of government bonds (gilts) or corporate fixed-income instruments like bonds or debentures. In the low-inflation environment that prevailed before the First World War, these were seen as safe and steady investments. These instruments were the norm, while equities were seen as speculative and risky, and at the time there was every expectation that this state of affairs would continue indefinitely. The idea that equities would eventually supplant bonds and gilts as the mainstay of the private investor would have seemed far-fetched. Equities were instruments either for reckless gamblers with fortunes to lose, or for those 'in the know' – usually the promoters or founding investors in a company. Almost every time private investors bought the shares of joint-stock, limited-liability companies, the results were disastrous. Fortunes were lost in the South Sea Bubble of 1720 and again in the mania of the 1820s.

Perhaps the first successful use of the joint-stock format was during the construction of the railways and the canals during the middle of the nineteenth century. These were bold engineering projects fraught with technological risks. Banks were often reluctant to fund such ventures, so the promoters turned to the stock exchange. Investors soon learned that if the construction phase was managed successfully and the asset built, income was then generated fairly reliably – in much the same fashion as the bond-type investments that were popular at the time. However, this was a small start. The successes were few compared to the continual failures, especially in mining or commerce. And the opportunities for investing in 'safe-once-built' enterprises like utilities were limited by the increasing municipal provision of lighting, electricity and telecommunications. Only at the end of the nineteenth century did investors turn their attention to joint-stock manufacturing and industrial companies – and when they did, it was often on a local stock market like Leeds, Manchester, Liverpool or Bristol.

The First World War changed the picture. It resulted in the national debt, which had been held steady for years, rising sharply. It also created millions of new investors who had subscribed to the various war bonds and gilts out of patriotism. Come the end of the war, they were ready to invest in equity securities, and there was no shortage of willing sellers. The largely unregulated equity market and the unscrupulous promoters within it combined with the world economic depression to create more ruined investors, although the scale of the collapse was nothing like that seen on Wall Street, and it was certainly not enough to snuff out the idea of equity investing altogether.

The aftermath of the Second World War, however, produced a quite different and much more dramatic outcome, because the monetary result was inflation, not deflation. That scenario suddenly rendered fixed-income investments, whose value could be eroded by inflation, less attractive than equities, whose value could rise or fall according to the prospects and the earnings capacity of the company involved. The post-war period was the true start of the equity culture in the UK.

US AND THEM

This did not mean that equity investing became a mass-market phenomenon, however. Investment in equities was still a pastime for the better off, and the way the City of London was run reflected the 'officers and men' class structure of British society almost exactly. Integrated investment banks along American lines were unheard of – instead there was rigid demarcation along mainly class lines, coupled with a system of regulation that relied primarily on a gentleman's word being his bond. (Gentlewomen were not a feature of the equity trading scene; women were not allowed on to the actual trading floor until 1973, at which point the provincial exchanges also amalgamated.)

> **The way the City of London was run reflected the 'officers and men' class structure of British society almost exactly**

At the top of the tree were the merchant banks, who were responsible for arranging flotations and rights issues. As such, they controlled the supply of new equity to the market. Immediately below them were the brokers, who took orders from buy-side investors, provided advice to them and were responsible for fulfilling their orders. They did this through 'jobbers', the market makers who traded for their own account and who were only as good as their last price. The jobbers were the foot soldiers of the City, drawn from grammar school graduates and East End barrowboys who had perfected their mental arithmetic in a more streetwise environment. The brokers and merchant banks were staffed by the officer class – usually educated at the private schools and Oxbridge.

The companies were all relatively small by the standards of today's global mega-banks, and were overwhelmingly run as partnerships. The partnership model meant that loyalty to the firm was strong, with half a century of service not unusual. Working conditions were relaxed, with long, boozy lunches, nice regular hours and usually a retreat to the countryside at the weekend. Competence with the fishing rod and the shotgun was often regarded as a prerequisite for working in such firms. Because it was a small world in which most people knew each other and in which most participants were men of integrity, self-regulation worked fairly well in the sense that there was rarely any outright fraud. Insider trading was of course rife, because disclosure standards were minimal, but that was perceived as part of the fun rather than anything more sinister. This state of affairs, which persisted from the creation of demarcation in 1908 until the early 1980s, has been best described as 'gentlemanly capitalism'.

LOADSAMONEY!

Two developments consigned the gentlemen to the dustbin of history. The first was the deregulation of the City, know generally as Big Bang. The other was the privatization of vast swathes of nationalized industry throughout the 1980s and 1990s, which created a new breed of middle-class equity investor.

The key feature of Big Bang as far as the stock market was concerned was that fixed commissions charged by brokers were ended. As a consequence, the demarcation was broken up. Previously, jobbers had dealt only with each other and the brokers and they traded for their own account – their profit was simply the difference between their bid and offer prices. Jobbers could not talk to clients other than brokers, who acted only as agents; that is, they did not trade for their own account. It soon became clear that in order to survive in a variable-commission environment, brokers would need to be able to trade for their own account as well as on an agency basis. The jobbers would be out of a job. There was a frenzy of consolidation, with high-street banks buying brokers, brokers buying jobbers and merchant banks buying both. Deregulation was attracting foreign capital too, so across came the US investment banks with vastly greater experience of managing integrated functions, and vastly deeper pockets. Partnerships were selling out left, right and centre, and some of the prices paid were crazy. One consequence of all of this was that by 2000 there was not a single major British-owned investment bank. The Americans in particular, who understood risk management and deregulated markets far better, cleaned up.

Meanwhile, the City was starting to attract some of the wealth being generated elsewhere in the country. While millions were thrown on to the dole in the massive industrial restructuring of the early 1980s, many took early retirement with a lump sum. Millions of people bought their own council houses cheaply, expanding the cult of property ownership. Wealth creation was in fashion. At the same time, the Government was busy selling off vast swathes of industry. Companies like BP, British Airports Authority, British Aerospace and British Airways were sold to the public via, for the first time, extensively publicized retail offerings. Perhaps the two most memorable were the marketing campaigns for British Telecommunications, privatized in 1984, and the 'Tell Sid' blitz that accompanied the sale of British Gas. This continued with the electricity and water companies in the 1990s, while at the same time many building societies – member-owned institutions originally established to help working-class people manage their finances – demutualized into public limited companies and floated on the stock exchange (*see* Table 2.1). Such floats usually saw members of the society – savers and mortgagees – issued with free shares. The 'carpetbagging' movement developed, with investors opening dozens of building society accounts in the hope of getting free shares.

Year	Companies sold	Year	Companies sold
1981	Cable & Wireless	1989	Anglian Water
1983	Association British Ports		Thames Water
1984	British Telecom		Wessex Water
	Enterprise Oil		United Utilities
1985	British Aerospace		Severn Trent
1986	British Gas	1991	PowerGen
1987	Rolls-Royce		National Power
	BAA		Scottish Power
	British Airways	1992	Forth Ports
1988	British Steel	1996	British Energy
1989	Hyder		Railtrack
	Yorkshire Water		

Table 2.1 UK privatizations, 1981 to the present

One end result of this was much broader ownership of shares: in 1980, there were 3 million private shareholders in the UK. Ten years later, the figure stood at 10.8 million. According to the Association of Private Client Investment Managers and Stockbrokers, over 12 million Britons now invest directly in stocks and shares. Although the proportion of shares held by individuals has fallen – reflecting the rise of the institutions in the post Big Bang environment – the raw value has increased massively. According to National Statistics, UK individuals held shares worth £290 billion at the end of 2000 – and that figure does not include shares held indirectly via unit trusts.

Another consequence was that share ownership became perceived as relatively normal, like owning a house or a car, rather than something that rich people did in their spare time. The adoption of 'shareholder value' renumeration packages for senior and middle managers, in which a large part of an employee's compensation package is composed of shares or options over shares, reinforced this, as did the end of punitive taxation rates on the very well-off, and the reductions in capital gains tax and stamp duty effected during these times.

THE LONDON STOCK EXCHANGE – WAKING UP AT LAST

Aside from the privately-run Ofex market for small companies, all shares in UK companies are traded primarily on the London Stock Exchange (LSE), which since Big Bang has cemented its position as Europe's biggest and highest-profile equity market. The LSE became a private limited company in 1986, and in 1991 replaced its Deed of Settlement with more normal Articles of Association and its Council with a board of directors. In 2001 it followed the well-established trend among terminal markets by demutualizing – switching from a member-owned organization to a for-profit public limited company. This came after a tumultuous year, during which it had seen its widely touted merger with Frankfurt to form iX fall apart, and had to fend off a hostile bid from Sweden's OM Gruppen.

The decision to demutualize resulted in a change in status. Because its shares trade on its own market, LSE is no longer deemed a competent listing authority. The role of approving listing applications and the contents of prospectuses has passed to the Financial Services Authority, the City's 'super-regulator'.

Market indices are compiled and calculated by FTSE International, a joint venture between the *Financial Times* newspaper and the Stock Exchange. The benchmark is the FTSE 100, usually referred to simply as 'the Footsie'. It used to represent the largest 100 companies by market capitalization; it now measures the 100 largest companies by free float. Its constituents are reviewed every three months. The broader index is the All-Share which is designed to capture around 98 percent of the market's total capitalization including.

Recent years have seen the introduction of some specialist indices, including the techMARK series in 1999. Designed to give London a benchmark for technology companies in the same way the Nasdaq Composite does in the US, the techMARK 100 and the techMARK all-share were launched just in time for the bubble in technology shares in late 1999 and early 2000. Since then, the indices have slumped, but are nevertheless used as benchmarks by some technology investment funds. In 2001 FTSE International introduced two indices designed for the growing ethical investment community.

Order execution in London is via two systems: SETS, the electronic order-driven system introduced in 1997, and the older SEAQ, which is price-driven. The larger and more liquid stocks tend to be traded via SETS, which simply matches buyers against sellers, while less liquid stocks tend to be traded by market makers, who post their bid-and-offer spreads on the SEAQ page of the relevant stock. Some smaller stocks are also traded in SEATS (a hybrid of SEAQ and SETS), as are all stocks listed on the Alternative Investment Market. This set-up is in contrast to many of Europe's smaller exchanges, which have entirely order-driven trading, and reflects the sheer depth of London's equity market and the large numbers of smaller, less liquid stocks.

Clearing and settlement in London is done by separate entities, unlike on many other exchanges where it is all done on one platform. Clearing goes through the London Clearing House (LCH), a mutually owned body that also processes the trades of other major markets like the London Metal Exchange.

Settlement has been the subject of intense argument over the past ten years, after the LSE's first attempt to implement a paperless trading system ended in humiliation and ignominious failure. The exchange spent £75 million on Taurus, which was supposed to replace the Talisman system, but failed to grasp the technological and organizational challenges the highly complex system posed, and, more significantly, tried to please too many factional interests at one time.

The successor to Taurus was CREST, which went live in July 1996. This, also a not-for-profit company, was established by the Bank of England, which, mindful of the infighting that had dogged Taurus, sent the most single-minded, plain-speaking, no-nonsense manager it could find to oversee the project. Iain Saville soon had plenty of explaining to do, because at first the system did not function as quickly or simply as had been envisaged and a large backlog of unsettled trades built up. By the spring of 1997, however, the system was starting to settle down and the big building-society flotations of that year passed off without a crisis. That was the turning point; even the old guard had to admit that Talisman would have keeled over under such a weight of transactions.

Information dissemination is one of London's strong points compared to many European exchanges, although it does not require quarterly reporting as the US exchanges do. All potentially price-sensitive information is at present divulged via the Regulatory News Service (RNS). The announcements – around 170,000 of them a year – are transmitted in real time to a variety of third-party information vendors, such as the wire services, and are increasingly available on the internet. This gives private investors access to company information at almost the same speed institutions receive it. Another strong point of RNS is that important announcements from sources other than listed companies are released over the system. Examples include rulings on the legality of takeovers, released by the Department of Trade and Industry at 11.00 am each day, or statements from the regulators of privatized utilities such as Ofgem (gas and electricity), Ofwat (water), the Strategic Rail Authority (train operating companies) and Oftel (telecommunications).

> Information dissemination is one of London's strong points compared to many European exchanges

Until April 2002, RNS was a monopoly operated by the Stock Exchange (www.londonstockexchange.com/rns), which received a subsidy for providing the service. After that date, news dissemination became commercialized, with a total of five organizations approved by the Financial Services Authority (FSA) to distribute company announcements. Companies will choose the best one for their needs and the subsidy to RNS will end. It is hoped that listing fees, from which subsidy is derived, will fall as a result. Most of the 'primary information providers' authorized by the FSA have pledged to continue supplying company announcements to investment websites free of charge, and the FSA itself has offered to step in and do so if this does not transpire.

THE SMALL-CAP ALTERNATIVE

When the Alternative Investment Market was launched in 1995, some institutional investors threatened to boycott it in protest at the diminished role for stock brokers and merchant banks in approving listings. Yet during 2001 London's junior market saw more initial public offerings than all the other 'second board' markets in Europe put together. AIM is without doubt one of the London Stock Exchange's success stories.

AIM was born out of the Unlisted Securities Market (USM), which was deemed a failure because it proved unable to attract sufficient liquidity. Listing rules are less stringent than for the Official List; there is no minimum trading record, no minimum free float and no minimum market value. Companies seeking an AIM listing also do not need a sponsor, just a nominated adviser – a firm approved by AIM for that role. There is no competent authority for vetting issue prospectuses – investors are obliged to trust the nominated advisers and heed the risk warnings emblazoned over offer documents. This makes listing much cheaper and remarkably quick; a company can announce its intention to float and be on the market literally within days. The LSE maintains that AIM's failure rate is no worse than that of comparable boards.

By the end of 1995 AIM had attracted 116 companies with a market capitalization of just over £2.2 billion. Towards the end of 2001 the number of listed companies had risen to over 600 and the total market capitalization was around £12.4 billion. During the height of the technology boom, AIM looked like it might be eclipsed by newer rivals, such as Deutsche Börse's Neuer Markt, but their stars faded after the collapse of the technology bubble and a range of insider trading and fraud scandals. 'All the continental exchanges have mimicked us with USM and AIM because we captured a real market with a really innovative product. They put it together badly – the Neuer Markt has been disastrous – whereas AIM is still very viable,' says Brian Winterflood of Winterflood Securities, a smaller brokerage that does a lot of business in AIM stocks.

What was the secret of AIM's success? It had its fair share of luck. It was created early on in a long bull market. Investing in AIM companies carried certain tax advantages, especially after the Labour administration was elected in 1997. Potential rivals like Easdaq never really got off the ground. Listing is cheap and easy, but London's relatively strong secondary market regulation affords investors better protection than other markets. But the most significant factors were its range of companies. AIM has its fair share of technology stocks, but it is also home to football clubs, penny-mining stocks, stock exchanges, even lap-dancing clubs. This variety left it less vulnerable to the implosion of technology stocks that began in 2000.

Trading on AIM is via SEATS Plus, a kind of hybrid between SEAQ and SETS. Market makers post their bid and offer prices on the screens as in SEAQ, but it is also possible to conduct order-driven trading. Given that AIM companies are often small and illiquid, it is no surprise that much of the trading is still done between market-makers. AIM has its own index.

Currently, the greatest threat to AIM comes not from a rival exchange, but from bureaucrats in Brussels. The Prospectus Directive, a piece of legislation designed to harmonize listing rules across Europe, could add substantially to the cost of listing and also spell the end for the nominated adviser system, which makes an AIM listing cheaper than a main-market quote. The LSE supports the directive as applied to larger companies, but thinks the one-size-fits-all policy inappropriate for smaller firms. It also objects to the proposed requirement that listed companies file a 'shelf registration' certificate every year, saying the £50,000 or even £100,000 this would cost is overly burdensome to the small and mid-sized companies that use AIM.

The UK Government has done little to head off the threat, saying that it is not an issue over which it has power of veto. Still, AIM aficionados can console themselves with the thought that another flagship piece of EU harmonization, the Takeover Directive, took 12 years to thrash out and was then scuttled by the European Parliament.

THE TAKEOVER PANEL

Perhaps one of the last remaining outposts of 'gentlemanly capitalism' is the UK's Takeover Panel, which regulates the procedural aspects of mergers and acquisitions. Unlike many other jurisdictions, the Takeover Panel is not a statutory body, and the legislation governing takeovers, the Takeover Code, does not carry much legal force. But in most cases the views of the Panel are respected and its supporters argue that the lack of statutory power actually leads to fairer, and certainly quicker, takeover battles.

The Panel was established by the Bank of England in the late 1960s after a series of takeovers in which minority shareholders were very poorly treated. Its first Director-General, Sir Ian Fraser, summed up the prevailing climate neatly: 'The takeover business had become an arena of complete lawlessness inhabited by cowboys who habitually kicked, punched and shot their opponents.' Like many others in the City, the Takeover Panel initially struggled to adapt to the seismic changes that occurred in the run-up to Big Bang – some of the most dastardly abuses of corporate power, such as the frauds of Robert Maxwell and the Guinness/Distillers scandal, took place in the early 1980s. But since then the Panel is generally perceived as having been equitable and effective.

The principles of the Takeover Code are fairly simple and clear. Every stake over 5 percent must be disclosed. If a company or an individual acquires more than 30 percent of another company's shares, it is obliged to make a general offer for the rest of the equity at the same price. Generally speaking, the timetable of a bid is dictated by the 'bid clock', which starts 'ticking' as soon as the formal offer document is dispatched. If a bid is allowed to lapse, the bidder is not usually allowed to make a second bid within 12 months, unless someone else bids for the same company.

The head of the Takeover Panel usually came from one of the old British banks, but since most of those have now fallen into foreign hands, the Bank of England has also moved with the times and the current director-general, Philip Remnant, is a senior banker at Swiss-American institution CSFB (although some things never change: he is an Old Etonian and the son and heir of Lord Remnant of Wenhaston).

As well as policing run-of-the-mill takeovers, the Panel is also occasionally required to rule on more controversial battles. It can, for instance, intervene to force a formal bid and prevent a 'phoney' bid battle being fought in the financial pages of the newspaper, but only if the target company requests that it do so. And it can also attempt to settle bid contests where there are two rival offers. This is more controversial territory and has led to criticism of the Panel from some quarters. An example was the battle in the summer of 2000 over Hyder, a heavily indebted Welsh utility that was eventually forced to put itself up for sale. There were two bids, one from the American firm Western Power Distribution (WPD), the other from the Japanese finance house Nomura. The Panel eventually called for sealed bids to be submitted in an attempt to break the deadlock, but bizarrely adopted an odd formula for determining the final price paid. The losing bidder, Nomura, claimed that WPD had broken the rules and submitted its bid late, and the whole process degenerated into acrimony and a general sense of farce.

But for every controversy, and every newspaper editorial calling for the introduction of statutory takeover supervision, there are a hundred bids that pass off uneventfully. Supporters of the Takeover Panel say that it can react flexibly to individual bid situations precisely because it is not hamstrung by law, and that, as a result, takeovers in the UK are not beset by legal shenanigans but settled quickly in the best interests of shareholders.

How much longer can the Panel hold out? Perhaps the greatest threat to its existence comes not from the Financial Services Authority, the 'super-regulator' created in 1997, but from the European Union's attempts to forge a Takeover Directive that would put takeover regulation on a common – and statutory – footing throughout the Union. But those attempts have so far come to nothing, and it seems the Takeover Panel will be policing UK mergers and acquisitions in its quiet and unobtrusive way for some years yet.

COMPANY CULTURE: HOW DO THEY DO IT IN THE US?

The UK's equity market is as deep as it is broad. There is a huge market in smaller quoted companies as well as in international blue chips. More than anywhere else in Europe, companies in the UK embody American tenets of capitalism. One aspect of this Anglo-Saxon model is that free floats among UK companies tend to be large, something that has benefited the exchange in the new world of indices based on free float, rather than total market value. Of the companies in the FTSE 100, only a very small number, such as British Sky Broadcasting and British Land, have substantial shareholders. Heavy family ownership of British listed companies is comparatively rare, especially among blue chips. Only among construction companies is it somewhat more common to have a family member as a large shareholder.

> More than anywhere else in Europe, companies in the UK embody American tenets of capitalism

Anglo-Saxon shareholder capitalism is first and foremost about shareholder value. There are relatively few concessions to other stakeholders like employee groups or national or regional governments. Companies are run by boards of directors. A chairman, who is usually non-executive, serves as a figurehead and is involved in setting the general corporate agenda. Implementation is largely the role of the chief executive, who is in charge of the day-to-day running of a company. Since the Cadbury Report of 1992, which set out the framework of modern UK corporate governance, combining the office of chairman and chief executive has become increasingly frowned upon. The interests of shareholders are protected by non-executive directors, who are not full-time employees of the company but are paid relatively nominal sums for their attendance at board meetings. It is the non-executives who are supposed to control committees that oversee things like executive pay and the choice of auditors. They also have the key role of advising shareholders, should an executive management team make an offer to take the company private.

Like so many aspects of UK regulation, compliance with the Cadbury code is voluntary, the theory being that the market, not the law, will impose the most effective punishment on those companies with poor corporate governance and disclosure. By that logic, it is difficult to know whether to credit Cadbury with the undoubted improvements in UK corporate governance since Robert Maxwell disappeared overboard with millions of pounds of shareholders' money, or whether to credit investors themselves for being more selective.

Another US import is incentive-based renumeration, either in the form of cash bonuses, shares or options over shares. In theory, such rewards are tied to the performance of the company or, more likely, its share price. In practice, the link is often less clear and one consequence of the downturn in markets during 2000 and 2001 is that executive pay is coming under more scrutiny than ever before. A series of UK companies, including market leaders such as Vodafone, Cable & Wireless, Royal Bank of Scotland and Billiton, have faced critical questioning at annual general meetings and elsewhere over the level of renumeration paid to executives and how that is linked to performance. There has emerged a general suspicion that com-panies are paying out bonanza sums on the basis of deals being done rather than on tangible results. In a few instances – Railtrack and Marks & Spencer being the two obvious examples – executives have forfeited their bonuses because of investor pressure. This activism is made possible, of course, by the amount of information listed companies are obliged to disclose and by the relatively high profile and power of UK institutional investors, who are not usually slow to demand change if they think it necessary.

One argument used to espouse high bonuses (other than the usual 'we need to attract the best talent') is that the risk of unemployment among UK executive managers is much closer to US levels than European ones. This is because takeovers, including hostile ones, are relatively commonplace. The first hostile bid in the UK happened in the 1960s. It is widely accepted that if a management of a company is not performing to expectations, a rival can table a proposal to run that company better and shareholders decide the outcome. Should shareholders plump for change, the defeated executives can usually expect to be vanquished forthwith.

The shareholder-as-king philosophy is not perfect, however. One criticism levelled at the UK, often by European politicians or left-leaning academics, is that the overwhelming focus on shareholder returns is short-termist and leads to low productivity and under-investment over the longer term. There is certainly plenty of evidence to back this up; productivity in the UK is weak compared with many other leading industrialized nations, and it is hard to see how frequent restructurings, rationalizations and takeovers can be good for employees. The desire to please the City, and be rewarded with rising share prices and ratings, can also produce constant about-turns in strategy that occupy disproportionate amounts of management time. In the 1980s, when being a conglomerate was fashionable, companies rushed to diversify and spent billions adding extra divisions and subsidiaries. By the mid-1990s, diversity was out – replaced by focus and 'core competencies' (management jargon being another of the UK's less desirable American imports). Thus much of the 1990s was spent selling off businesses acquired the decade before in order to get back to basics. Did shareholders profit from this? Not usually – as the case of GEC shows. Once a cash-rich defence and engineering business, GEC metamorphosized into Marconi, a manufacturer of telecommunications equipment, via a series of acquisitions. The company's debt ballooned and the company's most likely fate is to be taken over by a foreign competitor (*see* Fig. 2.1).

> **The desire to please the City, and be rewarded with rising share prices and ratings, can produce constant about-turns in strategy**

If that were to transpire, it would highlight another criticism of rampant shareholder capitalism – that the City's dispassionate bean-counters have allowed swathes of the UK corporate landscape to be sold off to foreign companies, in some cases ones that are still in partial or total state ownership. There is barely a sector of British industry in which foreign companies have not made inroads: two of the four mobile phone networks are owned by European firms; the UK car industry has been carved up by the Germans, the Americans and

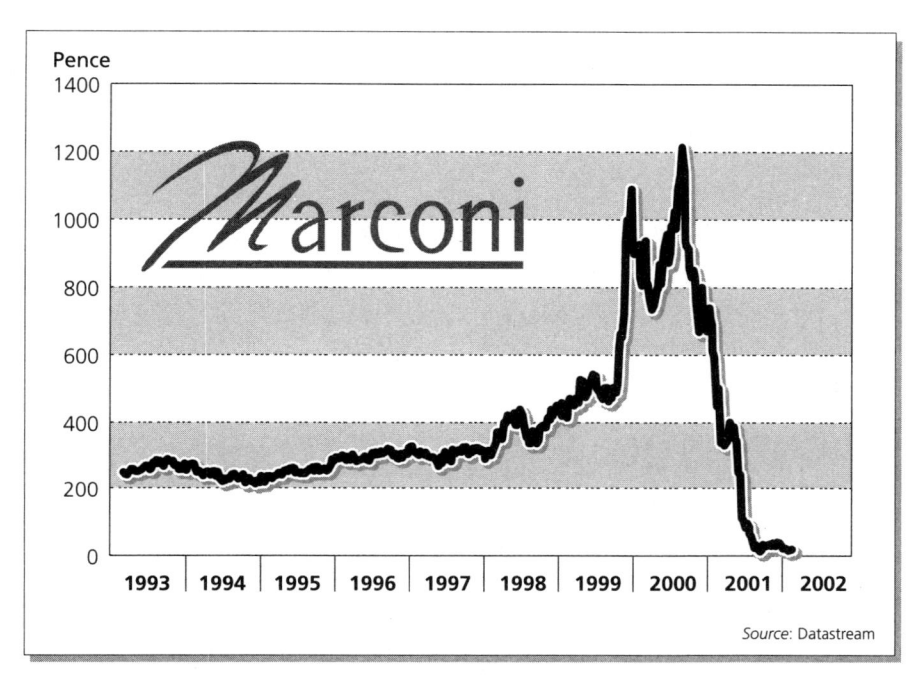

Figure 2.1 Marconi share price

the Malaysians (Lotus is owned by Proton); German, American and French utilities have bought up a number of the privatized utilities. None of the mainstream British political parties would regard the idea of the Government exercising a veto over any of these deals, or even commenting directly on them, as politically responsible.

So perhaps 'wide open' would be the best term to describe the UK equity market. It is home to the biggest players and some of the biggest companies, with relatively little of the domineering major shareholders and convoluted capital structures prevalent in some other jurisdictions. The shareholder is king. Company executives are merely there to do the shareholder's bidding, and can be rapidly dispensed with should they fail. Other stakeholders are rarely consulted unless there is a legal obligation to do so. While this system undoubtedly has its faults, it is the one we know – and it is the one increasingly being espoused by the bigger players in other markets. For better or worse, Anglo-Saxon capitalism is on the march. But some of the cultures and companies that it will come up against have a quite different structure.

> **Box 2.1 Equity investment in the UK**
>
> **Stock exchange**
> London Stock Exchange (www.londonstockexchange.com) operates the Official List and the Alternative Investment Market. JP Jenkins Ltd operates Ofex (www.ofex.com).
>
> **Clearing**
> Clearing is through London Clearing House (www.lch.co.uk), which is owned by its members.
>
> **Settlement**
> Settlement is through CRESTCo (www.crestco.co.uk) which was set up by the Bank of England and is owned by its members.
>
> **Regulation**
> The Labour administration, elected in 1997, consolidated all financial regulations under one roof, that of the Financial Services Authority (www.fsa.gov.uk). Part of the FSA is the UK Listing Authority, which approves listings now that the Stock Exchange is itself a quoted company. The FSA also supervises banks and insurance companies. It assumed its full powers in late 2001.
>
> **Takeovers**
> Takeovers are regulated by the Takeover Panel (www.thetakeoverpanel.org.uk), which is a non-statutory body run by representatives of the financial services industry.
>
> **Shareholders' groups**
> ProShare (www.proshare.org.uk) promotes share ownership within the UK. The UK Shareholders Association (www.uksa.org.uk) lobbies on behalf of private shareholders. Big institutions are often represented by the Association of British Insurers (www.abi.org.uk). Stockbrokers serving the smaller investor are usually members of the Association of Private Client Investment Managers and Stockbrokers (www.apcims.org).

TOP LISTINGS IN THE UK

BRITISH TELECOMMUNICATIONS AND VODAFONE – A TALE OF TWO TELCOS

The UK's two largest telecoms operators could not be more different. One still carries some of the millstones of state ownership, whereas the other has assumed the habits of the most American predator. British Telecommunications (BT) (www.bt.com), like most of its peers, was originally part of the Post Office. In 1984 it became one of the most significant privatizations of the Thatcher years, turning thousands of people into shareholders for the first time. It was not for some time, however, that BT was run like a quoted company, and even then its recent history has been characterized by strategic confusion and missed opportunities. The consequences of this was a huge debt pile, forcing BT to go cap in hand to its shareholders in 2001 for £5.9 billion.

There has never been any doubt about Vodafone's strategy (www.vodafone.com). It has become the world's biggest mobile phone company using skill and aggression in equal measure. Born out of a military engineering project in 1983, the company was already one of the UK's biggest mobile phone operators when it merged with AirTouch of the US in 1999. Barely had the ink dried on that deal before Vodafone announced a hostile bid for Germany's Mannesmann, one of the biggest and most significant takeovers ever (*see* Chapter 3 on Germany). This, and a raft of other deals, were mostly financed by the company's highly valued shares, a typically American mechanism. Vodafone's chief executive, Chris Gent, also likes American salaries – Vodafone has been criticized more than once for boardroom excess.

ANGLO AMERICAN – THE FOREIGN LEGION

The London stock market financed many of the gold mines in the Witwatersrand during the last century, but the introduction of apartheid in South Africa meant that international capital markets were closed to South African companies. Once the economy was opened up again, many of Johannesburg's bigger companies sought primary listings in London. One of the first was Anglo American (www.angloamerican.co.uk) – the sprawling conglomerate founded by Ernest Oppenheimer. Heavy family control, opaque disclosure and a tangled web of cross-holdings and subsidiaries were not features that endeared Anglo to the City, so it changed itself profoundly, selling off subsidiaries, making focused acquisitions and talking to investors as equals. It is not alone; the South African contingent in London now includes South African Breweries, Billiton, Old Mutual and Dimension Data.

ICI – LAST OF THE OLD GUARD

To the critics of shareholder capitalism, the story of ICI (www.ici.com) is a lesson in the shortcomings of the system. The once-mighty Imperial Chemical Industries, one of Britain's older listed companies, got bogged down in a swamp of debt after trying to impress the City with a big acquisition. It has spent the past few years refocusing on high-margin chemicals and paying down the debt. In the meantime, its market value has shrunk and most of its contemporaries taken over by foreigners.

ARM HOLDINGS – LEADER OF A NEW BREED

Perhaps no company epitomizes the judicious and responsible use of equity markets quite like ARM Holdings (www.arm.com). The company designs microchips and sells the licences to make its designs to big chipmakers. Its main assets are not buildings or machines, but people and ideas. As such, banks were not initially interested in backing it, and it turned to the stock market. Even then, it was the penny-share investors who bought it, rather than the big institutional investors. As the company grew at breakneck speed, so it began to pop up on bigger radar screens, and eventually became a member of the FTSE 100 index in 2000. Its growth would not have been possible without the equity market – and it rewards investors with lavish disclosure and communications. Most of its employees are shareholders, too.

3

GERMANY

All the management now understands we must sell shares as well as cars.
Bruno Adelt, chief financial officer, Volkswagen AG

NOT MUCH IS HEARD ABOUT the *Wirtschaftswunder* any more. After nigh on a decade of booming stock markets, soaring US productivity and the relentless march of shareholder culture, Germany's once-fêted bank-based finance system no longer looks quite so convincing. Indeed, with German unemployment remaining stubbornly high and the country's centre-left Government facing some increasingly unpalatable choices on welfare spending and taxation, it is frequently regarded – in some cases with more than a little *schadenfreude* – as a system that has had its day.

The central attraction of the German system was its long view. Historically, the chief suppliers of capital to German industry were the banks. In return for their long-term commitment, they had a say in the running of a company, often via seats on the board. This meant the relationship between a German company and its creditor banks was quite different to the arms-length one prevalent in the Anglo-Saxon economies. A bank was not just an adversary to be dealt with, but a major shareholder – someone who understood the business and its aims, indeed someone who owned a slice of it. German banks had teams of engineers and scientists on their staff who could evaluate new business proposals and advise bankers on whether to fund them or not – a far cry from UK banks, which have traditionally been ambivalent to new inventions, leaving that risk to the equity markets.

Furthermore, the bedrock of the German economy has, for many years, been the *Mittelstand*, the hundreds of thousands of small to medium-sized, privately owned enterprises. Often they are still owned by the founding families, or descendants of the founders. They and the banks, free from all the short-term targets of equity analysts, the demands of pension fund managers, the fashions and fads of the stock market and the glaring scrutiny of the financial media, have been free to plot their own course for decades. They have not tended to be expansionist, preferring to concentrate on producing a narrowish range of products well rather than empire-building overseas. Their productivity has been enhanced by a consensual approach to labour relations – the *Mitbestimmung* (co-determination) system established after the Second World War. Union representatives often sit on the advisory boards of companies and accept that their members' interests are best served by recognizing the role of the company as a profit generator. They see managers as equals rather than adversaries.

SHAREHOLDER CAPITALISM TAKES ROOT

Although there is no shortage of defenders for the old model, questions are now emerging as to whether the long-term, consensus-based system is the best to deal with the challenges of globalization and rapid technological change. Germany's relatively haphazard recovery from the recession of the early 1990s, coupled with the bull market in global equities, has awakened the capitalist demon within German society. And so an equity culture has begun to develop. In 1987, according to the Deutsche Aktieninstitut, a body that promotes share ownership, there were 1,111 listed companies in Germany. Ten years later, that total had more than doubled to 3,003. By September 2000, the figure had topped 10,000. Taking domestic shares only, the number rose from 679 in 1987 to 1,450 by September 2000; by comparison the UK, a smaller economy, had 2,371.

German companies were not slow on the uptake. Share issues by domestic companies were worth DM10.12 billion in 1987, at market prices. By 1997 that figure was DM18.80 billion, and during 1999 it rocketed to DM61.30 billion. The number of initial public offerings (IPOs) went from 19 in 1987 to 168 in 1999 (admittedly a boom year across the world).

The late 1990s rush into equities can be traced to two key events. One was the establishment of the Neuer Markt, of which more later. The other was the privatization of the German state telecoms monopoly, Deutsche Telekom. At the time, Telekom was the world's third largest phone company and the offering of its shares was Europe's largest-ever initial public offer. There was a massive advertising campaign, backed up with incentives for retail investors and reductions in fees. The issue was a roaring success, raising around DM15 billion, almost double the total of all new German issues during the previous year – and making hundreds of thousands of Germans shareholders for the first time.

But even at these growth rates Germany still lags behind more established shareholder cultures. Between 1986 and 1999 there were 470 domestic IPOs in Germany (and many of those came in 1999). In the same period there were 2,502 IPOs in the UK and a staggering 6,449 on Nasdaq. By August 2000 the value of companies on Germany's exchanges was US$1.420 trillion. At the same time London's quoted companies were worth US$2.82 trillion and the Nasdaq, by now well past its peak, was still worth US$5.82 trillion. As a percentage of gross domestic product (GDP), Germany's stock exchange was worth 67.8 percent by the end of 1999, the lowest proportion of any of the major industrialized economies. The US stock markets, bloated by technology valuations, were worth 181 percent and the UK's listed companies were worth three times its GDP.

Germany's first generation of shareholder capitalists have had something of a baptism of fire. The cult of equity took off just in time for the end-of-millennium boom in technology and telecom shares, which hugely inflated the value of 'new economy' stocks in fashionable sectors. Many Germans bought in at or close to the top of the market – the

State issued two more tranches of Deutsche Telekom shares to the market at values well above the first, and the offers were well subscribed. The subsequent collapse in valuations left many Germans sitting on heavy losses – even if they had managed to avoid the turmoil on the Neuer Markt. The slide revealed fault lines in the regulation and governance of even the biggest blue chips. By the end of 2001 Telekom itself was facing accusations that it had deliberately overstated the value of its property holdings at the time of its flotation. One official at the DSW, a shareholder rights group, told the *Handelsblatt* newspaper that Telekom's disclosure policy was 'unprofessional and unworthy of a blue chip company'. Telekom was reduced to placing advertisements in major newspapers bewailing its share price decline and assuring investors nothing had gone wrong.

> Germany's first generation of shareholder capitalists have had a baptism of fire

Meanwhile current and former executives at Mannesmann, including the head of the massive IG Metall union and Josef Ackermann, heir apparent to the top job at Deutsche Bank, were facing allegations that they had pocketed huge bonuses in return for acquiecing in Mannesmann's takeover by Vodafone.

The question is whether the growing pains of a relatively immature market will put traditionally risk-averse Germans off equity markets altogether. Not surprisingly, brokers, investment banks and agencies like the DAI say the upsurge in interest is not a passing fad. They are fond of pointing out that in the first half of 2001, despite sharp falls in stock markets around the world and the almost daily stream of scandal stories in the German press, the number of citizens owning shares via mutual funds rose by over a million. Furthermore, such cheerleaders can point to a number of demographic, legislative and cultural changes to back up their optimism.

THE DRIVERS OF CHANGE

The first, and one of the most important changes, is to Germany's system of pension provision. Historically, Germans have enjoyed pensions worth around 70 percent of their salary while they were working. Few other populaces in the world were so well rewarded in retirement. But the German Government has increasingly come to realize that such largesse at the end of working life, coupled with the great student gravy train at the start of it, is no longer affordable. The compromise, thrashed out after years of bitter argument, will not take Germany straight from a pay-as-you-go to a fully funded pension system. But it will reduce the benefits to wages ratio from 70.7 percent in 2000 to around 69 percent by 2010. By 2008, Germans will be able to invest up to 4 percent of gross wages in private pension savings instruments. Most observers think that this ratio will have to be increased further as state funding comes under more pressure.

The Government is also poised to end the punitive rates of capital gains tax charged when companies dispose of shareholdings in other companies. This could eventually unravel the endlessly complex system of cross-holdings that dominates the German economy (*see* Table 3.1). Schroder Salomon Smith Barney, an investment bank, calculated that German companies held around €170 billion of equity in cross-holdings at the end of 2001. It expected €14 billion of those cross-holdings to be monetized in 2002 alone. Not only could capital gains tax reform pave the way to far-reaching consolidation and restructuring among listed Germany companies, it could also end many of the de facto 'poison pill' shareholdings that make takeovers, especially hostile ones, so difficult in Germany. The protective shield of significant shareholders, who would face a big tax bill if they sold out, would be removed. The grandees of the Mittelstand would also be able to sell their businesses without incurring a hefty tax liability.

Change is also on the way for the hundreds of smaller retail banks, the *Landesbanken*. For decades, they have been able to borrow at preferential rates because their liabilities were guaranteed by the federal states (*Länder*). That guarantee will be phased out over the next five years, and many observers expect massive consolidation as the smaller players, many of them too small and inefficient to survive without the state cushion, are swallowed up into bigger regional groupings. Such far-reaching changes, and the restructuring they might bring, would be disastrous if implemented in a market not sufficiently mature to cope with the change. This is the final plank of the changes to the German system of capitalism. The Government is introducing several key pieces of legislation in 2002, aimed at tightening up disclosure and corporate governance, and providing a much improved system for regulating takeovers.

Holding company	Stakes in (%)
Allianz	Munich Re (23)
	HypoVereinsbank (13.7)
	MAN (13)
	Linde (12.5)
	BASF (11.9)
	RWE (11.6)
	E.ON (10)
	Schering (around 10)
	BMW (6)
	Bayer (5)
	Deutsche Bank (around 5)
Deutsche Bank	DaimlerChrysler (12)
	Linde (10)
	Continental (7.8)
	Munich Re (7.5)
	Allianz (4.2)
Munich Re	HypoVereinsbank (25.7)
	Allianz (21)
	MAN (6.5)
HypoVereinsbank	Munich Re (13.3)
	Allianz (6.8)
Commerzbank	Linde (10.7)
	MAN (6.5)
Siemens	Infineon (51)
	Epcos (12.5)
E.ON	Degussa (64.6)
	HypoVereinsbank (6.6)

Source: Reuters

Table 3.1 Major German cross-holdings

These initiatives represent a fundamental change to the established post-war order, and they will certainly be accompanied by energetic debate and the occasional messy compromise. There are bound to be more growing pains ahead. But the train is in motion and many strategists feel that Germany, whose stock market still accounts for a relatively small portion of its overall economy, could gain the most from Europe's increasing acceptance of equity culture.

FRANKFURT CONSOLIDATES ITS POSITION

As befits a federal country, Germany has seven regional stock exchanges as well as the Frankfurt bourse, known since 1992 simply as Deutsche Börse. The overwhelming majority of trade is now conducted in Frankfurt. Deutsche Börse listed its own shares in 2001, after pursuing a failed tie-up with the London Stock Exchange.

Trade is divided into different segments. Companies traded on *Amtlicher Handel*, loosely translated as the official list, must be admitted to the exchange through a formal listing process and must meet basic listing requirements. *Freiverkehr* is much more lightly regulated, and dealing on that segment is largely the preserve of *Freimakler* brokers. *Kursmakler* trade shares on the official list.

The main family of indices is compiled by Deutsche Börse. The benchmark index is the DAX 30, a capitalization-weighted index that tracks the 30 largest German blue chips (*see* Table 3.2). Its base was 1,000 at the end of December 1987. The broader market is measured by the DAX 100, which also has sub-indices for different industrial sectors, while the mid-caps are tracked by the MDAX.

Since 1997, trading on Deutsche Börse has been via the Xetra screen-based system. There is still some floor trading but Xetra now accounts for three-quarters of exchange turnover and over 85 percent of turnover in DAX-30 blue chips. Xetra is an order-driven system and like all such systems strives to preserve the anonymity of the counterparties. Trading can continue until 8.00 pm using Xetra, a policy that has irritated traders. They complain that there is no longer sufficient retail trade to keep them occupied in the evening.

Company (sector)	Weighting
Deutsche Telekom (telecoms)	11.69
Allianz (insurance)	11.00
Munich Re (reinsurance)	8.10
E.ON (utilities)	7.50
Siemens (engineering)	6.38
DaimlerChrysler (cars, trucks)	5.94
SAP (software)	5.57
Deutsche Bank (financial services)	5.53
RWE (utilities)	4.01
Bayer (chemicals, pharmaceuticals)	3.78
BASF (chemicals, pharmaceuticals)	3.69
BMW (cars, aero engines)	3.11
Volkswagen (cars, trucks)	2.74
Bayerische Hypothekenbank (financial services)	2.69
Metro (retailing)	2.16
Schering (pharmaceuticals)	1.84
Commerzbank (financial services)	1.74
Infineon (semiconductors)	1.71
Henkel (consumer goods)	1.71
Deutsche Post (support services)	1.42
Fresnius Medical (pharmaceuticals)	1.22
ThyssenKrupp (steel)	1.08
Linde (retailing)	0.90
Degussa (chemicals)	0.90
Preussag (leisure)	0.79
MLP (financial services)	0.72
Deutsche Lufthansa (transport)	0.71
MAN (vehicles)	0.51
Adidas Salomon (consumer goods)	0.42
Epcos (engineering)	0.39

Note: Weightings are approximate, as at September 2001.

Table 3.2 The DAX 30 index

Deutshe Börse believes in vertical integration, and early in 2002 it finally brought clearing and settlement completely under its own control. Before, it had held 50 percent of Luxembourg-based Clearstream, with Cedel International (owned by a consortium of banks) owning the remainder. It bought Cedel out for €1.6bn, and although Clearstream is still based in Luxembourg, it is now 100 percent owned by the German exchange. Deutsche Börse also owns 50 percent of Eurex, the pan-European derivatives exchange (SWX Swiss Exchange owns the other half).

Disclosure of price-sensitive information is made via Deutsche Börse's Ad Hoc system of company announcements. The feed is available on Deutsche Börse's website and is supplied to various third party information vendors such as VWD. Ad-Hoc is perceived as a very limited service; companies are free to choose their own interpretation of what is price-sensitive and what is not.

THE NEUER MARKT – EUROPE'S WILD WEST

When Rainer Riess, a senior executive of Deutsche Börse, went on a marketing tour of major financial centres in the summer of 2001, he asserted that the Neuer Markt was one of the leading stock exchange 'brands' anywhere in the world, rivalling even Nasdaq. He was quite right – although not for the reasons he had in mind.

The Neuer Markt has become known as a byword for all that was short-sighted, naïve and even criminal about the millennial technology boom. By the time Riess started on his tour, the benchmark index had fallen almost 90 percent from its March 2000 high, and was down 60 percent that year. For a technology-dominated index, that was hardly surprising – other technology benchmarks had also fallen heavily. But the fall of the Nemax all-share was accompanied by all manner of scandals over lax regulation, insider dealing and downright deceit. If Neuer Markt has a brand, it is one of damaged goods.

> If Neuer Markt has a brand, it is one of damaged goods

The Neuer Markt was established at a time when Easdaq, the fledgling European technology exchange, was considered a potentially formidable adversary. Deutsche Börse set up its own technology bourse to provide a domestic market for the kind of high-growth, young companies of which the banks were wary. In March 1997, Mobilcom became the first stock to list on the new exchange. Its shares rose 50 percent on the first day.

Thus the die was cast, and from that point on, the Neuer Markt grew at a rate that far exceeded initial expectations. By the end of the first year demand was such that the trading hours were extended and trading in the most liquid stocks was migrated to Xetra. In 1999 an index family was created for the new market, with the Nemax 50 being the blue-chip benchmark (see Fig. 3.1). The biggest stocks in the Nemax by September 2001 were T-Online (Deutsche Telekom's internet service provider) and biotechs Qiagen and BB Biotech. By the spring of 2001 it had 338 listed companies worth over £70 billion. By contrast, London's Alternative Investment Market (see Chapter 2) had secured 524 companies, but they were worth less than £20 billion. Even after its steep decline, the Neuer Markt was still worth more than all the other 'new' European markets put together. Furthermore, it had managed to attract 56 listings from overseas, more than the total number of companies listed on Easdaq.

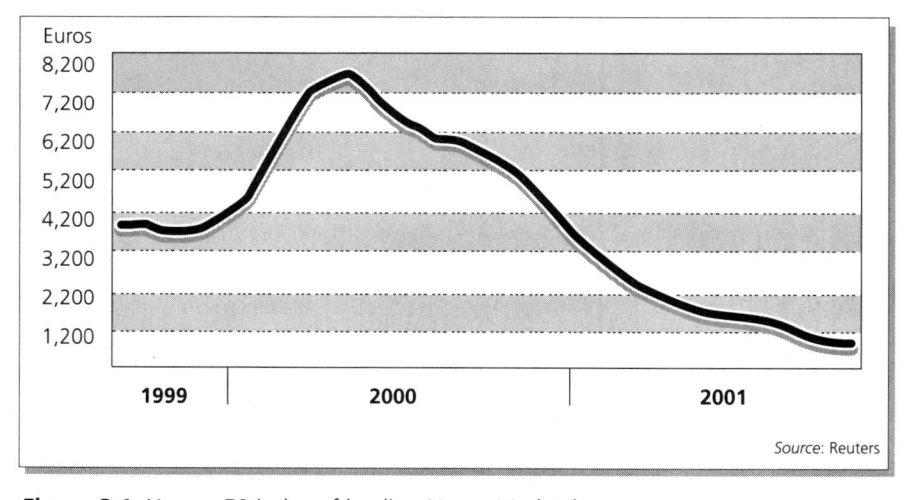

Figure 3.1 Nemax 50 index of leading Neuer Markt shares

While share prices were rising, few people were asking questions about the quality of some of these outfits, or the regulatory framework within which they were listing. But when the money ran out, the cracks soon appeared. One of the Neuer Markt's listing criteria was that companies offer the potential for double-digit growth. This led to some listing hopefuls submitting business plans that were in the realms of fantasy. Roland Oetker, president of the shareholder rights group DSW, said a large number of Neuer Markt companies 'were still in the venture capital phase and not really ready for a stock market listing at all'. Once they had secured their listing, they largely did as they pleased. 'At some Neuer Markt companies, nothing functions apart from the PR machinery,' he added.

After a summer of scandals, Gigabell, an alternative telecoms company, attained the dubious distinction of being the first Neuer Markt company to become insolvent in November 1999. Although Neuer Markt companies are required to prepare quarterly reports, these did not at the time have to include a balance sheet. So Gigabell managed to gobble all its listing proceeds without shareholders becoming aware of the fact until it was too late. Metabox managed to drive its share price up using exaggerated sales figures. Most investors' favourite Neuer Markt scandal, however, is that of EM.TV. It used easy cash from shareholders to go on an acquisitions binge, but somewhere along the way its executives had forgotten how to add up. It had to restate its interim results after including results from a subsidiary it had acquired subsequent to the period-end. Then, just weeks after insisting it would meet all its targets, it slashed its profit forecasts by 90 percent. Founder Thomas Haffa and his brother Florian, both of whom are alleged to have sold shares during a lock-up period, came under investigation for possible insider dealing.

Deutsche Börse knew it needed to rectify the Neuer Markt's image as the Wild West of Europe if it wanted to continue attracting international capital. It has implemented a number of measures, but even these have attracted criticism and controversy from various quarters. One particularly significant change was that from March 2001 directors were obliged to inform shareholders of their personal dealings within three days of the trade. Balance sheets were required with every earnings report, and fines for non-compliance with listing requirements were raised substantially. But the reforms cut little ice with the market's critics; the SdK, a small shareholders' society, described the penalties as 'laughable' – a €100,000 fine is hardly going to deter a director who could pocket millions from an illegal share sale – and pointed out that while directors' dealings had to be disclosed, those of their immediate family did not. Another proposal was that bombed out companies whose share prices had slid below one euro should simply be delisted. This caused major protests, with many arguing the deletion criteria should be market capitalization rather than something as crude as the share price value.

In a report produced in the autumn of 2001, the exchange effectively admitted that mistakes had been made in the rush for growth. But it also defended the Neuer Markt's record, and pointed out that comparisons with Nasdaq, established over 30 years ago and operating in a completely different regulatory environment, were not entirely valid. 'A comparison of the early days of both markets reveals that companies on the Neuer Markt performed on average better than those on Nasdaq,' it claimed. It is certainly true that an exchange cannot be responsible for the recklessness of investors or the dishonesty of company directors. It is also true that in the early years of its equity culture Germany lacked a single powerful regulator like the Securities and Exchange Commission. But what is less certain is whether the European technology leaders of the future will still want to be associated with a market so tainted with scandal.

MINDING YOUR OWN BUSINESS

Although equity shareholder culture is expanding, and the biggest companies aspire to be as open and transparent as their US or British equivalents, the way many German companies are structured, operated and regulated owes much to a previous modus operandi. One obvious manifestation of this is in the cross-holdings, detailed earlier, that characterize even the biggest listed companies.

Another issue is the relative lack of depth to the equity markets. In the UK there are thousands of quoted smaller companies across a whole spectrum of market segments. That simply does not exist in Germany. Most of the companies on the Neuer Markt have a distinct technology bias; they are relatively young and therefore likely to have a higher failure rate than more established concerns in so-called 'old economy' sectors. Most of the smaller and mid-sized companies that in the UK would be quoted remain in private hands in Germany.

Furthermore, those that did go public often did so by selling only a minority stake, with the family taking a controlling stake. Subsequent capital increases were often effected by issuing non-voting or preferred shares so as to protect that control. In bigger companies these have mostly gone, but some fairly substantial concerns like truck-maker MAN or car manufacturer Volkswagen still have preference share structures.

There are valid reasons as to why the situation might change in the years ahead. One of the most compelling is simple demographics. The patriarchal figures that run many of the smaller companies are advancing in years. They may have a younger generation that can take over, but this is not always the case. In these circumstances an equity market flotation is one exit route. The company is effectively sold to investors, with professional management installed, allowing the vendors to cash in on a lifetime's hard work.

In practice, however, the experience of the *Mittelstand* on the equity markets so far has been a mixed one. Many companies with a hundred years or more of history behind them have been disappointed at the indifference shown towards their shares by a new generation of investors more interested in the casino stocks of the Neuer Markt. It is possible that the mood of greater realism, coupled with an increasing tendency to buy shares via mutual funds rather than directly, could make such value stocks more attractive. But even then there are liquidity issues. Big remaining family shareholdings and capital structures designed to maintain family control are not going to attract institutional shareholders, who generally like an independent management and a big free float.

❝ Big family shareholdings and capital structures designed to maintain family control are not going to attract institutional shareholders ❞

Germany's banks-and-families system has also left its fingerprints all over the country's disclosure habits. Family-run businesses traditionally do not want outsiders poring over their financial affairs – which is fine when a company is in private hands, but is less satisfactory in a publicly quoted firm. Unfortunately, bad disclosure habits are not confined to the *Mittelstand* – they pervade some of the very biggest companies in Germany. Investors were to some extent prepared to overlook this when share prices were rising, but falling markets have made investors' collective gaze turn very critical.

Even those that do try to be more open face challenges. Germany's native accounting system, the Handelsgesetzbuch (HGB), is designed with the interests of creditors, not shareholders, at heart. Investments have to be carried at cost, not market value, except when the market value remains beneath the cost over a long period. There are also widely differing practices between HGB and International Accounting Standards (IAS) or US Generally Accepted Accounting Principles (GAAP) when it comes to revenue recognition and depreciation. Investors want companies to switch to IAS or GAAP because those systems are more in tune with the needs of equity investors. Most German companies have obliged, led by Daimler Benz in 1993, but HGB is still the basis of German company law. Quarterly reports in particular, which are not usually audited, can be a confusing mish-mash of the two standards.

Deutsche Börse is starting to force better accounting standards, most notably by insisting on quarterly reporting for bigger companies, in line with US practice. This has caused some interesting frictions – carmaker Porsche refused to comply, saying its business was seasonal and that quarterly reporting could cause such seasonal factors to be misinterpreted as a downturn in sales. These claims were mostly met with derision in the investment community, and Deutsche Börse stuck to its guns and threw the prestigious company out of the MDAX index.

Director shareholdings are another area where the 'none-of-your-business' approach tends to dominate. In March 2001, amid much fanfare, Deutsche Börse introduced for Neuer Markt companies compulsory disclosure of management shareholdings (but not those of close family members) and required reporting of any dealings, however small, in company shares. But these requirements do not as yet apply to the main market. The annual reports of German companies do not contain detailed breakdowns of management pay and stock options. They are not obliged to disclose such information.

Progressive factions within Germany are fond of saying that perception is the problem. 'Germany corporate governance is already of a high standard ... However, the problem for foreign investors so far is that they are not fully aware of all the German regulations because they are scattered throughout a number of laws,' said Gerhard Cromme, the chairman of ThyssenKrupp who also chaired a government commission into improving corporate governance (www.corporate-code.de). His draft proposals call for the enshrinement of one-share, one-vote, more accessible annual general meetings, a more carefully defined role for the Aufsichtsrat or supervisory board, along with measures to safeguard its independence, plus much better disclosure of directors' salaries, pensions and bonus entitlements. Companies will not be obliged by law to comply with the code, but will have to explain their reasons if they choose not to. The theory is that the market will punish miscreants with lower share ratings.

However, Dr Cromme did not venture onto the hallowed ground of the German company management system, known as *Mitbestimmung* (co-determination), saying only that 'in practice, the two-tier system and the board of directors system, are converging'. *Mitbestimmung* allows trades unions and other stakeholders to enjoy a significant role in running companies. This is exercised courtesy of the Germany system of corporate governance, under which a company has two boards – a management board (*Vorstand*) and a supervisory board (*Aufsichtsrat*), whose function is to act as a check and balance on the managers. This structure is a legal requirement for all companies employing more than 500 people; and in all those with more than 2,000 employees half the members of the *Aufsichtsrat* must be elected by employees – reducing the ability of shareholders to influence company management via the annual general meeting.

The *Aufsichtsrat* is not there to perform the function of non-executive directors in the Anglo-Saxon sense, although the chairman does represent shareholders and has a casting vote. Its function is to represent the interests of a number of stakeholders, including unions and the company's creditor banks. A good example is the board of ThyssenKrupp, one of Europe's biggest steelmakers. There are ten shareholder representatives, including bigwigs from Siemens, Deutsche Bank, MAN, Commerzbank, Westdeutsche Landesbank, Allianz and Dresdner Bank. Then there are ten 'employee representatives', including six heads of works councils and three senior trade unionists. It is very difficult to imagine even the most moderate shop stewards being invited into the boardroom of a British or US company.

The system of *Mitbestimmung* is admired by progressive factions in many other societies and there can be little doubt that harmonious industrial relations made an immense contribution to Germany's postwar industrial recovery – a recovery that was delivered within a bank-based system of finance. The relationship between *Mitbestimmung* and equity shareholders, who would generally demand that a company be run overwhelmingly for their own benefit, is a less cosy one. But attempting to water down its principles would be political suicide for a German government of any hue.

However, the German Government is tackling other shortcomings in the system through the *Viertes Finanzmarketförderungsgesetz*, the fourth in a legislative series designed to bring German market regulation into line with that of other countries. Its main aims are to end demarcation on the stock exchange, increase levels of protection for minority shareholders, improve disclosure of company information and substantial shareholders, and crack down on insider trading. Oversight of the stock market and listed companies will be centralized at federal level, rather than being split between the BaWE, the Stock Exchange and the federal *Länder* as they are at present.

HOSTILE TAKEOVERS? *NEIN DANKE!*

In the spring of 2000 Vodafone pulled off a truly historic deal by becoming the first foreign company to take over a German company against its will. It bought Mannesmann, an engineering conglomerate turned telecommunications giant, in a massive all-share deal. Pundits caught up in the white heat of the technology boom hailed the transaction as the dawn of a new era, in which no company would be safe from Anglo-Saxon predators and the inexorable march of shareholder value.

The reason the bid was such a landmark is that hostile takeovers remain practically unheard of in Germany – and it is not hard to see why. The confrontational nature of an unsolicited approach is an anathema to Germany's consensual system of management and corporate governance. The idea that a management can be ejected en masse by shareholders runs against the grain of its bank-based, long-termist finance system, where shareholder banks stand by company managements through thick and thin. Any hostile bidder would also have had to negotiate Germany's woeful system of takeover regulation. Like the UK, Germany's takeover code was voluntary – but while adherence to the Takeover Code in the UK is near-universal, its equivalent in Germany commanded nowhere near the same respect or authority. Companies chose whether to recognize the code or not; the Uebernahme Kommission website detailed those that did, as if grateful to them for doing so. There was no requirement to make a general offer once a major shareholder exceeded a certain level of ownership, nor was the principle that all shareholders be treated fairly and equally enshrined in the code. Nor did bidders have it all their own way, because there was no squeeze-out rule. This meant that a bidder who had acquired 97 percent of the equity could not oblige the remaining minorities to sell up – a significant weakness given the power that minority shareholders wield in some matters.

> "The confrontational nature of an unsolicited approach is an anathema to Germany's consensual system of management"

Vodafone was able to capture Mannesmann primarily because, unusually among Germany companies, its shares were widely held by overseas institutions rather than en bloc by German banks and insurance companies. The bid battle was fought largely on an international stage as a result of this, and did not test Germany's archaic takeover legislation. However, it did make Germans aware of the issues arising from takeovers, and eventually led to a much more solid takeover regime.

Chancellor Schröder, mindful of the controversy that the Mannesmann deal had aroused among his more left-leaning supporters, set up a panel of experts not long after the transaction was completed to consider the issues. Among the panellists was Klaus Esser, the company's vanquished chief executive.

The result has been a bill broadly disappointing to the investment community. The framework is broadly similar to other countries; any shareholder acquiring more than 30 percent has to make a general offer to all shareholders at the same price, and once acceptances top 95 percent, that shareholder can compulsorily acquire the remainder.

The biggest remaining sticking point is hostile takeovers, and the use of 'poison pill' type defences to thwart them. Many investors wanted the right to shareholder consultation over bid defences enshrined in law. But company management can still put in place takeover defences with just the assent of the supervisory board (which, stacked with employee representatives fearful of job losses, would be only too keen to see hostile bids frustrated).

This is a highly political issue in Germany, as was demonstrated when Chancellor Schröder visited his old stomping ground in Lower Saxony early in 2002. 'Any efforts by the Commission in Brussels to smash the Volkswagen culture will meet the resistance of the federal government so long as we are in power,' he told car workers at VW's Kassel plant. The 'Volkswagen culture' he referred to is the blocking stake of the regional government, which makes the company immune to takeover. He justifies the resistance by claiming that golden shares and disproportionate voting rights are still in use in other countries. But the speech shows that stakeholders other than shareholders have real power in Germany, and they aren't about to prostrate themselves before the archbishops of shareholder value.

But the new law does plug many of the loopholes in the old regime. Dr Franz-Joerg Semler, a lawyer at CMS Hasche Sigle Eschenlohr Peltzer Scaffer, says that most of the people who opposed earlier takeover legislation and the proposed EU directive have fallen in behind the domestic law. He concedes that legal action based on technicalities may be increasingly used to thwart takeover bids – a common criticism of statutory regulation – but nevertheless believes that takeovers will be settled quicker and minority shareholders treated better. The abolition of capital gains tax on the disposal of corporate shareholdings, and the consolidation that is expected to trigger, will probably result in the new law being put to the test in 2002.

But small shareholder organizations were annoyed over the watering down of the poison pill provisions. 'Executive and advisory boards are being given carte blanche to put in place highly restrictive takeover defences for years, without any further agreement from shareholders,' said three leading organizations in a joint statement.

> **Box 3.1 Equity investment in Germany**
>
> **Stock market**
> The main marketplace is Deutsche Borse (www.deutsche-boerse.com) which operated the Frankfurt Stock Exchange and the Neuer Markt (www.deutsche-boerse.com.nm).
>
> **Clearing and settlement** is done through Clearstream International (www.clearstream.com).
>
> **Indices**
> The DAX30 is the blue chip index. The top 50 growth stocks are tracked by the Nemax 50 index.
>
> **The federal supervisor** is the Bundesaufsichtsamt für den Wertpapierhandel (BaWE, www.bawe.de), which controls company news disclosure and combats insider trading. The regional authorities are responsible for regulating banks and brokers.
>
> **Company news**
> Disclosure is through the Ad Hoc system (http://www.vwd.de/news/adhoc/main.html; many statements are in English). Ad Hoc is also available on the exchange's homepages.
>
> **Advocates for the small shareholders** include Deutsche Schutzvereinigung fur Wertpapierbesitz (DSW: www.dsw-info.de) and the Schutzgemeinschaft der Kleinaktionare (www.sdk.org). The Deutsche Aktieninstitut (www.dai.de) promotes equity ownership.

Government initiatives on corporate governance and takeover law indicate that the administration is keen to embrace shareholder capitalism – which it needs to deliver its pension and welfare reforms – while preserving the most cherished elements of the bank-based system. But there is still nobody to speak up for the rights of the shareholder. One healthy aspect of the increased interest in equity markets is the emergence of several bodies dedicated to rooting out bad governance and opaque disclosure, lobbying for better protection and if necessary pursuing the worst offenders through the courts.

TOP LISTINGS IN GERMANY

FINANCIALS – WANNABE CONSOLIDATORS

Germany's big banks have been trying to merge with each other for years. Thus far, the only big deal between two banks has been the merger of Hypothekenbank and Bayerische Vereinsbank to create Bayerische HypoVereinsbank, since renamed HVB Group.

Currently, the biggest player is Deutsche Bank (www.deutsche-bank.com), kingmaker in many a German deal by virtue of its web of industrial shareholdings. It has expanded heavily into investment banking, as all the big German banks have. Disagreements over the future of investment banking were the primary reason for the collapse of its proposed merger with Dresdner Bank (www.dresdner-bank.com) early in 2001. Dresdner has instead hitched up with Allianz, the insurer, in a deal that will make Allianz (www.allianz.com) the largest listed German company. Allianz owned 20 percent of Dresdner before the deal, and it will get more equity from Munich Re, another insurance firm, which is swapping its stake in Dresdner for Allianz's holding in HypoVereinsbank.

That leaves Commerzbank (www.commerzbank.com), the fourth largest listed bank, out of the party. It too has tried to merge with Dresdner, but the talks fell apart. The company is widely thought of as a takeover candidate, because it is considerably smaller than the other banks and because it has struggled to improve its profitability and control its costs. Many investors have been critical of the strategy of former chief executive Martin Kohlhaussen, who, after the collapse of the Dresdner talks, insisted the bank was viable as an independent player. The most likely outcome for Commerzbank now is that it will be taken over by a bigger European group looking for a presence in the German market. A number of suitors have been rumoured.

AUTOMAKERS – *VORSPRUNG DURCH* ACQUISITION

Is there any more potent symbol of Germany's manufacturing and engineering prowess than its mighty motor industry? Across the world, Mercedes and BMWs are renowned as superbly engineered luxury cars, while Volkswagen is perceived as one of the most solid and reliable middle-market cars available. In stock market terms, however, the motor manufacturers have a less sterling reputation.

DaimlerChrysler (www.daimlerchrysler.com) is the biggest of the three main manufacturers. Partly because of its 1998 merger with America's Chrysler, its shares are more widely held, although Deutsche Bank does still hold a considerable stake. Substantial shareholdings are a big feature of the other two. Bayerische Motorenwerke (BMW) (www.bmwgroup.com), based in Munich, is still heavily influenced by the Quandt family, which owns 46 percent of the shares, while some 18 percent of Volkswagen (www.vw.com) shares are held by the government of the state of Lower Saxony, where its manufacturing operations are based. Volkswagen has a poor reputation for disclosure and a disdain towards the equity market – there is a consensus that the company's top priority is looking out for the interests of its main shareholder. Bernd Pischetsrieder, the former head of BMW, was appointed chief executive in 2001.

An interesting feature of the industry is its misadventures in the field of mergers and acquisitions. Volkswagen has fared better than the other two, successfully turning around Spain's SEAT and Skoda of the Czech Republic. But BMW's ownership of Rover group, which it bought in 1994 for £1 billion and sold in 2000 for just £10 – having absorbed hundreds of millions of pounds of losses along the way – was a disaster that cost the company's chief executive his job.

That fate has not yet caught up with Juergen Schremmp, boss of DaimlerChrysler, although many would argue it should have. In 1998, DaimlerBenz unveiled a plan to merge with Chrysler, the smallest of the US's volume car makers. The logic was to give Chrysler luxury brands and a distribution and marketing foothold in Europe, while Daimler would get middle-market vehicles to complement its luxurious ranges. The significance of such an ambitious foray into the home of shareholder capitalism was not lost on corporate Germany, either. Two years later, the deal looked little else other than a disaster. The management styles of the two companies were poles apart. There was bitterness, there were recriminations and lawsuits. By the end of 2000 the combined company was worth less than DaimlerBenz alone had been worth before the deal. Schremmp had been outfoxed. Chrysler sold up because it knew that it could not afford the costs of developing new model ranges alone. Then it succeeded in securing a 'merger of equals' style deal, with all the compromises that implies, when a straightforward takeover would have been better.

CHEMICALS – DON'T MENTION THE WAR

Germany's big three chemicals companies, Bayer, BASF and Hoechst, were once one giant concern, and not a particularly pleasant one at that. IG Farben, formed in 1925, happily used slave labour during the Second World War and developed and manufactured Zyklon B, the poison gas used in the death camps of eastern Europe. Accusations and lawsuits dating from this era are still levelled at the three companies today.

Badische Anilin und Soda-Fabrik (www.basf.com) is how BASF started life, producing the synthetic dyes that would eventually replace more expensive organic ones. When IG Farben was broken up under the Potsdam Agreement after the war, BASF was reborn as an independent company and profited handsomely from demand for basic chemicals during the rebuilding of Germany. A string of acquisitions has given the group its current shape (with five divisions) and size – it is Europe's largest chemical company. One interesting feature is its *Verbund* strategy, whereby plants and divisions are suppliers and customers of other divisions within the company.

Bayer (www.bayer.com), founded by Friedrich Bayer in 1863, also had its origins in synthetic dyes and also played a role it would rather forget in the wartime IG Farben. After the war it branched out into plastics and polyurethanes and merged its Agfa photographic business with that of Belgium's Gevaert, only to buy back the combined business a few years later and subsequently spin off the unit into a separate company. These days, much of the company's big research-and-development spend goes into drugs and healthcare – Bayer invented aspirin and owns other leading over-the-counter brands like Alka-Seltzer.

DEUTSCHE TELEKOM'S EQUITY HANGOVER

There was much comment in the German press one week in September 2001, when, for the first time, the value of Deutsche Telekom's shares slipped below the price at which they had first been offered to the public in 1996 (*see* Fig. 3.2). It seemed to symbolize all that had gone wrong with Germany's equity market adventure.

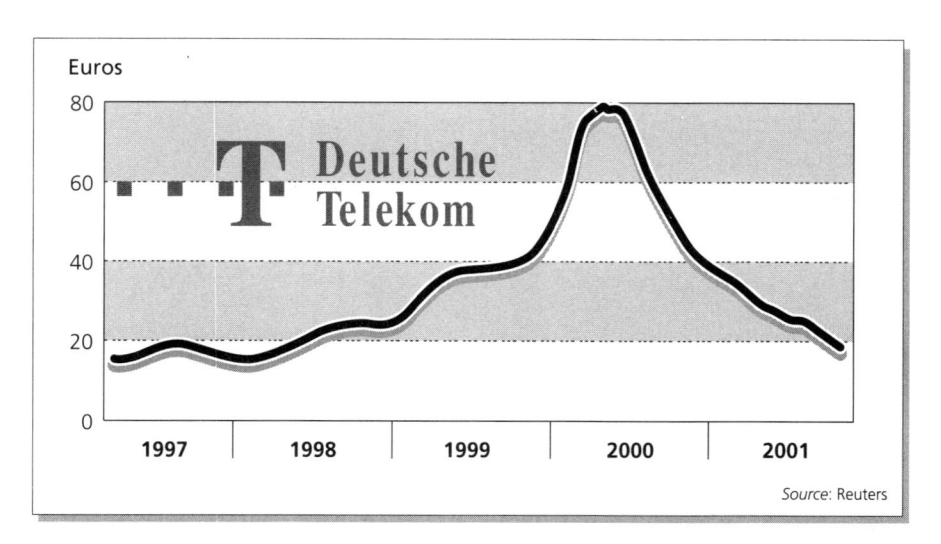

Figure 3.2 Deutsche Telekom share price

Telekom (www.telekom.de) attracts intense scrutiny precisely because it holds such a dominant place in the minds of German investors.

Investors have often not liked what they found, particularly concerning the valuation of the company's property holdings at the time of the initial public offering. But one of the main reasons for the collapse in Telekom's share price was its massive overhang of shares. Although three tranches have been offered to the public, companies and institutions still own huge blocks, and whenever these are released on to the market the price is depressed. So it was when Deutsche Bank placed out some of its holding, and the market is now bracing itself for shares owned by investors in Voicestream, a US phone company that was taken over by Telekom in 2000. Voicestream shareholders were paid in Telekom stock, and they have begun dumping it as the share price slid.

4

FRANCE

Shareholder value is the most important concern, but we try to temper a bit the adoration of shareholders.

Marc Vienot, former chairman of Société Générale

THE PARIS BOURSE BUILDING with its elegant neo-classical columns and sweeping stairs is now a museum after electronic share dealing rendered the building's trading floor redundant. But just a few yards away is Espace Bourse Wargny, a day trading centre where France's growing band of investors can key in their buy and sell orders for shares. It is visible proof that an equity culture is gaining ground in a country whose dirigiste economy was run for centuries by an all-powerful state and its servants, dating back to King Louis XIV and his finance minister Jean-Baptiste Colbert, who nationalized the tobacco industry.

The State still has sizeable, even controlling stakes in some of France's biggest listed companies like France Telecom, Air France, Thomson Multimedia, Renault and Crédit Lyonnais. But France also has a vibrant and international stock market – Europe's second largest after the UK. Foreign investors hold 36 percent of total French market capitalization (*see* Fig. 4.1), rising to more than half of the CAC 40, the French blue chip index of top 40 companies. Almost 10 million French citizens, or more than 20 percent of the population, own shares directly or indirectly. France's biggest companies have also become much more international in their outlook. Ten years ago global insurance giant Axa and telecoms equipment maker Alcatel were small, domestic-focused businesses. Vivendi Universal, one of the world's biggest media companies, grew out of a domestic utility. In 2000 it bought Canadian Seagram's Universal music and movie-making business for $34 billion, a deal of global proportions by anyone's standards.

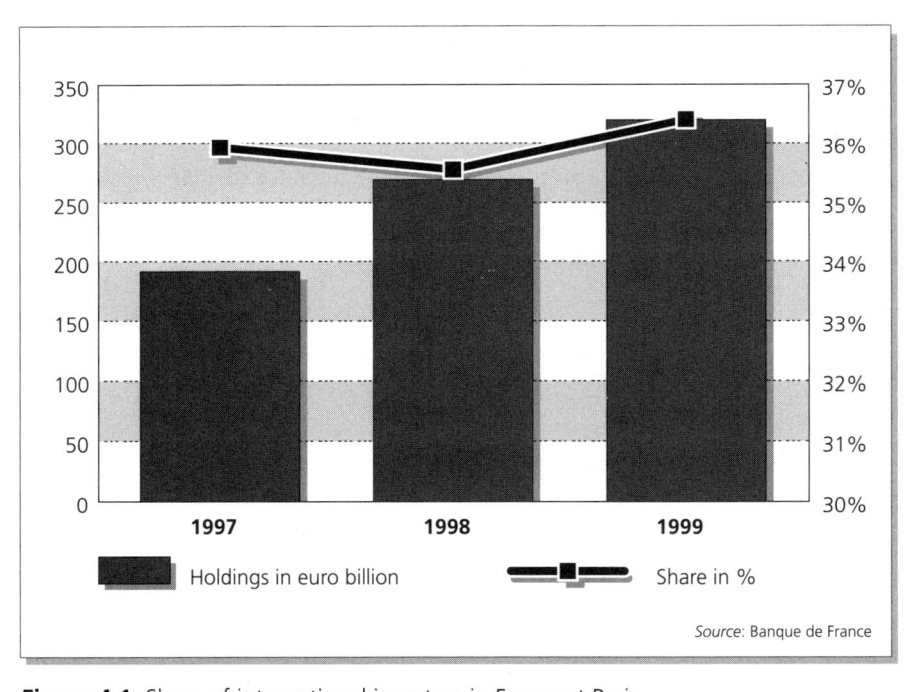

Figure 4.1 Share of international investors in Euronext Paris

But state ownership of key services, which have already been privatized in other countries, remain a feature of French everyday life. For instance, the two main utilities, Electricité de France (EdF) and Gaz de

France, are state-owned but also profitable. The State also owns the rail system, the nuclear industry, most of Air France, the national flag carrier, Paris airports and chunks of companies like carmaker Renault, and Crédit Lyonnais bank. But the French State is expected to continue scaling back its ownership of such key companies as its role comes under scrutiny. EdF's stake in Italy's privatized Montedison utility angered Italy. Critics accused EdF of having continued dominance of its domestic market while also being able to enter other markets by taking big slices of utilities elsewhere because those markets were more open.

Progress has also been made on creating a more favourable mindset towards equities. 'Shares have a much better image now, and the fact that many of the small investors are young is a sign of a change in culture,' said Arnaud de Bresson, who runs Paris-Europlace that promotes the French capital as a financial centre.

AMERICAN STYLE

The image of equities in France has been fashioned by some of the country's top bosses adopting a very American style of cultivating public profiles, more akin to the legendary Jack Welch, former head of US General Electric than the traditional, low-key continental European CEO.

Bernard Arnault, chairman of the LVMH, the world's top luxury goods group, is referred to as the wolf in cashmere clothing, though he was not cunning enough to outmanoeuvre France's richest man, retail tycoon François Pinault, from taking control of Italian luxury fashion house Gucci. The two tussled from early 1999 to late 2001 over who should control Gucci, taking the warring parties to a court in Amsterdam where Gucci is listed. Both sides in the handbag war later made efforts to resolve the dispute behind closed doors, giving Pinault control of Gucci and Arnault a fat cheque.

Vivendi boss Jean-Marie Messier is called J6M and *maître du monde*. Serge Tchuruk, head of telecom equipment maker Alcatel, is another example of France's newer breed of CEOs.

France is one of Europe's most diverse markets for investors, offering wide sector representation from technology, media, telecoms and pharmaceuticals to financials, industrials and consumer companies.

> **France is one of Europe's most diverse markets for investors, offering wide sector representation**

A traditionally high savings rate among the French could help underpin equities in future if the stock market's image improves further and the need to save for retirement grows. The nation's thrifty citizens save about 16 percent of their disposable income, though some economists argue that the high rate has partly been a result of the fear of being out of work as unemployment raced higher in the 1990s.

Between 1970 and 1998 household savings more than doubled, but the amount held in the form of shares is still small, between 12 and 17 percent of the total. As foreign investors continue to buy more shares in French companies, the percentage of domestic market capitalization held by the French had fallen to about 33 percent by 2001 from 48 percent at the end of 1995. 'The French do not invest enough in shares,' French fund management association AGF concluded in a report that came out in 2001. Europlace estimates that half of all small investors are young, with 80 percent trading online. France has about 400,000 online accounts, and more than 1 million online orders were executed in January 2001, or a fifth of all transactions on Euronext in Paris.

But only ten years ago when the longest stocks bull run on Wall Street was getting underway, it was all very different in France, a country where bonds ruled and shares were a distrusted sideshow.

MOVE OVER BOND

France's shift to an equity culture did not come about because of some sudden love affair with shares, but because of pure self-interest. During the 1990s it made sense to buy bonds because interest rates were high, but then two things prompted a shift into shares.

In the early 1990s interest rates across Europe began to converge and establish themselves at lower levels ahead of the euro single currency. Poorer gains from interest-rate linked bonds spurred institutional investors to move from money markets and into equities to look for higher returns. The second push to shares came in the late part of the decade when a wave of privatizations made chunks of well-known companies available for smaller investors. Strong economic growth in France after 1993 boosted corporate earnings and made shares in the companies more attractive. Also during the 1990s many companies, which has been burnt by the pricking of a real-estate bubble, began to clean up their balance sheets and focus on the core business to improve their performance. Unwinding the *noyeaux durs* or cross-holdings between companies unlocked big parcels of shares for the market.

'The French market was also cheap compared to other international markets and foreign investors knew this before the French investors did, which is why the part of foreign investors in the market is very high,' said Florent Brones, head of equity research at BNP Paribas in Paris. In a global equities bull market, it was also an easy way for French companies to raise money by going to the stock market rather than the traditional bank route. Rising share markets make it easier for companies to float or return to the market with a secondary issue.

A new law in 1998 made it easier tax-wise for companies to buy back some of their shares. This triggered a huge increase in shareholder-friendly buybacks, especially in the oil and banking companies.

The market capitalization of the Paris stock exchange grew dramatically to €1.54 trillion by 2000, equivalent to 110 percent of gross domestic product (GDP), compared with just 27 percent back in 1990 (*see* Fig. 4.2). French equities analysts would like to see the total rise to 150 percent of GDP and in line with US levels. 'Dirigisme is not completely dead but it's changing. The market is really becoming much more influential than any dirigisme as the civil servants lose influence,' said one senior Paris banker. 'Everyone has finally understood it's the market that is leading and not the Government.'

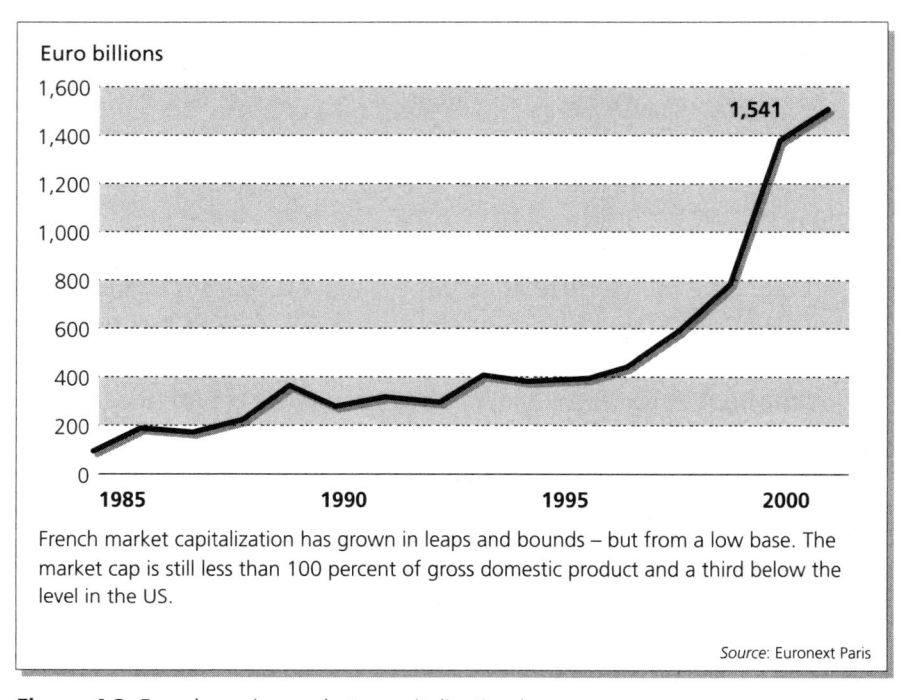

> Euro billions
>
> 1,541
>
> 1985　1990　1995　2000
>
> French market capitalization has grown in leaps and bounds – but from a low base. The market cap is still less than 100 percent of gross domestic product and a third below the level in the US.
>
> *Source:* Euronext Paris

Figure 4.2 French equity markets: capitalization leaps

Echoes of dirigisme came to the fore in the three-way merger attempts by Banque Nationale de Paris (BNP), Paribas and Société Générale which critics say highlighted the Government's unease of the market determining changes in corporate control. In the tussle, BNP grabbed rival Banque Paribas from under the nose of Société Générale. BNP's plan in 1999 to buy Paribas and Société Générale to create the world's first trillion-dollar bank failed, because Société Générale shareholders played hard to get. 'Foreign bidders were also discouraged informally, as the French government preferred consolidation over European integration in financial services,' Deutsche Börse CEO Werner Seifert and a group of academics and consultants wrote.

One key problem for the French market is the lack of pension funds that provide such huge pools of money for stock markets in the Netherlands, the UK and the US (*see* Fig. 4.3). France is strong in funds, but they mainly hold their assets in government bonds, and only a small portion of their holdings have been diverted to equities. Still, over half the money flowing into life assurance companies is now finding its way into the stock market or to products linked to stocks.

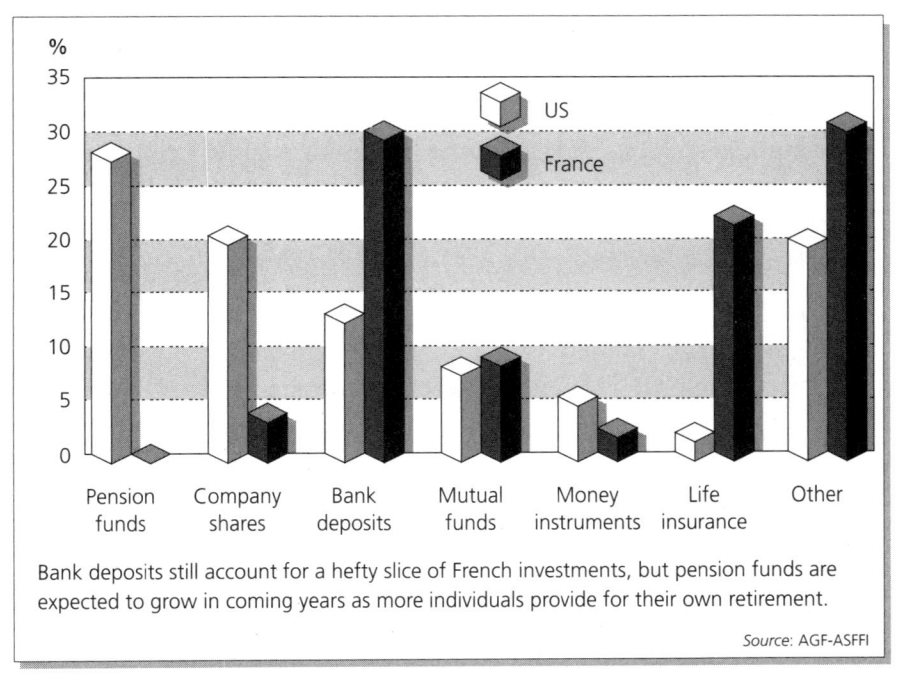

[Chart showing breakdown of investments in France and the US across categories: Pension funds, Company shares, Bank deposits, Mutual funds, Money instruments, Life insurance, Other. Y-axis in %, ranging 0-35. Legend indicates US and France.]

Bank deposits still account for a hefty slice of French investments, but pension funds are expected to grow in coming years as more individuals provide for their own retirement.

Source: AGF-ASFFI

Figure 4.3 Breakdown of investments in France and the US 2000

Many of France's big listed companies also encourage employees to own shares in their company, and around 3 percent of the CAC 40 market capitalization is held in employee stock plans. Buying a company's shares helps to demystify equities and spread knowledge about the stock market to ordinary people, so fostering a deeper equity culture. For example, the typical employee of Société Générale bank holds about 400,000 francs worth of stock in the company. But stocks remain a bit of a mystery to the older generation, which prefers state bonds to shares. It is the younger people, who dominate online share trading in France, who are the real hope for building an equity culture.

The French Government has also been taking steps to encourage investors to buy shares. In 2001 the Government was proposing a more favourable tax treatment of the Plan d'Epargne en Action (PEA), a savings scheme which invests in shares. When PEAs were first introduced in 1992 there were 2 million with €10 billion under management. There are now over 6 million active PEA accounts, holding assets worth nearly €100 billion. The Government was planning to allow investors to buy any European and not just French shares under the savings scheme, to raise the investment ceiling for the product, and to make growth stock funds eligible for investment. 'As the savings rate remains at a very high level, the equity culture currently being developed is unlikely to be undermined,' said equity analyst Alain Bokobza of Société Générale in Paris.

Not surprisingly, the 2000–1 sharp global pullback in stocks, led by the technology-laden Nasdaq in the US, slowed the push towards a broader equity culture in France. Lingering distrust of equities was also evident in skirmishes between companies and politicians over issuing stock options to loyal employees. France Telecom has blamed government opposition for its decision not to offer stock options in the state-controlled company to staff. Companies are still trying to educate lower levels of staff that stock options are not a lottery simply for top bosses.

> **Companies are still trying to educate lower levels of staff that stock options are not a lottery simply for top bosses**

During the huge new economy shares boom that ended in March 2000, younger people left safe jobs in French government administration or with big companies to start up their own business. But the technology crash sent them back to their old jobs as many of those new start-ups in the internet sector crashed. Such start-ups are a typical part of the economic cycle in Anglo-Saxon style economies, but were a new phenomenon in France and some initial, harsh lessons were learned.

Despite these problems, the French mentality toward shares is shifting from distrust to a more European outlook based on Anglo-Saxon underpinnings of shareholder value and more transparent ways of running companies and corporate governance.

CORPORATE GOVERNANCE – *JE VOUS AI COMPRIS?*

French political warhorse General de Gaulle once ambiguously said in a famous speech in Algeria, 'Je vous ai compris' – I have understood you. France's top bosses now say the same thing to their shareholders, but just as it was with de Gaulle, there remains some ambiguity as to how far the country's corporate rules want to go to please investors.

French corporate governance has come a long way in a short time, however. Many of today's standard practices stem from the two reports published in 1995 and 1999 by Marc Vienot, former chairman of the bank Société Générale and now a board member of five French companies – the maximum recommended in his reports. As Vienot said:

> When we published the first report, nobody believed in it. But the pressure of the market would pressure the companies to follow the recommendations, especially the companies in the CAC 40. There are things to be improved, but the atmosphere in board meetings now is quite different. We have more meetings and people feel more responsible to shareholders.

France is now ahead of continental rival Germany in terms of corporate governance, and closing in on the UK, seen as the European benchmark. Most top companies have appointed independent directors, and bosses' pay is increasingly vetted by committees that are dominated by the non-executive directors. However, with around 40 percent of French stock market capitalization held by foreigners, non-French directors are generally still thin on the ground. Some of the corporate governance recommendations contained in Vienot's two reports remain voluntary, but companies are adopting them – though some more so than others. Many French companies still have too few or no independent directors on their boards compared to Anglo-Saxon peers.

Oddball corporate set-ups are becoming rarer. For example, Michelin, the world's biggest tyre maker is a member of the elite CAC 40 blue chip group, yet it is still effectively run by the Michelin family even if it does not own most of the shares. Recruitment firm Korn/Ferry reported that Michelin was the only CAC 40 constituent that has shown little regard to the Vienot reports. Michelin boss Edouard Michelin is known as *l'americain* inside the company, but for many investors the tyre maker's corporate governance is still too far removed from the American model that many shareholders want European firms to copy. However, Michelin is rapidly becoming the exception among France's leading companies rather than the norm it would have been maybe five to ten years ago.

Other recommendations included in the second Vienot report were that companies should state in their annual reports how much their top officials have been paid, and also disclose any stock-option or stock-purchase plans. In July 2001 the French Parliament agreed to the bill of *nouvelles regulations economiques* – a range of measures drawn from the second Vienot report to tighten up procedures in corporate takeover battles and make company bosses more accountable. Some 75 percent of companies in the CAC 40 French index have a single board of directors, with the chief executive and chairman the same person. A Vienot recommendation passed into law by the *nouvelles regulations* gives single-board companies permission to separate the duties of chairman and chief executive officer. Only a quarter of the CAC 40 companies have a supervisory and an administrative board, but the trend is in this direction. Companies are also now under pressure to spell out in their annual reports how they comply with the recommendations in the two Vienot reports and why any of those recommendations have not been followed.

With foreign investors accounting for such a big slice of French market capitalization, more international companies are feeling the heat from their big foreign investors, like the American funds, to improve corporate governance. A study by Korn/Ferry showed that 97 percent of the CAC 40 companies now comply with local recommendations in the two Vienot reports on corporate governance. Back in 1995, only 37 percent of companies observed the corporate governance recommendations.

Shareholder value is also becoming more defined, but Marc Vienot, like many senior financial figures in other continental European countries, questions to what extent the Anglo-Saxon model of shareholder dominance should be copied:

Shareholder value is the most important concern, but we try not to forget the other competences of the company. We try to temper a bit the adoration of shareholders – they are important in the game but they are not the only actors. Should we comply totally with the Anglo-Saxon model of shareholder value before anything else?

Some key problems in corporate governance still remain, particularly the concern among shareholders that one share does not always mean one vote as it does in the Anglo-Saxon corporate world. Because of a 1960s corporate law, companies are allowed to distribute voting rights among shareholders on a less-than-equal basis – widely seen as a de facto 'poison pill' mechanism to thwart hostile takeover bids. Oil company Totalfina's successful takeover of rival Elf Aquitaine, which had a clause limiting votes, is seen by some as proof that hostile bids can still succeed.

Most of France's blue chips have the right to give more votes to some shareholders than to others. For example, in 2000 Société Générale bank put a 15-percent lid on the votes of any of its shareholders. There is certainly still some way to go in France to ensure that one share equals one vote.

France also has the practice of double votes, whereby if an investor holds a share for two years or more, it can count for two votes instead of just one or none at all. This option is used by more than half of the CAC 40 companies as a way of rewarding loyal shareholders, but critics call the facility a hidden anti-takeover poison pill.

Thus although there is a gradual elimination on the voting limits and other anti-takeover devices that companies use, for some international investors more progress is still needed.

MANNING THE BARRICADES: SHAREHOLDER ACTIVISM

Shareholders who own minority stakes in companies are taking up the cudgels with firms that ride roughshod over them. The investor lobby group Adam, or Association pour la Défense des Actionnaires

Minoritaires and corporate governance consultancy Deminor (www.deminor.com) are among those groups that act on behalf of institutional investors in France.

Adam successfully intervened in the €7.9 billion friendly takeover bid by Schneider Electric in 2000 for rival domestic low voltage equipment maker Legrand. Instead of ordinary shares, some of Legrand's shareholders held preference shares that are eligible for an additional dividend because they bear no voting rights. Schneider offered these preference shareholders a much smaller premium for their shares than the premium it offered to Legrand's ordinary shareholders. Angered, the preference shareholders, many of them institutions, hit back, deploying Adam to take their case to the Paris Appeals Court, and in a rare move the judge annulled a decision by the Conseil des Marches Financiers (CMF) market regulator to approve the bid. This forced Schneider to extend the offer deadline and gave it little choice but to improve the terms.

An embarrassed CMF then had to ensure that Schneider gave better terms to holders of preferred shares in Legrand. The revised offer valued the preferred shares at a 20-percent discount to the common shares, compared with a 43-percent discount seen in the original offer. The better terms cost Schneider an extra €200 million. Adam had argued in court that in a similar case – retail giant Carrefour's offer for domestic peer Promodes – there was only a 16-percent discount compared with the ordinary shares.

Forcing Schneider to make a better offer to Legrand's preferred shares owners marked a significant coup for minority shareholders across Europe, who are developing a growing confidence and expertise in tackling unfair treatment. Legrand's initially blinkered view was almost certainly due to having a board of directors stuffed with family members and with no outside directors. In the event, it didn't matter – in October 2001 the European Union vetoed the merger, saying the combination would be too dominant in the market.

Another example of successful shareholder pressure was when utilities giant Suez had to withdraw its €53 billion takeover bid for Air Liquide. Normally, shares in the company being taken over jump on

> The problem is not so much the lack of modern corporate governance rules but ensuring that companies pay attention to them

news of a takeover bid, but Air Liquide's stock dropped sharply when the bid was made public, because shareholders in the company believed a merger made no industrial sense. After Suez retreated, Air Liquide's shares rose again on investor relief that Suez's bid had failed.

Colette Neuville, the doughty head of Adam shareholders group, has said the problem in France is not so much the lack of enlightened and modern corporate governance rules but ensuring that companies pay attention to them:

> It's not so much the existence of preference shares or double votes, but the poor application of the laws. The Vienot rules are not sufficient but are a step in the right direction. The problem is how to ensure that the company boards carry out their responsibilities and it's almost impossible to force them to do this.

The French economy has made the transition from dirigisme of the old days to a market economy, but Neuville believes the country's legal mindset is still steeped in dirigisme, which makes the costly and time-consuming process of taking companies or their directors to court even more difficult:

> There is a problem with the functioning of the legal system, with delays in the process too long, as nobody wants to open a case that lasts for five years. The judges have also not reached a stage where they consider that company directors have responsibilities. You never get any big fines in these matters.

EURONEXT – A TALE OF FOUR CITIES

Euronext is Europe's first successful attempt to consolidate the region's plethora of national stock exchanges. These have flourished in the wake of the euro, which has encouraged the buying and selling of shares from across the region, often by industry group rather than along national lines. The Paris Bourse, Amsterdam exchanges and the Brussels exchanges announced in March 2000 they would join together to form Euronext, which became a fully-merged exchange in September 2000. In 2002, the Lisbon stock exchange merged with Euronext.

Euronext was a defensive move by Paris at a time when euro-zone arch-rival Deutsche Börse in Frankfurt and the London Stock Exchange were in the throes of merging themselves. Brussels was too weak to continue on its own and Amsterdam needed a bigger partner too. A Paris–Amsterdam merger also made good business sense because Paris is strong in equities but its derivatives business failed to take European markets by storm. In contrast, Amsterdam has a flourishing derivatives market but its equity business is still small by European standards, even though the country has a mature equity culture. Paris also wanted to press ahead with a European project because it was miffed after the Deutsche Börse jilted the French exchange and turned its attention to London. However, the Frankfurt exchange failed there too and the Anglo-German plan to create iX was unceremoniously buried around the same time that Euronext was officially born.

Euronext's chief executive Jean-François Theodore has made no secret of his wish to see Euronext and London merge to create a European superbourse. Euronext became a publicly traded company in July 2001 by listing on its own market, raising a decent warchest for acquiring or merging with another exchange.

Euronext is Europe's second largest stock exchange after London. It has a market capitalization of over €2.4 trillion and over 1,600 companies listed on it. Paris is the dominant partner, gaining 60 percent of the Euronext holding company that is registered in the Netherlands. Amsterdam exchanges hold a 32-percent stake, while Brussels was given a meagre 6 percent.

Euronext uses Paris' NSC technology as its trading platform. By the end of October 2001, the Amsterdam, Brussels and Paris equities markets had integrated on to the same trading system, making it Europe's first exchange allowing investors to trade cash equities from three countries on a single platform. Brokers and other stock-market intermediaries only need one access point to trade shares from all three countries. Euronext has also signed cross-membership agreements with the Luxembourg stock exchange and with the Helsinki stock exchange. Such links allow for two-way access to trade listings on each other's platforms, helping to cut costs.

The back office clearing and settlement functions from all three countries have also been streamlined. Paris' Clearnet provides clearing and a central counterparty – a system that guarantees that trades are completed and everything is done anonymously, so neither side of the trade nor other players in the market know each other. Settlement is centred on Euroclear in Brussels. French settler Sicovam was merged with Euroclear, and the Dutch Negicef and Belgian CIK settlement houses will also be merged with Euroclear by 2003. All clearing and settlement is done electronically with no paper certificates. Stock market regulators in Paris, Belgium and the Netherlands have also signed a memorandum of understanding to forge a common approach to Euronext.

The three national blue chip indices, France's CAC 40, the Dutch AEX and Belgium's Bel 20 have been retained, but a new set of Euronext indices were launched too. France's Nouveau Marche (www.nouveau-marche.fr) segment for growth companies is among the largest of its kind on the continent after Germany's Neuer Markt and Italy's Nuovo Mercato. Euronext has also created the Next Economy market segment that will include all the growth stocks from Amsterdam, Brussels and Paris. Its listings will comply with standards such as quarterly reporting – including an English language version that conforms to International Accounting Standards.

Euronext admits new members, defines listing requirements, lists and suspends companies, defines the market's operating rules, and organizes trading and records transactions. It also calculates the main CAC 40 benchmark.

TOP LISTINGS IN FRANCE

TOTALFINAELF
www.totalfinaelf.com

An oil and gas company with oil reserves in the Middle East. Created by Total's acquisition of Belgium's PetroFina in 1999 and Elf Aquitaine of France a year later. The company has upstream exploration and downstream refining and service station operations.

VIVENDI UNIVERSAL
www.vivendiuniversal.com

A tale of a 150-year-old Compagnie Générale des Eaux utility which has turned itself into a global media giant by acquiring Canada's Seagram, the owner of Universal Music Group and Universal Studios. It also owns Canal+, the French pay-TV provider. Vivendi is headed by Jean-Marie Messier. It is the world's second-largest media company after AOL Time Warner.

AVENTIS
www.aventis.com

Created by the merger in 1999 of France's Rhône-Poulenc and Germany's Hoechst. The company, now one of the largest drug firms in the world, has some 80 percent of its operations in pharmaceuticals, with about a third of this sector's sales in the US. The rest of the business is in agricultural research, but Aventis has announced plans to divest CropScience and Animal Nutrition businesses, along with other non-core units.

FRANCE TELECOM
www.francetelecom.fr

Dating back to 1851, it provides local, long-distance and international calling services, wireless phone services and data transmission. A former monopoly, the company is still 54-percent owned by the French Government after it sold an initial 20-percent chunk in 1997. The company owns UK mobile-phone operator Orange. France Telecom also controls Equant, which provides international data and voice services to business customers.

AXA
www.axa.com

One of the world's largest insurance companies. It also has reinsurance, investment, banking and real-estate management activities spanning Europe, the US, Canada and South-East Asia.

L'ORÉAL
www.loreal.com

The world's biggest cosmetics company, owning brands like Laboratoires Garnier, Maybelline and Lancôme. The founder's daughter, Liliane Bettencourt, and her family own just over half of Gesparal, a holding company that owns 54 percent of L'Oréal. The company has a minority stake in French drugs company Sanofi-Synthelabo.

BNP PARIBAS
www.bnpparibas.com

France's biggest bank since Banque Nationale de Paris grabbed rival Banque Paribas from under the nose of Société Générale. BNP was privatized in 1993, setting it free to extend its operations to New Zealand, Brazil and the US. BNP's plan in 1999 to buy Paribas and Société Générale, to create the world's first trillion-dollar bank, failed because Société Générale shareholders played hard to get.

CARREFOUR
www.carrefour.com

Europe's biggest retailer and the creator of hypermarkets. It operates across 27 countries under many names. It has many stores in Latin America and Asia. Carrefour become the world's second largest retailer, after Wal-Mart of the US, following its acquisition of French rival Promodes for $16 billion in 1999. It opened its first shop in Japan in 2001.

SUEZ
www.suez.fr

Formerly called Suez Lyonnaise des Eaux, it was created by the 1997 merger of Compagnie de Suez and Lyonnaise des Eaux. The conglomerate focuses on water services, waste treatment and energy. It owns Belgium's Tractebel energy company. The company has been expanding outside its French and Belgian bases and has bought US water treatment operations. The founding Suez company built the Suez canal in Egypt under Napoleon in the nineteenth century.

STMICROELECTRONICS
www.st.com

One of Europe's biggest computer chip makers. It makes memory chips and many different types of circuits used in communications, computers and consumer electronics. It supplies components to Nokia, Sony, Bosch and Nortel Networks. Over half its sales are generated outside Europe. France Telecom has a minority share of ST, along with Italian aerospace company Finmeccanica.

SOCIÉTÉ GÉNÉRALE
www.socgen.com

Privatized in 1987, Société Générale, or SocGen as it is often known, has tried to build an international presence ever since. A planned friendly merger with domestic peer Paribas collapsed after a third player, Banque Nationale de Paris, stepped in to try and merge all three. This also failed, but BNP was left with Paribas in the bag and Société Générale chose to stay out in the cold. It has a strategic alliance with Spain's Banco Santander Central Hispano. It has also acquired units in Germany and the US.

SANOFI SYNTHELABO
www.sanofi-synthelabo.fr

Created by the merger of two French drugs firms, Sanofi and Synthelabo in 1999. French oil group TotalFinaElf has a stake of around 30 percent, while cosmetics group L'Oréal has a smaller share.

LVMH
www.lvmh.com

The luxury goods group Louis Vuitton Moët Hennessy is 48-percent owned by one of France's most colourful finaciers, billionaire Bernard Arnault. LVMH owns brands such as Givenchy, luxury watch maker Ebel, and champagne names like Moët & Chandon and Dom Perignon. It has a minority stake in Italian luxury goods group Gucci, although it lost out after French conglomerate Pinault-Printemps-Redoute snapped up a big chunk of Amsterdam-listed Gucci, triggering a legal battle in the Dutch courts. LVMH sales are spread throughout the world.

ALCATEL
www.alcatel.com

An international company whose core business includes telecommunications, railroad and energy transportation systems. The group's cable subsidiary is the largest producer of power transmission cables in the world. Alcatel CEO, Serge Tchuruk, is considered to be one of France's leading corporate figures, although his reputation was dented in 2001 as the company failed to take over troubled US rival Lucent's fibre optics business, and Alcatel was forced into a restructuring amid falling global demand for telecom equipment.

Box 4.1 Equity investment in France

Stock exchange

Euronext (www.euronext.com), created by merger of the Paris Bourse, Amsterdam exchanges and Brussels exchanges in September 2000. Merged with Lisbon and Oporto Exchange in 2002.

Clearing and central counterparty

Clearnet, owned by Euronext.

Settlement

Euroclear Sicovam, part of Euroclear Group.

Regulation

Conseil des Marches Financiers (CMF) (www.cmf-france.org), founded in 1996 – the supervisory body for all financial markets in France. It defines rules for securities houses and banks, oversees the placement of new listings, and approves general principles for the organization of equities. It has a mandate to protect investors and ensure orderly transactions. It also regulates takeovers. The French Government plans to merge CMF, Commission des Opérations de Bourse and asset manager supervisory body Commission de Discipline de la Gestion Financière into a single super watchdog called the Autorité des Marches Financiers, akin to the US regulator Securities and Exchange Commission (SEC) or Britain's Financial Services Authority (FSA). The Commission des Opérations de Bourse (COB) (www.cob.fr) was founded in 1967 and has broad powers to probe, fine and verify information published by listed companies. It also investigates complaints from the public.

In spring 2002, COB and CMF were looking to update their takeover code for French companies to avoid a repeat of the embarrassing tussle seen during the failed three-way banking merger moves in 1999. Following a consultation with the market, one of the key changes eyed would be to force bidders to give far more detail of their bids from the outset to improve transparency, so that all investors have as much information as possible. In the past, details of a bid were not revealed to the public until the deal had been cleared by the CMF, a process that could take several weeks. A crackdown on poison pills was also expected.

Shareholders' group

E-mail adam.bp.208.chartres@wanadoo.fr.

5

BENELUX

THE NETHERLANDS – PUNCHING ABOVE ITS WEIGHT

The basis for shareholder activism is still the Anglo-Saxon winds that have blown over Europe, and they reached the Netherlands first because it's an internationally focused country.
Peter Paul de Vries of the shareholders' lobby group VEB

WORLD ONLINE, THE INTERNET SERVICE PROVIDER that floated in March 2000 amid much fanfare, only to crash shortly afterwards and leave a trail of burnt investors, was a sobering experience for small investors in the Netherlands. The dot bomb's impact was all the more shocking because the country's equity culture and stock market are among the most developed anywhere, though investors on both sides of the Atlantic were having to come to terms with tumbling new economy shares.

The Netherlands has the world's oldest stock exchange, set up in Amsterdam at the start of the seventeenth century with the Dutch United East India Company, the world's first firm to raise cash by issuing shares to the public. The Dutch success story in equities has been based on an open, liberal economy. It is home to some of the world best-known companies, like Philips, Royal Dutch/Shell and Unilever, which have attracted international investors in droves for many years. But World Online, and recent problems with high-profile companies like KPN, the telecoms group, and United Pan-European Communications, as well as clashes over corporate governance, have underscored the need for further improvements.

NOT TOO TAXING

The equity culture in the Netherlands was given a big lift by the 1988 privatization of the chemical company DSM, and later privatization of the telephone operator KPN in 1994. The stock market also benefited from a tax system that favoured shares over bonds. Bonds were also becoming less attractive as yields fell while interest rates in Europe began converging ahead of the euro's launch. Investors who took their dividends in the form of more stock, rather than cash, paid no tax. But the Government has recently moved to ensure that shares and bonds are treated equally by the tax man.

ABN Amro bank estimates there are 600,000 small investors in the Netherlands who have bought shares directly, and that 150,000 of those, or 10 percent of the population, are active (*see* Fig. 5.1). Many of the Dutch listed blue chips earn half or more of their income from outside the country, which has helped to shape how companies operate. The Netherlands places no major obstacles to direct foreign investment. According to Jelle Mensonides, investment director at Algemeen Burgerlijk Pensioenfonds (ABP), a large pension fund: 'We were dominated in the past by multinationals like Shell, Unilever and Philips, and they brought in the Anglo-Saxon corporate culture here, which we are now more familiar with than say Germany or France are.' The Netherlands long-standing tradition as an international trading-based economy has also made it receptive to US and UK style corporate rules, but with some notable exceptions like its two-tier board structure.

Number of households × 1,000

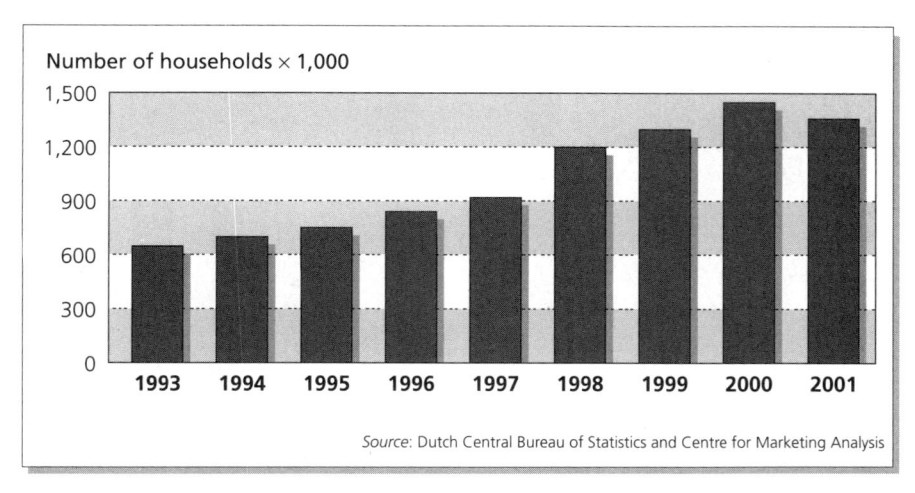

[Bar chart showing values approximately: 1993: 650, 1994: 700, 1995: 760, 1996: 840, 1997: 910, 1998: 1200, 1999: 1280, 2000: 1430, 2001: 1380]

Source: Dutch Central Bureau of Statistics and Centre for Marketing Analysis

Figure 5.1 Securities investors in the Netherlands

The presence of such international companies and a relatively developed equity culture has allowed the Dutch market to punch above its weight for many years, despite having a population of only 15.8 million (see Fig. 5.2). 'It served as a proxy to invest in Europe – the first stop was the Netherlands for US investors,' explains Jan de Ruiter, managing director of ABN-AMRO Rothschild, part of the Netherland's biggest bank, ABN AMRO. Dutch stock market capitalization reached a peak of 150 per cent of the country's gross domestic product, a ratio similar to the US, whereas most continental European countries are around 100 per cent or below. But according to de Ruiter: 'This phenomenon is gradually disappearing as France, Germany and Italy develop an equity culture, and their markets become more liquid and more in keeping with the size of their economies.'

Many of Holland's biggest companies are actively traded in the US on the New York Stock Exchange. Worries surface from time to time that the bulk of trading in the multinationals will shift to New York. These concerns have proved unfounded so far, but having two centres of active trading in the same company gives rise to arbitrage, whereby traders exploit the differences in prices between the two listings.

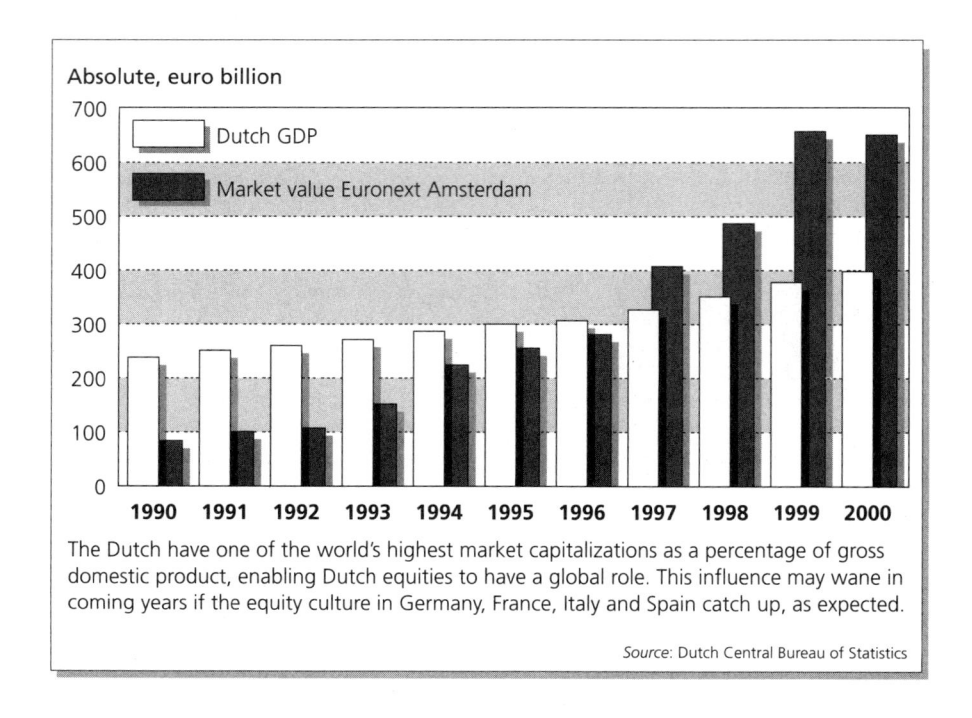

> Absolute, euro billion
>
> [Bar chart comparing Dutch GDP and Market value Euronext Amsterdam from 1990 to 2000, values ranging from 0 to 700 euro billion]
>
> The Dutch have one of the world's highest market capitalizations as a percentage of gross domestic product, enabling Dutch equities to have a global role. This influence may wane in coming years if the equity culture in Germany, France, Italy and Spain catch up, as expected.
>
> Source: Dutch Central Bureau of Statistics

Figure 5.2 Dutch GDP versus market value of Dutch shares

FULLY-FUNDED

The role of large pension funds that invest in shares has helped the Netherlands to develop a liquid stock market and a more advanced equity culture than Germany, Italy and France where there is no real pension fund industry. The Netherlands is one of the few countries in Europe where pension provision is fully funded. Huge pension funds like ABP and PGGM have became too big for the Dutch market to offer enough investment opportunities, and so they must diversify their investments across many markets in Europe and the US.

ABP, the world's second largest pension fund, has scaled back dramatically its investments in Dutch shares. Until 1987, Dutch funds had to invest every guilder in domestic listings but the euro zone created one enlarged 'home' market. ABP, which has a portfolio worth €150 billion with 40 percent in equities, now invests only between 5 and 8 percent of its equity investments in the Dutch market, the rest going into foreign companies. As ABP's Mensonides has said: 'Dutch pension funds have a very international orientation, so what you saw with the introduction of the euro was that a number of funds have now made the reallocation towards Europe instead of focusing on the Netherlands.'

But it is also a case of swings and roundabouts for Dutch shares, just as it is for all markets in the single currency area. Mutual and pension funds elsewhere in the euro zone have also scaled back their national exposure and topped up on shares from neighbouring countries, with Dutch blue chips like Royal Dutch/Shell or Philips a staple for many of their investment portfolios.

WATCHDOG TOO WEAK?

Investors worry that Dutch market regulation is not strong enough. There have been persistent complaints, especially from the shareholders' lobby group Vereniging van Effectenbezitters (VEB) that the Dutch securities watchdog Stichting Toezicht Effectenverkeer (STE) was too feeble and unable to tackle insider trading properly.

Some commentators see insider trading as a particular problem in the Netherlands. For example, in 2000 the STE was probing former Philips chairman, Cor Boonstra, for suspected insider trading. Another example of apparent watchdog weakness was the once highflying Dutch software house Baan that fell to earth after it was forced to restate its accounts. But it was the US regulator Securities and Exchange Commission, and not the STE, that initially forced Baan – which was also listed in the US – to present accurate accounts.

The STE has gradually taken on more supervisory powers from the Amsterdam exchange as the bourse merged with exchanges in Paris and Brussels to form Euronext. Investors now have to tell STE if they hold more than 5 percent of a company. But STE has shown little appetite for acquiring more substantial powers that would turn it into a Dutch copy of the US super-watchdog Securities and Exchange Commission, even though stiffer powers have clearly been needed at times.

Finally, in March 2002, the STE was renamed the Netherlands Authority for the Financial Markets and armed with broader powers that were taken from the Dutch central bank (consumer credit). The enlarged body will also be responsible for investment funds, making it a more all-encompassing supervisor like the UK's Financial Services Authority. But time will tell if the beefed up Dutch watchdog will use its bigger teeth more effectively.

World Online – now owned by Italy's Tiscali – also caught Dutch regulators and the Amsterdam stock exchange on the hop. World Online managing director Nina Brink sold most of her shares in the company three months before it went public, and at a fraction of the offer price. Small investors were furious, alleging the initial public offering (IPO) prospectus had been misleading about the sale of Brink's shares. Brink said she did not even read the prospectus until the month of the launch. The Dutch public prosecutor later cleared Brink of suspicion of criminal wrongdoing in the IPO. Three civil cases against World Online and its bankers, ABN AMRO, Goldman Sachs, were filed, but it is still difficult to present a watertight case that conclusively links the drop in World Online shares to the prospectus, since this was a time when the global internet sector was crashing.

> World Online played a symbolic role in denting Dutch small-investor confidence in new-economy shares

Whatever the rights and wrongs of World Online, it played a symbolic role in denting Dutch small-investor confidence in new-economy shares. 'We had the introduction of World Online in the Netherlands which was a real disaster. There were lessons to be learned there,' Mensonides said. 'The regulator has seen some lessons there too.'

Membership of the Dutch shareholders' lobby group VEB surged from 7,500 to nearly 30,000 in 2000, as small investors lined up to sue World Online. VEB is generally seen as being well organized and acting effectively on behalf of small investors, though some critics feel the lobby group puts too much emphasis on shareholder demands that can be short-sighted.

After the collapse of World Online, the Dutch finance ministry unveiled tighter controls for listing new companies, including stiffer rules on disclosing financial information and closer monitoring of the so-called grey market where shares of soon-to-be-floated companies are given a preliminary value.

CORPORATE GOVERNANCE – A MIXED BAG

Corporate governance in the Netherlands took a leap forward after a report headed by former Aegon chairman Jaap Peters in 1996. The report looked at the openness of companies, or transparency, as well as accountability to shareholders, and made about 40 recommendations, most of them implemented. According to Peter Paul de Vries, director of VEB:

> The weak recommendations have been followed, but the ones that give influence to shareholders have not been followed. The basic principles for good share trading is that shareholders have voting rights and a reasonable position within a company, that the company sets clear objectives and provides good information to shareholders. In all these elements, a lot of work has to be done.

For example, VEB said that in 2000 some 40 percent of Dutch companies listed on the Amsterdam bourse still do not report on a quarterly basis.

Dutch corporate governance is a mix of Anglo-Saxon and continental European models, but is less strict than in the US or the UK. Dutch companies have a two-tier board – the supervisory board oversees and advises the management board. What many companies find uncomfortable is that the supervisory board chooses its own members, but this is likely to change to give shareholders more influence in appointing new supervisory board members. Mensonides of ABP explains:

> Shareholder protection is a little bit debatable because of the supervisory board, but companies are more and more aware of shareholder value and work according to that. The bad news is there are still some companies where the supervisory board and management board neglect shareholders, but that is being reflected in the share price. Most of these sort of companies are domestic-oriented and a number of them will be taken over.

A classic example of this was in 2001 when Dutch construction company Hollandsche Beton Group (HBG) repeatedly spurned a fat takeover bid from rivals Heijmans and Boskalis. Even though HBG's shareholders liked the initial offer, HBG looked for ways to thwart it. Shareholder lobby group VEB was able to convince a court to stop HBG's spoiling tactic of setting up a joint venture with another company, Ballast Nedam. The court also forced HBG to open talks with Heijmans. This battle was seen as a key test of just how committed the Dutch were to building a more shareholder-friendly Anglo-Saxon style of corporate governance. Following the HBG episode, politicians debated if tougher rules were needed to ensure companies respect shareholder wishes.

Another thorny topic for shareholders is the Dutch fondness for holding stocks with administration or trust offices, which issue certificates to investors that bear no voting rights. There are a substantial number of large blocks of shares held by such administration offices that are often controlled by boards of the companies the offices hold, creating a situation ripe for conflicts of interest. Among the most extreme examples, ING Groep has placed all its voting stock into such a trust office, and the office in turn issues certificates that are traded on the stock exchange (*see* Fig. 5.3). The certificates represent all the cash-flow rights of the underlying shares but none of the voting rights. The trust office is controlled by the (self-appointing) board of ING.

Some Dutch companies are trying to introduce better corporate governance. Dutch food group Numico in early 2002 changed its rules to allow its shareholders the chance to request voting rights from the trust office that holds the shares. But if shareholders failed to ask for these rights, the trust office would still be able to use those rights to vote against hostile takeovers. Shareholders in Numico were also given the right to vote by proxy and to vote on members of the supervisory and executive boards, though with nominations still being made by the supervisory board. The changes were demanded by a group of pension funds which complained that the new rules did not go far enough to allow hostile takeovers to take place. Food giant Ahold also introduced similar changes to shareholder rights.

```
                    ┌─────────────────────┐
                    │ Certificate holders │
                    └─────────────────────┘
            100% capital    │    0% votes
                            ▼
                    ┌─────────────────────┐
                    │  ING trust office   │
                    └─────────────────────┘
            100% capital    │    100% votes
                            ▼
                    ┌─────────────────────┐
                    │        ING          │
                    └─────────────────────┘
```

The Netherlands provides a means for achieving complete separation between ownership of cash-flow rights and voting power – the trust office. Dutch insurance and financial services group ING has placed all its voting stock into such a trust which, in turn, issues certificates that are traded on the stock exchange.

The certificates represent all the cash-flow rights of the underlying shares but none of the voting rights. The trust office could be controlled by a family, but in the case of ING it is controlled by the self-appointing board of ING.

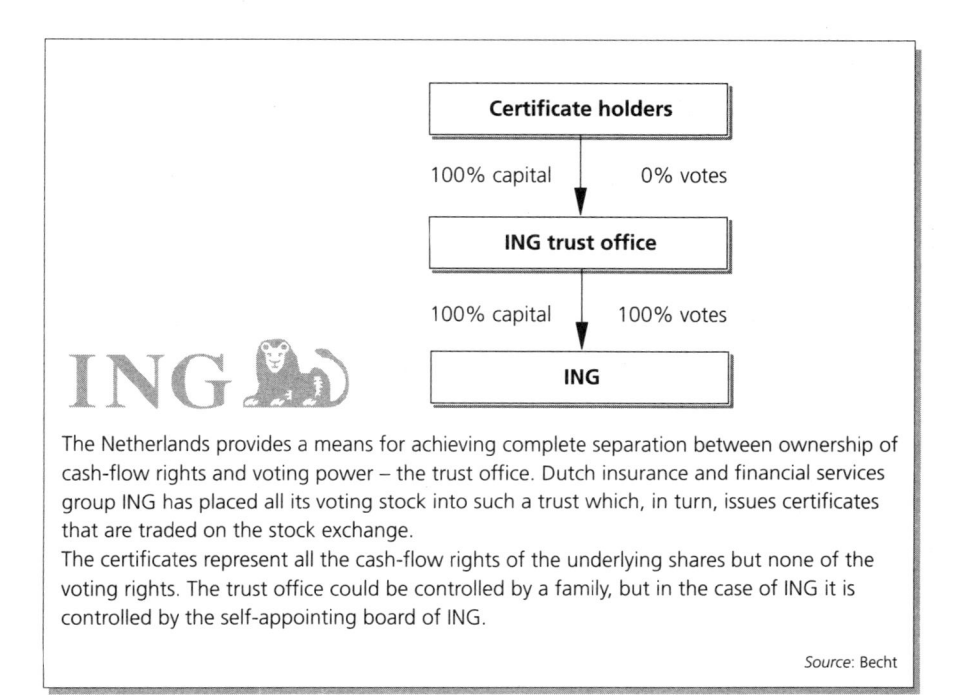

Source: Becht

Figure 5.3 Private control bias through dual-class stock

Ordinary shares with full voting rights are, however, the most common form of shares in issue, but about one third of Dutch companies have certificates. Critics liken certificates to a hidden anti-takeover measure or poison pill because holders of certificates would not be able to vote in favour of any bid that the company itself may find unpalatable. Some companies also have preference shares, which also carry no voting rights. Certificates are likely to be phased out over time, but not preference shares, though their use as a possible poison-pill tool will most probably be severely restricted in future. Even where certificates or preference shares are in issue, if a company is faced with an attractive takeover bid, it will increasingly feel duty bound to give strong reasons to its shareholders if it wanted to turn down the offer. This will be increasingly the case after the HBG saga in 2001 and as VEB clocks up more legal wins against backward-looking companies.

> **Box 5.1 Equity investment in the Netherlands**
>
> **Stock exchange**
> Euronext (www.euronext.com) (*see* Chapter 4).
>
> **Clearing**
> Clearnet, owned by Euronext.
>
> **Settlement**
> Dutch settlement house Necigef is merging with Euroclear Group (the chosen settlement house for Euronext).
>
> **Regulation**
> In March 2002, former watchdog STE was renamed the Netherlands Authority for the Financial Markets (www.autoriteit-fm.nl). It now also supervises consumer credit and investment funds as well as the stock market.
>
> **Shareholders' group**
> Vereniging van Effectenbezitters (VEB), in the Hague (www.veb.net, e-mail info@veb.net).
>
> **Investor complaints**
> Klachtencommissie (Complaint Board), Dutch Securities Institute, PO BOX 3861, NL-1001 AR Amsterdam.

TOP LISTINGS IN THE NETHERLANDS

UNILEVER
www.unilever.com

Anglo-Dutch Unilever is listed in Amsterdam and London, and operated under two separate holding companies but with the same board members. It is one of the world's top consumer goods companies, with leading brand names from foods (Hellmann's and Knorr) to personal hygiene products (Mentadent toothpaste and Vaseline). The company was created from the 1930 merger of the UK's Lever Brothers and the Dutch Margarine Union. The company is in the process of rationalizing its stable of brands and centralizing production.

ROYAL DUTCH/SHELL GROUP
www.shell.com

Among the world's top oil and gas groups, Royal Dutch/Shell Group has operations in more than 130 countries. The company is a joint venture between Royal Dutch, which holds 60 percent, and the UK's Shell Transport and Trading (40 percent). Royal Dutch shares are listed in Amsterdam, while Shell is traded in London.

ING GROEP
www.ing.com

One of the world's leading diversified financial groups, involved in insurance and banking, as well as asset management, securities and investment services. It has exposure to the US after its purchase of Aetna financial services. ING has a complex ownership structure which leaves shareholders with little power (*see* Fig. 5.3).

AEGON
www.aegon.com

Large insurance group with growing presence abroad, especially in the US and UK, making it one of the largest insurance groups in the world. In the US it bought J.C. Penney's marketing unit to improve its direct reach to customers.

PHILIPS ELECTRONICS
www.philips.com

Europe's biggest consumer electronics company and the world's third largest in a sector dominated by Japan's Matsushita and Sony. It manufactures television sets, telephones, compact disc players and other gadgets. It also makes light bulbs, personal computer screens and is a major semiconductor chip maker. It has a strategic partnership with ASM Lithography, also listed in Amsterdam.

ABN AMRO
www.abnamro.com

As the top Dutch bank, it provides a wide range of services, from investment banking to retail and private banking. It has operations in many countries and owns Standard Federal Bank in the US Midwest. ABN AMRO also has operations in Brazil and Asia. The bank was created in 1991 by the merger of Algemene Bank Nederland and the Amsterdam-Rotterdam Bank. It also has asset management divisions.

ROYAL AHOLD
www.ahold.com

One of the world's top retailers, it has thousands of supermarkets in Europe, Asia and the US, competing with large rivals like Carrefour of France and Germany's Metro.

ELSEVIER
www.elsevier.com

Just like Royal Dutch and Unilever, Elsevier is also an Anglo-Dutch company with its UK partner Reed. The company is a global giant in educational, legal, business and scientific publishing. It operates LexisNexis, a legal information provider in the US.

HEINEKEN
www.heinekencorp.nl

The world's third largest brewer and a top brand in Europe, owning Murphy's and Amstel. It also has brands in the US and Asia, and is a distributor of soft drinks.

BELGIUM – LEFT BEHIND IN THE EQUITY RUSH

Belgium suffers from a particular sickness which can be called the fetishism of the reference shareholder.
Eric de Keuleneer, chairman of the Belgian Directors' Foundation

Belgium may be at the heart of political Europe, but in equities it is firmly on the region's periphery, largely through its own fault.

When the Euronext merger of stock exchanges in Brussels, Paris and Amsterdam was drawn up in 2000, the Brussels exchanges ended up with a tiny stake in the new tri-country holding company, compared to Amsterdam taking about a third, and Paris taking the dominant stake. Belgium's miserly slice reflected the weakness of its equity base after years of decline in the grip of a few, powerful holding companies that stifled any move to a more liberal Anglo-Saxon style of corporate governance.

The Belgians had a long-standing love for the fixed income market, with many buying bonds in nearby Luxembourg where they did not have to pay a withholding tax, though falling interest rates have now made bonds less attractive. Even though the lure of bonds may have waned in Belgium, the alternative of equities has scarcely been exploited. There are still deep-rooted problems that hinder the creation of a flourishing equity market, despite Belgium being a relatively affluent country with plenty of companies. The country's stock market is summed up by Hugo Pauwels, a member of the Belgian small investors' clubs association, VFB: 'Poor liquidity and low market capitalization are the weak points of the market, and transparency and communication are the weak points of companies.'

POOR LIQUIDITY SINKS GLOBAL BEER CAPITAL

Few countries brew beer better than Belgium, but the small nation's stock market has lacked fizz for years, leaving investors saddled with shares they were unable to offload. Little wonder many investors preferred buying Dutch or US stocks. Belgian shares have been cheaper than elsewhere, but only because of the poor market turnover and unattractive corporate governance. On any given day, the volume traded in one Dutch share, like Unilever in Amsterdam, can be greater than all the shares traded on the Belgian market.

> ❝Belgian shares have been cheaper than elsewhere, but only because of the poor market turnover and unattractive corporate governance❞

Three financial stocks, Fortis, Dexia and KBC, account for over 60 percent of Belgian market capitalization, making the bourse hostage to interest rates. Without a deep pool of trading volumes, large investors are afraid of stepping in to buy shares, because thin liquidity makes them more difficult to sell in a hurry, if need be.

The pan-European stock exchange Easdaq, specializing in growth companies, was located in Belgium, but it floundered from its birth because its location outside Europe's main financial centres robbed it of precious liquidity. Easdaq also failed to capitalize on the lively high-tech sector in the Flemish area of Belgium. The exchange was finally taken over by US Nasdaq in 2001 and rebranded Nasdaq Europe.

The liquidity or share-trading volume problem is intertwined with the stranglehold of cross-holdings between the big companies that created listings on the bourse with a free-float, or a portion of total shares not being closely held as low as 20–25 percent. Belgium also lost more than half a dozen of its largest listings as a result of mergers and takeovers in the late 1990s, robbing the exchange of a big chunk of trading volumes and leaving it with many small and medium-sized companies. One of the country's industrial scions, Société Générale de Belgique, was snapped up by Suez Lyonnaise des Eaux, a utility based in neighbouring France. Suez also added insult to injury by grabbing Belgian electricity generator Tractebel, a deal that minority shareholders in Tractebel failed to stop.

The lack of pension funds in the market also denies Belgium the fuel that drives more liquid markets in the UK, the US and the Netherlands. Belgium also suffered from a lack of high-profile technology and telecom companies that attracted so much retail and institutional investor interest in other European countries during the technology boom.

Many of Belgium's smaller to mid-sized companies are family owned, and the family members are loathe to give up their control, which would happen if private companies went public, or those who are already listed raised their free-float. To get round this reluctance to give up control, Belgian bourse officials have suggested that companies could issue certificates that would have no voting rights for shareholders – as many Dutch companies do. Alternatively, they could mirror the French who grant double-voting rights for certain stock. Both these remedies have been dubbed back-door anti-takeover measures that fall well short of the Anglo-Saxon style corporate governance that is increasingly becoming the international standard. Vincent van Dessel, Euronext Brussels' executive director of market supervision, has said: 'We are telling companies that when they come to the market, if they want to grow, then they have to put themselves forward in the spirit of growth before the spirit of holding on to their control.' He added that there was no one easy solution to the Belgian market's structural problems that lead to low liquidity and poor minority shareholder rights. Some companies like Interbrew have been successful in nurturing a management that is not beholden to the dominant shareholder.

In 2002 Euronext launched a new Next market segment for the non-blue chip Belgian, French and Dutch companies. Those that want to be listed on it will have to meet stricter codes of conduct, such as quarterly reporting, operating a website, allowing more openness and observing International Accounting Standards to make it easier for foreign investors to compare the companies with peers elsewhere. Belgian firms are slowly accepting that listing is not a one-way street: to keep attracting investors after going public calls for harder work than in the past, as trading in Europe moves from a national to a regional and even global perspective. As van Dessel has said: 'Five years ago, no company would be in favour of more constraints, but now you feel companies are asking for help and asking what they have to do and are prepared to make an effort.'

Planned changes in how the Belgian market is regulated may also help to reassure smaller investors. Euronext Brussels is responsible for monitoring market manipulation and insider trading, but moves are underway to shift these powers from the exchange to the Banking Commission, the country's main watchdog. The move was spurred by the European Union's push to gather all the key regulatory powers in each country under one authority. Watchdogs were concerned that with exchanges like Euronext becoming publicly traded companies on their own markets, the bourses needed to be shorn of some regulatory powers to avoid possible conflicts of interest.

EURONEXT THE SAVIOUR?

Belgian companies hope that Brussels exchanges' decision to merge with peers in Amsterdam and Paris to create Euronext will finally attract some real interest in their listings, but the hope may remain just that for a while. Euronext was officially launched in September 2000, but its first year was spent combining trading from all three members on to one platform operated by Paris. The three clearing systems also needed to be switched over to Clearnet, the Euronext-owned clearing system and central counterparty. The merger of Belgian settlement house CIK with Euronext's chosen settlement group Euroclear will be completed in 2003.

Once Belgian, Dutch and French shares are on the same trading and back-office platforms and operating under the same cost structure and fees, access to Belgian shares by Dutch, French and foreign members of Euronext will be much easier – so the argument goes. Critics say that the opposite will equally be true – that Belgian investors will find it easier to avoid domestic shares and buy stocks from elsewhere that are more attractive because of their deeper liquidity. 'It will be a one-way activity – Belgians will look abroad, while the French and the Dutch don't have enough reasons to look at Belgium,' shareholder activist Hugo Pauwels has said. 'I am afraid for a lot of the small Belgian companies as they are too small to survive in that kind of environment.'

In the Euronext 100 index of top 100 blue chips from the three member countries, there were only about nine Belgian listings in 2001, with about 30 Dutch and the rest French. Even in the Next 150 index, there were only about 20 Belgian companies. What makes matters worse for Belgium is that the Euronext indices have yet to garner any real following as they languish between the active national indices like the CAC 40 in Paris and AEX in the Netherlands, and the truly pan-European indices like the Euro Stoxx 50 or Eurotop 300.

> "It is up to the companies themselves to make the most of the potentially wider investor audience they have on a three-nation exchange"

Euronext Brussels has said that it is up to the companies themselves to make the most of the potentially wider investor audience they have on a three-nation exchange, but the need to good corporate governance still applied. As Euronext Brussels' van Dessel said: 'The role of the exchange is to improve access to the companies but we are not managing them or their communication. They have to take the opportunities.'

REFERENCE SHAREHOLDERS RULE

Belgium's lip-service to corporate governance over the years has created a company mindset that it closed and hostile to minority shareholders. Over the past 15 years the big holding companies have run Belgium's equity show. Foreign ownership is an important feature of Belgian corporate control, in particular from France and Luxembourg, with a range of anti-takeover devices employed, for example at Solvay. It has also been commonplace for reference or dominant stakeholders to appoint most of a company's board of directors to do their bidding.

The dominant shareholders usually control up to 70 percent of a company, but often less than half the ownership base. Even though minority shareholders collectively can add up to most of a company's shares, they are often still neglected and abused. According to Eric de Keuleneer, head of Belgium's Directors' Foundation, 'The aim of the government over the last five years has been to reduce the role of the reference shareholders through the introduction of independent directors.' But the Belgian Banking Commission has also insisted that companies publish a list of board members according to whom they represent, thus going against another Anglo-Saxon corporate governance rule, that board members are not beholden to any narrow interest. 'It is the reason for the shallowness and inefficiency of the Belgian stock market,' de Keuleneer said. 'Belgian boards of directors are full of conflicts of interest.'

Some argue that one reason why Belgian shares perform badly is because shareholder rights are not protected. The concern among controlling shareholders to safeguard their influence has hindered the takeovers that would dilute their clout, leaving minority shareholders sidelined. Hugo Pauwels, a member of the Belgian small investors' clubs association, VFB, explains:

Minority shareholders have very little influence on the functioning of the companies. Most of the members of the board of directors are appointed by the families. There is a law imposing independent directors on the board, but I am a little bit doubtful about the independence of these directors. It's more of a case of 'I'll take someone from your family if you take someone from my family'. It's a first step, but all those independent directors are general managers or major shareholders from other companies and Belgium is not a large country.

The VFB or Vlaamse Federatie van Beleggingsklubs en Beleggers is a voluntary organization comprising 500 clubs with about 5,000 individual members confined to the Dutch-speaking Flemish parts of Belgium. Unlike the Dutch shareholder lobby group VEB or Germany's DSW, the VFB does not initiate legal cases against companies that flout shareholder rights. Instead, disgruntled shareholders in Belgium hire a commercial consultant like Deminor if they want to file a complaint. The VFB presses a more general agenda of trying to persuade companies to improve communication with shareholders and in turn to improve turnover in their shares by attracting foreign investors. Quarterly reporting, for example, is a fairly recent development in Belgium, though more companies now have websites that are updated regularly. Pharmaceutical company UCB and chemical group Solvay are considered among the more open Belgian companies.

Attempts to raise the profile of equities in Belgium suffered a big setback in 2001 when former high-tech star Lernout & Hauspie crashed and wiped away nearly $10 billion in shareholder value, forcing the speech-recognition company into bankruptcy protection. Lernout's former chief executive Gaston Bastiaens was left facing charges of fraud, insider trading, stock-market manipulation and accounting law violations on both sides of the Atlantic. In contrast, Belgian brewer Interbrew has become one of the country's more dynamic companies, gathering a clutch of global beer brands, from Stella Artois to Beck's, as it strives to rival Heineken in neighbouring Netherlands.

Box 5.2 Equity investment in Belgium

Stock exchange
Euronext (www.euronext.com) (*see* Chapter 4). All share dealings are handled on the Euronext NSC trading system, which is also used by Paris and Amsterdam.

Clearing
Clearing 21, operated by Euronext-owned Clearnet.

Settlement
Steps are underway to merge the settlement operations of CIK, the Belgian central securities depository, with Euroclear, the settlement house aligned to Euronext. CIK's custodian operations are to remain in Belgium.

Regulation
The Banking Commission is the national watchdog for the equity market, responsible for initial public offering prospectuses, and ensuring that companies issue annual reports. The Brussels Exchanges are responsible for monitoring against market manipulation and insider trading, but moves are underway to give these responsibilities to the Banking Commission as Euronext itself had become a publicly listed company on its own market. The stock market regulators from all three Euronext member countries, Belgium, France and Netherlands, are working closely to devise a consistent approach to regulation.

Complaints
Ombudsman de l'ABB, Rue Ravenstein, 36, bte 5, B-1000 Bruxelles (e-mail ombudsman@abb-bvb.be).

Company news
Released by companies directly to the press, and posted on the Euronext website.

Shareholders' group
VFB or Vlaamse Federatie van Beleggingsklubs en Beleggers (e-mail emvb@village.uunet.be) is a voluntary organization comprising 500 clubs, mainly in the Dutch-speaking parts of Belgium.

TOP LISTINGS IN BELGIUM

The Bel 20 blue chip index comprises Belgium's 20 leading companies, but market capitalization is concentrated in the top three or four.

FORTIS
www.fortis.com

A Belgian-Dutch financial services firm which merged its listings in December 2001. The company is a major provider of insurance and banking services across the world. Its roots can be traced to a burial fund set up the nineteenth-century Netherlands.

DEXIA
www.dexia.com

A Franco-Belgian bank, closely involved in city government lending, with operations in Italy and Spain, as well as South America and Asia. In 1999 the company decided to merge Dexia Belgium and Dexia France into a single Belgian holding company, which makes it easier to have a single listing on Euronext.

KBC
www.kbc.be

As Belgium's biggest financial group, it operates branches around the world, covering high street banking and insurance services. It is two-thirds owned by the Almanij holding company (www.almanij.be).

INTERBREW
www.interbrew.com

One of Belgium's more dynamic companies, Interbrew has a big thirst for acquisitions which have triggered clashes with competition authorities in Europe. The world's second-largest brewer holds some of the best-known brands in the business, including Bass Ale and Stella Artois, and has also swooped down on Germany's Beck.

DELHAIZE 'LE LION'
www.delhaize-le-lion.be

One of Belgium's global success stories, Delhaize has food retail operations across Europe, Asia and America, but well over half of the company's sales come from the US. Eastern Europe has been a recent focus of expansion.

LUXEMBOURG – THE INDEPENDENT MINNOW

With a population of only about 400,000, it is no surprise that Luxembourg's stock market is tiny, with a market capitalization of €35 billion, the equivalent to a handful of blue chips on Europe's bigger markets. Created in 1928, the Luxembourg Stock Exchange (www.bourse.lu) lists some 20,000 instruments, but international corporate debt makes up about 70 percent of these. The exchange is also active in investment funds, where Luxembourg ranks second in the world with net assets of €875 billion. Dealings in equities, however, are thin, with little foreign investor interest. However, one of Luxembourg's few equity listings, steelmaker Arbed, merged in 2002 with French steel giant Usinor.

Neighbouring stock exchanges in Belgium, the Netherlands and France have merged to form Euronext. The Luxembourg stock exchange said it would remain independent, though in September 2001 is signed a cross-membership agreement with Euronext that allows members of both exchanges to trade in each others listings. The tiny bourse felt it would be the loser in any merger deal, which could also jeopardize Luxembourg as a financial centre.

The Luxembourg Government tried to promote an equity culture by its Rau law which enabled citizens of the Grand Duchy to deduct some €3,000 from their taxes if they invested it in funds that mainly held Luxembourg shares. Many thousands of people did so, and the Government hoped this would encourage the companies listed to expand their market capitalization by issuing more shares. However, since this has not happened, the Rau law is due to be phased out.

> **Box 5.3 Bourse de Luxembourg**
>
> **Exchange**
>
> Bourse de Luxembourg (www.bourse.lu).
>
> In 2001 the exchange's listings totalled 23,438, comprising 16,447 bonds, 5,407 undertakings for collective investment, 1,306 warrants and rights, but only 278 shares. Trading in bonds accounted for 67 percent of turnover in 2001, with trading in shares 33 percent.
>
> In November 2000, the bourse signed an agreement with the Franco-Benelux bourse Euronext to allow for cross-membership between the two exchanges.
>
> **Settlement**
>
> Clearstream International (www.clearstream.com).
>
> In early 2002 the Deutsche Börse was planning to buy the half of Clearstream it did not already own.
>
> **Regulator**
>
> Commission de Surveillance du Secteur Financier (CSSF), part of the Luxembourg government.
>
> **Shareholder lobby group**
>
> Investas – Association Luxembourgeoise des Actionnaires Privés (www.investas.lu).

RTL RANKLES

Small investors were lulled out of their slumber in 2001 when one of the bourse's most popular listings, the RTL group, was taken over by Germany's unlisted media group Bertelsmann. RTL is Europe's leading broadcasting and production company, which owns 24 television channels and 17 radio stations across the region.

In April 2001 Bertelsmann bought a 30-percent stake in RTL that was held by Belgian billionaire Albert Frere's Groupe Bruxelles Lambert, giving Bertelsmann 67 percent of RTL's equity as the German company had already built up a 37-percent stake in RTL. In exchange, GBL gained a 25-percent stake in Bertelsmann. However, analysts estimated that a 30-percent stake in RTL was worth about €4 billion, while the stake in Bertelsmann it was swapped for was worth about €12 billion. Luxembourg's small shareholders in RTL were furious, arguing that GBL won a massive premium for its shares in RTL while they did not.

The small investors felt so short-changed they filed a lawsuit in late 2001 against RTL, Bertelsmann and GBL, backed by top Luxembourg officials who held shares in RTL like Joseph Weyland who became Luxembourg's ambassador to the UK. The lawsuit was the first by a group of Luxembourg shareholders and is seen as a sign that minority shareholders in the small nation are waking up and that the Duchy's equity culture is finally developing, though it may be too late.

RTL is also listed in Brussels and London, but because so much of its shares are closely held, its free-float is too small for it to be included in the UK FTSE 100 blue chip index.

Luxembourg's small investors were angered at the way control of RTL was passed to Bertelsmann. Jean-Paul Hoffmann of Investas, the Luxembourg small investors' association, explained:

> We wanted to be treated in the same way as Groupe Bruxelles Lambert was. We have received nothing except stock whose price has tumbled. The issue of minority shareholder rights is a serious one in Luxembourg. If RTL was a Belgian company, a deal like that could not have been done.

The final insult for Luxembourg's shrivelling equities role came in January 2002 when global stock index compiler MSCI said it was removing the Duchy from its indices because of the loss of Arbed listing. MSCI said the two remaining Luxembourg shares in its indices, RTL and Cegedel, were too illiquid and had too small free-floats.

6

SWITZERLAND

I see the same stereotyped chairman wherever I go. A man, nearly always. Upper middle aged, no strong deputy ... His fellow directors are all like him, friends from the military, the golf club or local politics. You can just hear them say: 'Of course we're modern-thinking – didn't we give the vote to women more than 20 years ago?'
Iain Martin, Geneva-based management consultant

SWITZERLAND IS INDELIBLY ASSOCIATED with money. Ever since the religious conflicts that tore through Europe in the sixteenth and seventeenth centuries, it has been the destination of choice for the relatively well-off refugee. The Huguenots, who fled to Geneva to escape persecution in France, were particularly instrumental in bringing wealth into the country for safekeeping (and for establishing the country's other big industry, horology).

Following the defeat of Napoleon, Switzerland declared itself a federal republic, and its independence and neutrality were guaranteed by the 1815 Treaty of Vienna. Neutrality has served it well, and today the country has around a 10-percent share of the global private banking market. Because its own population is so small (around 7 million), it has achieved this position by appealing to an international client base. By some estimates, the country accounts for 35 percent of all private assets held across borders.

Another factor in this growth has been the country's reputation for financial secrecy and discretion. In reality, banking secrecy is not quite as sacrosanct as many outside observers believe. Swiss authorities regularly co-operate with investigations into criminal activities and money laundering. There is no such thing as an anonymous bank account – the identities of all account-holders are known, and legislation against money-laundering and organized crime is highly developed. However, there are two complicating factors. One is that Switzerland refuses to pass on information that could then be forwarded to a third party, a point that has been tested at the country's highest court. A second is that it does not recognize tax evasion as a crime, and thus is unable to hand over bank details to foreign tax bodies such as the UK's Inland Revenue or the US Internal Revenue Service. This insistence has particularly irked the latter organization, since Americans living abroad and earning above a certain amount are still obliged to pay federal taxes back home, and maintaining a Swiss bank account could enable them to avoid this obligation. The country's banking secrecy laws are also under pressure from the Organization for Economic Co-operation and Development and the European Union, which like the US wants withholding taxes to prevent its citizens squirrelling away undisclosed funds.

Like its banking citadels, Switzerland's stock exchange has long recognized the need to look to the world as well as to its small but affluent domestic market. This is reflected in its flagship companies – Switzerland is home to two of Europe's five biggest banks, as well as a disproportionate number of international giants like drugs companies Novartis and Roche, and food producer Nestlé. It is also evident in its various co-operations with other European capital markets, most notably in the creation of virt-x. It merged its derivatives markets with Germany's DTB to form Eurex in 1998, while it is also a partner in Stoxx (*see* Chapter 9), the family of indices set up for European equity benchmarking.

Traditionally, the Swiss have been relatively ambivalent to shares, preferring safe investments like property, fixed-income instruments and cash. The country has also not seen the waves of privatization that other countries have. Only the federal telecommunications firm, Swisscom, has been privatized so far, and even then the Government hung on to two-thirds of the shares. There has been talk of privatizing the state rail network, the post office or the state-owned cantonal banks, but only in the medium to long term. It seems Switzerland is not in a hurry to start a boom in mass share ownership. But there has been some change. Recently, consistently low interest rates on bank accounts, coupled with a growing tendency to pay part of salaries in shares, or options over shares, have led to renewed enthusiasm.

> **Switzerland is not in a hurry to start a boom in mass share ownership**

Changes to the pension schemes are also planned. The Swiss Government wants to move towards funded pension schemes run by external fund managers, and as a result the proportion of equities held by the average Swiss pension fund is set to rise to around 14 percent from around 10 percent during the 1990s. What the exchange wants next is a reform of Switzerland's tax regime, which levies a fixed stamp duty of 0.15 percent on domestic transactions (0.3 percent on foreign ones). The tax regime for foreign investors is even more draconian; Switzerland levies a witholding tax of 35 percent on bank deposits and income from investments, such as dividends. This is designed to discourage individuals from abusing Switzerland's banking secrecy laws, and overseas shareholders can obtain relief under the relevant double taxation laws – providing, of course, that they declare the investment in the first place.

THE MARKETS

The first stock exchange in Switzerland was established in Geneva in 1850, followed by two more – in Zürich (opened in 1873) and Basle (1876). The three were merged in 1995 to form the current Swiss exchange, SWX. The trading floor was abolished in 1996 with the introduction of electronic trading. In 1998 a comprehensive new securities law came into force, superseding the former cantonal exchange laws.

In 1999 SWX introduced its own version of the Neuer Markt – unimaginatively titled the New Market. Like its similarly named counterparts elsewhere in Europe, it is primarily aimed at growing technology companies. The rules for New Market listings are similar to those of AIM, the Neuer Markt and other growth company boards, although there are some variations. Shareholders' funds must total at least SFr2.5 million, there must be a free float of at least 20 percent and a 12-month operating record (although there are no minimum requirements for revenue or profit). Flotation must occur as part of a capital increase, which in turn must be at least 50 percent of the offering. There is a six-month lock-in period for existing shareholders, and quarterly reporting to US GAAP or International Accounting Standards is compulsory.

The blue chip index is the Swiss market index or SMI, which now comprises 27 of the largest and most liquid companies listed in Switzerland (see Table 6.1). It captures some 90 percent of the exchange's trading volume. A broader index is the Swiss performance index or SPI, which is made up of all listed companies on the main or secondary segments, and domiciled in Switzerland or Liechtenstein. The all-share is even more comprehensive, comprising every listed company. The New Market has its own index.

Company (sector)	Weighting
Novartis (pharmaceuticals)	21.6
Nestlé (food)	18.3
UBS (financial services)	13.3
Roche (pharmaceuticals)	10.9
Credit Suisse (financial services)	9.04
Swiss Re (insurance)	5.76
Zürich Financial (financial services)	3.69
Compagnie Financial (financial services)	1.97
Serono (pharmaceuticals)	1.29
ABB (energy, engineering)	1.90
Swisscom (telecoms)	1.59
Adecco (support services)	1.53
Holcim (building materials)	1.32
Schweizerische Lebensversicherung (insurance)	0.69
Syngenta (chemicals)	1.32
Baloise Holdings (insurance)	0.71
Ciba Specialty Chemicals (chemicals)	0.96
Lonza (chemicals)	0.50
Givaudan (speciality chemicals)	0.50
Baer Holding (financial services)	0.52
Clariant (chemicals)	0.63
Swatch bearer shares (consumer goods)	0.67
Swatch registered shares (consumer goods)	0.30
Kudelski (electronics)	0.34
Unaxis Holding (IT hardware)	0.21
SGS (testing, support services)	0.24
Sulzer (engineering)	0.16

Note: Weightings are approximate, as at March 2002

Table 6.1 The Swiss market index

Computerized trading took over in Switzerland in 1996. Alongside Paris, the SWX is reckoned to have one of the most sophisticated trading platforms of any exchange in Europe. Trading, clearing and settlement is fully integrated and completely computerized, although only the actual trading platform is run by the SWX. Clearing is via Secom and trades are settled via SegaInterSettle.

THE VIRT-X PROJECT

When the SWX introduced electronic trading in 1996, some 14 percent of trading in Swiss securities actually took place in London. By the end of 2000, that proportion had almost doubled. SWX's response to this was basically: 'If you can't beat 'em, join' em.'

The Swiss had long been aware that their bluest chips were big international fish in a relatively small domestic pond. Swiss companies knew that in order to raise their international profile, they needed to be traded on a deeper, more liquid and more international market. London, the financial centre of Europe and one of the three most important markets in the world, was the logical choice. It is widely rumoured that SWX courted the London Stock Exchange (LSE) about a tie-up, but found the LSE unreceptive to the idea. Maybe London thought it could carry on stealing turnover in Swiss stocks without going to the trouble of a merger. So SWX reversed itself into Tradepoint, a small quoted UK stock-market operator that had for some time had ambitions to take on the staid LSE. The transaction resulted in SWX owning around 40 percent of Tradepoint, which was duly renamed virt-x (for virtual exchange). The remainder was held by a consortium of investment banks and public shareholders.

Why should one of Europe's top ten stock markets, with some of the best technology in the business, place such faith in a relative tiddler? It's a question that Antoinette Hunziker-Ebneter, chief executive of virt-x and the driving force behind the project, gets asked a lot. She identifies three main reasons. One is that Tradepoint had RIE (recognized investment exchange) status in the UK, something that would reassure major institutional traders. Another is that the people running Tradepoint had vital experience of running a trading platform. The third is that it was part-owned by investment banks, who could be called upon to endow their offspring with vital extra liquidity.

For a new trading platform, liquidity is key. If there is no depth to the market, then big institutions will be wary of trading it, since normal-size deals will have a disproportionate effect on the price, increasing volatility and making risk management more difficult. Virt-x set itself a target of snaring 10 percent of trade in the constituents of the pan-European Dow Jones Stoxx 600 index by the end of its first year in operation. It got a head start courtesy of the Swiss blue chips, with trading in all 29 constituents of the Swiss market index transferred from SWX to virt-x on day one of its operation. The Swiss members of the Stoxx 600 alone account for around 7 percent of the index, so all virt-x had to do was grab the remaining 3–4 percent from other markets. It managed that target in about two weeks, helped by trading from its investment bank shareholders, but has found it difficult to maintain this.

Virt-x makes no bones about its primary attraction to institutional players – cost. It puts the cost of trading, clearing and settlement – all integrated – at around €2 per trade, and says it can cost up to 40 times that going through national trading and clearing systems. Courtesy of its investment bank shareholders, it also says it provides two-way prices that are as good as any available on SETS, Xetra or any of Europe's other order-driven trading systems.

Will the gamble work? Only time will tell whether SWX lives to regret its decision to hand over trading in its most prestigious stocks. If virt-x does not attract consistent volume outside Swiss blue chips, then another exchange could well simply snap it up for its technology platform, leaving the Swiss playing second fiddle to a larger foreign institution. However, if virt-x does take off, it could be the trigger for a fresh wave of consolidation attempts among the established exchanges – and SWX's stake in virt-x will give it a seat at that table.

REGULATION

Regulation of securities trading in Switzerland is clear and modern, with the cantonal laws now replaced by the 1997 Stock Exchange Act. The stock exchange is expected to regulate trading and admissions, but the ultimate regulator is the Federal Banking Commission (FBC), which also regulates banks and investment funds.

Takeovers are regulated by the Takeover Commission, made up of bankers, investors and securities dealers and established by the SWX. Although it cannot force compliance – only make recommendations – the FBC is empowered to implement them. Shareholdings of over 5 percent must be disclosed, and a major shareholder is required to make a general offer if the major shareholder's stake rises above a third. However, the price is not guaranteed – it must be at least as high as the market price, and not lower than 25 percent of the highest price paid by the offeror during the last year. This means it is quite possible that some shareholders will get better treatment than others – but that is simply characteristic of the Swiss system.

The disclosure regime contains some of the same loopholes as the German one, most notably in that it is up to the company to decide whether a new fact has the potential to influence the price substantially. Profit warnings need only be issued if the revised profits will fall materially below the company's own guidance; in the event of unjustified exuberance among analysts, the company is not obliged to say a word. However, companies are cautioned against trivializing stock-exchange announcements with news of minor acquisitions, conclusion of contracts, heavy expenditure and so on. This is designed to prevent announcements turning into public relations exercises.

WE KNOW BEST

Switzerland's corporate scene is one of great contrasts. For such a small country with limited natural resources, it is home to a disproportionate number of world-scale companies. The greatest of these is probably Nestlé, for which the domestic market accounts for just

1 percent of sales. But the country also punches far above its weight in banking, pharmaceuticals and building materials. The surprise is that so many of these companies are effectively run by a clubby, tight-knit circle of executives, bankers and grand old families. This elite uses a variety of archaic corporate structures to keep outsiders away from Swiss boardrooms.

Even by European standards, Swiss companies are generally very difficult to take over because of their capital structures. Most of these were devised with the specific intention of keeping predators, especially foreign ones, at bay. Bearer shares and participation certificates were created; these had their attractions for investors, too, since they could be kept anonymously in a bank account. Many Swiss companies have abandoned the different share classes, but a fair sprinkling survive, among them elevator maker Schindler and regional airline Crossair. However, one share one vote is certainly not a core principle in Switzerland and various restrictions on voting rights are routinely used to maintain family control, even when only small proportions of the ordinary share capital are in the hands of the family. Nowhere is this more apparent than at Roche, the pharmaceutical company where the Hoffman families control over 50 percent of the votes with just 10 percent of the shares.

This system is starting to come under pressure, both from domestic troublemakers like Martin Ebner (*see* below), and from overseas investors, some of whom have mounted legal challenges. A veteran US corporate raider, Asher Edelman, bought a 28-percent stake in Baumgartner, but those shares carried only 3 percent of the voting rights because of rules laid down in Baumgartner's articles of association. Edelman argued that since he only had 3 percent of the votes, he should not be obliged to make a general offer to all shareholders if his stake were to rise above 33 percent, the usual trigger for such an offer. The Takeover Commission and the FBC ruled in his favour, but the court of appeal disagreed and said the FBC had exceeded its powers. The decision was a major disappointment to those who want Switzerland's share registers opened up.

Another characteristic of Swiss companies is their 'heavy' share prices. This is a result of a quirk in Swiss company law, which until recently stipulated that the minimum par value of a share should be SFr100. In May 2001 that was cut to 1 cent, and a steady procession of share splits has been the consequence. However, some monsters remain – shares in publishing group Neuer Zürcher Zeitung still command SFr170,000–200,000 each.

> **Beneath the arcane capital structures and voting restrictions lay the assumption that Swiss managers were a class above others**

Beneath the arcane capital structures and voting restrictions lay the assumption that Swiss managers were a class above others, so that there would basically never be any need for a takeover. This belief might have held true a few years ago, but after a growing number of scandals and corporate catastrophes, many are wondering if it is time for a change of the guard, or even the system.

Switzerland is in the process of drafting a corporate code of conduct. Until recently, it was the only major European industrial country not to have one. Like its German equivalent, it has no force in law. It stresses the paramount rights of shareholders and suggests companies review how their 'articles of association (like a constitution) 'can make it easier for shareholders to exercise their statutory rights'. It recommends that a board of directors 'be sufficiently few in number to enable an efficient decision making process', a reference to the large boards of many Swiss companies, and adds that there should be separate committees for audit, renumeration and nomination. Like the UK's Cadbury Report, it advocated the splitting of the job of chairman and chief executive, but stops short of urging that the chairman of the executive board should not hold the same post at the supervisory board.

There have been some successes. In early 2002, Rolf Huppi was forced to give up the chief executive role at Zurich Financial after months of investor pressure, although he did remain as chairman. But there have been many setbacks too, where potentially innovative overseas executives have been forced out by the old guard. One outspoken critic of the Swiss boardroom network is Iain Martin, who runs a management consultancy in Geneva and Zurich. He argues that the system of patronage which has served Switzerland well in the past is not appropriate for the future, urging boards instead to follow the example of companies like Nestlé and Novartis – appoint more women, more foreigners and more people with international backgrounds. He thinks the stipulation that a majority of directors be Swiss is outdated and should be scrapped.

The clubby atmosphere at the top has made direct criticism rare, and frequently given rise to conflicts of interest. It is also difficult for ordinary shareholders to challenge boardroom cosiness. Mounting legal action against Swiss companies is prohibitively expensive, and minority shareholders have few rights compared to the big family shareholders. It is noticeable that when heads have rolled at Swiss corporations, it has usually been at the instigation of large outside shareholders. A case against Swissair was brought by a lawyer, Hans-Jacob Heitz, who assembled fed-up shareholders into an action group. But he was backed by the federal government and the cantonal government of Zürich. Another row over who ran Kuoni was also eventually settled by the intervention of the Zürich cantonal government. Not only did these episodes cause embarrassment for the Swiss, they also reflected poorly on the corporate governance regime generally, since governments were obliged to stand up for shareholders' interests.

The one event that laid bare many of the faults in Swiss corporate governance was the humiliating collapse of national airline Swissair in late 2001, with recriminations set to last for years. Swissair was not one of Switzerland's biggest blue chips – its rating in the SMI was modest even when it was at its peak value – but it was a national icon. Even economy-class passengers sat in leather-trimmed seats. The inflight service was outstanding. The punctuality record was enviable. For Swiss and non-Swiss alike, flying Swissair was an 'I've made it' statement.

Perhaps echoing its country's tradition of neutrality, Swissair did not become part of the global airline alliances that sprung up during the 1990s. Instead, it started building stakes in smaller European airlines like France's Air Liberté and AOM, and Belgium's Sabena. The intention was to create a network of partners. The money used to acquire these stakes, a process that started in 1995, was largely borrowed. But Swissair did not have management control over any of its investments and in some cases – notably Sabena – it laid itself open to significant extra funding requirements.

Swissair collapsed under the weight of its debt shortly after the World Trade Center attacks (*see* Fig. 6.1), but the savage downturn in global aviation that followed the outrages was merely the *coup de grâce* for an airline that was already in terminal trouble. It was not making enough money to service its debts, its staff costs had risen and its market value had shrunk. Already, investors were fuming. A lawyer set up a shareholders' action group and soon fellow shareholders were flocking to his internet site. Some 5,000 of them turned up at the company's annual general meeting.

Swissair tried to implement a restructuring, furiously selling non-core assets in order to pay off its debts. A rights issue was being planned when disaster struck in New York. Even the attempt to rescue the company was a farce. UBS and Credit Suisse put together a package to keep the planes flying, but it was too late. One of the world's premier airlines was grounded, unable to pay its staff or its

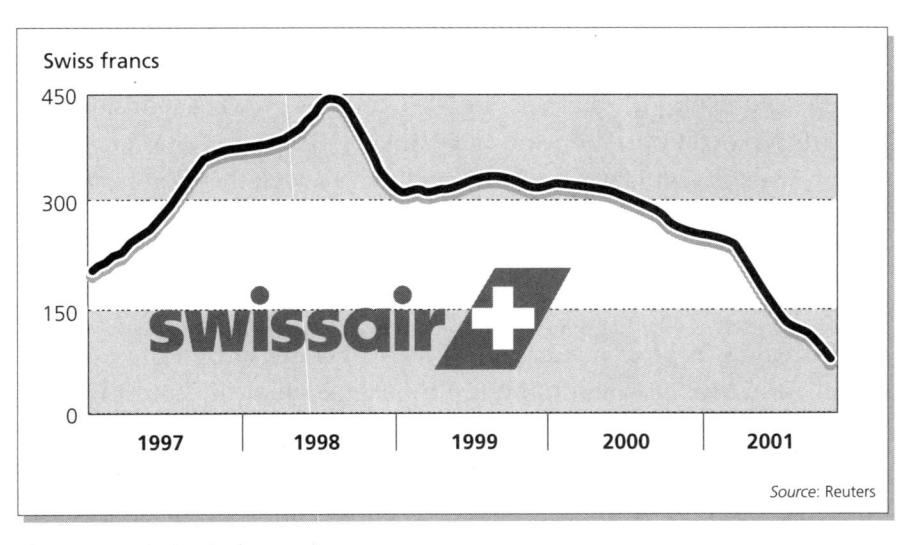

Figure 6.1 Swissair share price

fuel bills. Stranded passengers at Zürich airport were served meals by charities and drank apple juice supplied by local farmers. The national humiliation was comprehensive; the planes could only fly after the Government stepped in. The recriminations were bitter – UBS staff received death threats, and effigies of the company's chairman, Marcel Ospel, were burned in the streets.

What makes the Swissair debacle particularly significant is that the company's board of directors, as befits a totem of national pride, was made up of the great and the good among Switzerland's elite. Lukas Mühlemann, the chief executive of Credit Suisse, sat next to Thomas Schmidheiny, boss of Holderbank, who rubbed shoulders with Andres Leuenberger, vice-chairman of Roche. These titans of Swiss industry seemed impotent as the carrier's troubles multiplied. Even after a mass of directors resigned, the man brought in to save the airline was another member of the club, Nestlé's Mario Corti.

Criticism of the nation's favourite company was not tolerated. When an analyst at Credit Suisse's investment banking arm CSFB, Cristopher Chandiramani, warned of the coming cash crunch at the airline, he was promptly sacked. But amid the controversy are signs that the old order is starting to break up. Corti was harshly critical of some of the country's top bankers. 'I never had an insight into the plans of the banks which ended in Project Phoenix [the proposed rescue plan]. I felt betrayed at the end of last week – the solution was dictated to me,' he told reporters. The country's finance minister publicly scolded Ospel for being on board a private jet to New York while Swissair jets sat idle. Non-Swiss creditors also felt they had been kept in the dark, and may mount legal action.

DER BÖRSENHAI

If lasting improvements do eventually come to Swiss corporate governance, one man lining up to take some of the credit will be Martin Ebner, the founder of BZ Bank. Ebner is the *bête noire* of Switzerland's old guard, a corporate raider and shareholder activist who has shaken up the boards of some of the country's oldest and grandest institutions.

Ebner never wanted to be anything other than a millionaire financier. After studying law in Switzerland, he familiarized himself with the tenets of shareholder value in the US before returning to Zürich to found BZ Bank Zürich. While in the US, he also learned a thing or two about derivatives, and it was success with these enormously risky instruments that propelled BZ Bank on to investors' radar screens. Ebner became a millionaire, and a self-made one at that, in contrast to the family fortunes that enfranchise most of the country's elite.

Ebner's targets have been numerous, but his technique is basically the same. The investment funds controlled by BZ will buy a substantial stake in a company's shares. Usually, BZ will become the biggest or second-biggest shareholder. Ebner will then demand board representation and make quite clear what his agenda will be if he attains that goal. Most companies, not surprisingly, want nothing to do with him, and Switzerland's clubby boardroom network and its convoluted capital structures mean that it is often not difficult to keep him out. Some are less hostile; ABB invited him on board as a non-executive director, and his presence chimed usefully with the company's drive to become more international and more open.

Perhaps Ebner's single biggest coup was as the catalyst for the merger in 1998 of UBS with its smaller, but more aggressive rival, Swiss Banking Corporation. This was not directly his doing, but it is fairly clear that his constant and public criticism of the staid UBS put that institution firmly on the defensive. Many of the measures he espoused were implemented by the merged group not long after.

He has had less luck with Roche, the pharmaceutical company. Despite accumulating a fair chunk of the shares in the group, the preferential voting rights held by the Hoffman and Oeri families made it certain that Ebner would get nowhere near the boardroom. His demands were distinctly unpalatable – an end to the archaic voting structure that enables the families to keep their control, and a full spin-off of Nasdaq-listed Genentech. Eventually, Ebner sold his shares to Novartis, Roche's rival, fuelling long-held speculation that the two will eventually merge. That at least will give the Hoffmans something else to think about.

There are many people, not just within Switzerland's corporate elite, who consider Ebner to be a ruthless operator – a *hai* (shark) who is addicted to the pastime of making a nuisance of himself. He would argue that this is not always the case. For instance, BZ Group for a long time owned shares in Intershop, a property agency, and Rieter, a maker of car parts; Ebner did not publicly interfere in either of these companies and left their managements to get on with it. But there can be little doubt that he relishes the David-versus-Goliath challenges of taking on the old guard – and the spate of Swiss corporate catastrophes over the past few years suggests that many more of the old guard will be on shark-alert in the years ahead.

Box 6.1 Equity investment in Switzerland

Exchanges

The 27 blue chips in the Swiss Market Index are traded on virt-x (www.virt-x.com) in London. Virt-x is owned by the SWX Swiss Exchange, a consortium of banks, plus private shareholders. Other stocks are traded in Zürich on the SWX (www.swx.ch).

Regulation

Financial services in Switzerland, including equity trading, are regulated by the powerful Federal Banking Commission (www.ebk.admin.ch).

Clearing and settlement

Virt-x follows the horizontal integration philosophy, so trades can be cleared through a choice of clearers, including the London Clearing House and Euroclear. Settlement is through SegaInterSettle (www.sisclear.com).

Indices

SWX compiles the Swiss Market Index (SMI) for the blue chips and the all-share Swiss Performance Index (SPI).

Others

The Swiss Banking Institute (www.isb.unizh.ch) does surveys into levels of share ownership. The Swiss Business Federation (www.economiesuisse.ch) has co-operated with SWX on the corporate governance code. Financial news in English is available from Swissinvest (www.swissinvest.com). The site set up to coordinate legal action against Swissair is www.sairschutz.ch.

TOP LISTINGS IN SWITZERLAND

UBS AND CREDIT SUISSE – THE GNOMES OF ZÜRICH (AND GENEVA)

Befitting its status as a world financial centre, Switzerland's corporate scene is dominated by banks. Two giants have emerged over the past few years as a result of merger activity, but there are still smaller listed private banks and still more that are privately-owned partnerships.

Top of the tree is UBS (www.ubs.com), one of the biggest financial institutions in Europe. Formed by the merger of the Bank of Winterthur and the Bank of Toggenburg in 1912, it expanded steadily throughout the early part of the twentieth century, and happily took deposits from both Jews and Nazis during the Second World War. International expansion followed, although it was not all plain sailing. The group's London operation was hit hard by the 1987 stock market crash, while its US business was damaged by the collapse of Drexel Burnham Lambert and the junk bond market in 1990. Despite these setbacks, the acquisitions continued both at home and abroad, and by 1994 the bank had overlapping operations, sprawling bureaucracy and heavy exposure to real-estate lending. Profits collapsed, leading Martin Ebner (him again) to wage a war of attrition against the company's management. After fighting off a bid from Credit Suisse, the group embarked on a draconian restructuring and rationalization programme, which gathered pace after its 1999 acquisition of Swiss Banking Corporation, its smaller and leaner rival.

Switzerland's 'other' bank, Credit Suisse (CS) (www.credit-suisse.com) started life in 1856 as a venture capital firm. The switch to commercial banking came in 1867 and by 1871 it was the country's largest bank. Like UBS, CS played a role it would rather forget in handling plundered gold during the Second World War, and gold trading and foreign exchange became important earnings streams after the war. The association with First Boston began in 1978 when CS bought a stake in the Wall Street firm, but the full merger did not come until 1988 (forming CSFB). In reality, it was more of a rescue as First Boston had been damaged by the 1987 crash and required a capital injection and surgery to its loan book. Almost a decade later came another major deal – the acquisition of Winterthur, Switzerland's second-largest insurer, and at the close of 2000 it bought another Wall Street firm, DLJ.

CSFB's reputation was tarnished in the early years of the twenty-first century by a series of regulatory run-ins. James Archer, son of the disgraced novelist and one of the self-styled 'Flaming Ferraris', was sacked for manipulating the Swedish stock market, and there were also mini-scandals in Japan and the US. By 2001 the wild days were over; a former Morgan Stanley executive with a reputation for savage cost-cutting was installed as head of the key investment banking business.

Private banks in Switzerland are divided between those that are listed, like Julius Baer and Vontobel, and those that still operate as partnerships, like Pictet. In the latter, the partners carry unlimited personal liability, which proponents say makes for more responsible asset management.

NOVARTIS AND ROCHE – OLD VERSUS NEW IN PHARMACEUTICALS

The two giants of Swiss biotechnology and pharmacy sit glowering at each other from opposite banks of the Rhine in Basel. Although in some ways they could not be more different from each other, many commentators remain convinced that in the long run grand old Roche (www.roche.com) will merge with the upstart Novartis (www.novartis.com) and create a massive Swiss drugs powerhouse.

Novartis (Latin for 'new arts') was formed in 1996 from the merger of Ciba-Geigy and Sandoz. In some ways it was a reprise of an earlier combination; between the two world wars Ciba, Geigy and Sandoz founded a Basel AG cartel to take on the might of IG Farben, the German chemicals giant. It was under the auspices of the Basel cartel that the three companies, which hitherto had produced natural and synthetic dyes, diversified into pharmaceuticals. After the Second World War the cartel voluntarily dissolved itself back into its three components, although not before Geigy's Paul Müller had won a Nobel prize for inventing the pesticide DDT. Ciba merged with Geigy in 1970. Both the merged company and Sandoz pursued a series of US

SPAIN: MADRID BOURSE DURING FIRST DAY OF EURO TRADING A man uses a calculator in front of a panel showing the euro conversion rate for the peseta at Madrid's Bourse on the first day of trading in euros, 4 January 1999. Spanish stocks soared and brought a rush of investors to Spain's biggest companies. Traders, analysts and fund managers reported no technical problems with dealing in euros, but were at a loss to justify investors' sudden enthusiam for Spanish stocks when the economic fundamentals were unchanged. (Photo by Andrea Comas; © Reuters 1999.)

UK: NEWLY APPOINTED CHIEF EXECUTIVE OF LONDON STOCK EXCHANGE
Clara Furse, newly appointed chief executive of the London Stock Exchange, smiles to photographers as she stands in front of a board at the entrance of London's stock exchange, 24 January 2001. Furse was the first ever woman chief executive in the LSE's 200-year-history. (Photo by Yiorgos Karahalis; © Reuters 2001.)

NETHERLANDS: EURONEXT LAUNCH EVENT IN AMSTERDAM Euronext chairman and CEO Jean François Theodore (centre), Euronext Chief Operating Officer George Moller (left) and Euronext Secretary General Olivier Lefebvre cheer on their new company during the Euronext launch event in the Park Plaza in Amsterdam, 22 September 2000. Euronext is the European Exchange created by the merger between Amsterdam exchanges, Brussels exchanges and the Paris Bourse. (Photo by Fred Ernst; © Reuters 2000.)

NETHERLANDS: WORLD ONLINE EXECUTIVE CHAIRWOMAN TOASTS CHAMPAGNE Dutch Canadian executive chairwoman Nina Brink raises a glass of champagne after signing the listing agreement at the Amsterdam stock exchange, 17 March 2000. The launch was the biggest initial public offering ever in Amsterdam and the biggest internet offering in Europe. The share opened at €50.20, just over €7 above the issue price of €43. In the first four minutes 7.5 million shares were traded. (Photo by Jerry Lampen; © Reuters 2000.)

BELGIUM: BEER AT THE BRUSSELS BOURSE Pedestrians walk past a giant Jupiler beer can placed in front of the Brussels Bourse to publicize the stock market debut of the world's number two brewer, Belgium's Interbrew, 1 December 2000. Interbrew listed 21 percent of its capital, with shares opening at €34. (Photo by Thierry Roge; © Reuters 2000.)

SWITZERLAND: EMPTY BAGGAGE CARRIERS PILE UP AT ZÜRICH AIRPORT
Rows of empty baggage carriers are piled up at Zürich airport as Swissair's entire fleet remained grounded, 3 October 2001. The collapse of the flag carrier was a national calamity and led to widespread recriminations. (Photo by Andreas Meier; © Reuters 2001.)

US: TELEFONICA SERVICIOS MOVILES LISTS AT NEW YORK STOCK EXCHANGE
Telefonica International chief executive Luis Lopez-Van Dam (centre), poses with New York Stock Exchange chairman Richard Grasso (left) and NYSE president William Johnston before ringing the opening bell as part of ceremonies marking the initial listing of Telefonica Services Moviles at the NYSE on 22 November 2000. European companies are looking increasingly to top the large US pool of investors for money by having a listing in the US. (Photo by Peter Morgan; © Reuters 2000.)

UK: LONDON AND FRANKFURT CONFIRM BOURSE MERGER Deutsche Börse chief executive Werner Seifert looks past the chairman of the London Stock Exchange, Don Cruickshank, during a news conference to announce the merger of the London and Frankfurt bourses, 3 May 2000. The merger was broken up by a hostile bid for the LSE from Sweden's OM Group. (Photo by Kieran Doherty; © Reuters 2000.)

acquisitions during the 1980s and 1990s, taking them further into biotechnology and pharmacy, as well as into seeds and agrochemicals.

Novartis in its current form has a very recent history. In contrast, Roche goes back 105 years, to when Fritz Hoffman founded the company in 1896. Perhaps the group's most recent heyday was in the 1960s and 1970s, when Librium and its successor Valium were spectacular successes. When the patents on Valium expired in the mid-1980s, Roche went shopping, buying US biotechs like Genentech and spending $10 billion on diagnostics group Boehringer Mannheim. It was products from these companies, rather than formulations developed in-house, that allowed the company to keep growing. Profits were also swelled by the financial wizardry of Henri Meier, the group's finance director, who was so skilful at capital management that Roche came to be known as a bank with a pharmaceutical business attached.

But as the twenty-first century dawned, so Roche began to get left behind. Unpleasant side-effects caused sales of its Xenical treatment for obesity to stall, while the US Government fined the group's vitamins division $500 million for price-fixing, and several high-profile compounds failed late-stage clinical trials. Roche's market capitalization drifted, so the company that in the mid-1990s had come close to becoming the world's biggest pharmaceutical company was by 2001 a mere eleventh. Meier's successor as finance director, Anton Affentranger, was fired within a few months.

In the midst of all this, financier Martin Ebner sold his 20 percent holding to Novartis, piqued that he had been unable to gain a seat on the board or influence Roche's strategy. Novartis teases Roche by describing its stake as a 'financial investment', but the logic of a merger and the potential for massive cost reductions is obvious. That puts the Hoffman families in a difficult position. They could easily block a takeover with their votes. But the more it becomes apparent that the company is run for their benefit rather than that of all shareholders, the lower Roche's share rating will sink.

NESTLÉ – GLOBAL FOOD GIANT

Nestlé (www.nestle.com) is another characteristically Swiss company with a long history and a dominant position as the world's biggest food company. It also makes contact lenses and pet food and has an indirect stake in cosmetics company L'Oréal. The company was founded in 1843 by Henri Nestlé, but he sold out in 1875. The modern giant that is Nestlé had its genesis in 1905 when it merged with Anglo-Swiss Condensed Milk Company. Nescafé, the revolutionary instant coffee, hit the shelves in 1938. By the 1980s, the company's tentacles had spread across the world, and in the 1990s it branched into new areas such as mineral waters and deluxe ice-creams. Like its peers, it is perceived as as 'defensive' stock, and its stable earnings, massive financial power and strong brands find themselves much in demand during times of market uncertainty.

7

SCANDINAVIA

In 1996 there were fewer than half a million shareholders in Sweden, today four out of five Swedish adults – almost seven million people – invest in shares and investment trust funds.
Sten Trolle, chairman, Swedish shareholders association

IT'S HARD TO THINK OF SCANDINAVIA as an investment destination. Strong social democratic traditions, rigorous protection of the environment, absurdly generous welfare systems, high taxes and well-protected workers suggest that ruthless pursuit of shareholder value is an anathema to the area's well-heeled inhabitants.

To an extent, that's still true of Norway and Denmark. Norway is a traditionally protectionist country, fearful of its corporate scene being overwhelmed by bigger companies from much bigger countries. Its people voted against joining the European Union, and its government has only very recently started privatizing state-owned companies, selling minority stakes in Telenor in 2000 and Statoil in 2001. However, there are signs of change. The Oslo stock exchange has demutualized and signed up to the Norex alliance (*see* below), and the Government has at last allowed one relatively high profile Norwegian company to be taken over by a foreign one.

Denmark is also relatively unfamiliar with the cult of equity. For many years, its financial systems have been based around bonds and other fixed-income instruments, a trend dating back to the Fire of Copenhagen in the late eighteenth century. Much of the rebuilding of the city was financed by mortgage credit institutions, and much of Denmark's capital investment is still financed that way today. Relative to the size of the country, Denmark's bond market is one of the biggest in the world. Other factors putting investors off equities were a fairly punitive rate of taxation and the lavishly generous welfare state it provided. Only very recently have some Danes begun to wonder whether the system will always be able to take care of them. Again, though, there are signs of greater enthusiasm. The Copenhagen stock exchange has seen a sharp increase in membership and turnover since it became part of the Norex regional link up. The Danish shareholders association has also seen membership increase. E-trade, the US online broker, is setting up operations in Denmark in 2002.

If Norway and Denmark are the laggards, Sweden is the regional leader. The shareholding promotion society, Aktiespararna, estimates that by 2000 80 percent of Swedes owned shares, either directly or through mutual funds. Direct ownership of shares stood at around 41 percent of the population, up from around 30 percent two years before.

There are many reasons for this. One is that from 1870 to around 1970 Sweden enjoyed a growth rate that, on average, was among the best in the developed world. A strong industrial tradition, good education system, heavy government investment in industry and technology and neutrality in two world wars helped nurture a crop of companies that punched well above the country's weight on the international stage. Government policy has also played a part. According to Lars-Erik Forsgårdh, managing director of Aktiespararna: 'Back in the 1970s, the Government created a tax-subsidized savings system for mutual funds. When the social democrats were returned to power in 1982, they did not dare dismantle it. This contributed towards the rapid growth in equity ownership – you simply couldn't afford not to be in this system of saving.'

More recently, radical changes were implemented to the country's pension system, effectively changing it from one of defined benefits to one of defined contributions. Swedes who once knew that their pensions would be based on their best 15 years of earnings now know only that they must pay in 18.5 percent of their salary into a pension scheme that will pay out based on their total earnings since the age of 16. Furthermore, citizens are being given a choice over how some of that money is invested. Of the 18.5 percent, 16 percent goes into a state pension scheme, but the remainder goes into a premium pension account managed by a commercial fund manager. A significant proportion of these funds are likely to end up in equities.

> A significant proportion of these pension funds are likely to end up in equities

Allied to all of these reforms was the explosion of interest in equities generated by technology. Sweden is one of the most wired countries in the world, with the latest internet and mobile phone technology enthusiastically adopted not just by consumers but also by companies. Parts of the country have been compared to Silicon Valley, and the similarities are clear: government investment in the basic infrastructure, as well as a supply of bright young graduates from technical universities.

Technology has also played a big part in creating an equity culture in Finland, a country that industrialized at a far later stage than its neighbours and which for many decades was criticized for being over-reliant on national resources. The astonishing rise of Nokia, which now accounts for a sizeable share of Finland's exports, has spawned a generation of high-technology companies.

However, Finland is in several respects the odd man out in Scandinavia. Its language is radically different from the others and it has orientated itself towards Europe and even Russia as much as it has the rest of Scandinavia. Finland is the only Scandinavian country to have signed up to the euro – Sweden is waiting and seeing, Denmark voted 'No', and Norway is not even in the European Union.

Equity culture in Finland took off in a big way with the rise of Nokia at the close of the millennium. Share trading volumes on the Helsinki Stock Exchange were puny until 1998, when turnover topped €50 billion for the first time. In 1999, it topped €100 billion and the following year cleared €200 billion. It remained above that mark in 2001, even as technology stocks fell back. Despite the increase in local share ownership, the majority of Finland's stock market capitalization is in foreign hands – some 65 percent, according to the Finnish Foundation for Share Promotion.

THE MARKETS

Sweden is the leading stock exchange in Scandinavia. A stock exchange was constructed in 1778, but for many years goods, bills and marine insurances dominated the products traded. Between 1853 and 1860 only six trades in shares were recorded, since share trading was conducted on an over-the-counter basis at the banks. The stock exchange proper opened in 1863, although in the first years following its inception trading was dominated by one man, Carl Gustav Hierzeel. It was a similar story in the inter-war years, when the suicide of one Ivar Kreuger caused the stock exchange to close for nine days. Kreuger had literally built an empire on matchsticks. He offered massive credits to countries financially strained by the First World War in return for the monopoly on match production and sales in that country. The credits were financed by share issues in Sweden, but the Wall Street crash of 1929 hit the over-geared company hard and it became insolvent.

The 1990s was a decade of radical change for the Swedish bourse, starting with the introduction of electronic trading in 1990. In 1993 the exchange reorganized itself as a joint stock company, thus becoming the first exchange in the world to demutualize and become a for-profit entity. In 1997 it merged with OM, which had developed into a powerful player in derivatives trading since it was started in 1985. In 1998 the market set up a second board for growth stocks, the Nya Marknaden.

Admission to the stock exchange is approved by the exchange, based on regulations issued by Finansinspektionen, the financial supervisory authority. There are two lists: the A list, for blue chips, and the O list, which is for younger companies without enough trading history to satisfy A-list requirements. Those requirements are a minimum market value of SKr300 million and 2,000 investors holding 25 percent of the shares or at least 10 percent of the votes.

Although non-voting shares are not permitted in Sweden, differentials in voting rights are. Many companies issue A and B shares, with the B shares generally having fewer votes. In most cases the ratio is around one-to-ten, but in some cases it is a lot more.

Sweden's benchmark index is the OMX, which tracks the 30 largest blue chips (*see* Table 7.1). Clearing and settlement is via the Värdepapperscentralen (VPC), the central securities depository. Owned by four of Sweden's biggest banks, it moved to book entry in 1990 and trades are cleared and settled on the third business day following the trade. Trading itself takes place on OM's SAXESS system. Major shareholders need to disclose their stakes starting at 5 percent, and then in increments of 5 percent. The obligation to make a general offer to all shareholders is triggered at 40 percent, and there is a squeeze-out rule above 90 percent. There is no central mechanism for distributing information; most companies use either their own websites or a specialist information distributor.

Company (sector)	Weighting*
Ericsson (telecoms equipment)	15.57
AstraZeneca (pharmaceuticals)	12.04
Nordea (financial services)	10.01
Telia (telecoms)	7.52
Hennes & Mauritz (retailing)	6.98
Svenska Handelsbanken (financial services)	5.44
ForeningsSparbanken (financial services)	3.59
Securitas (security services)	3.08
Skand Enskilda Banken (financial services)	3.04
Skandia (financial services)	2.83
Sandvik (engineering)	2.67
Investor (financial holding company)	2.58
Nokia (telecoms equipment)	2.27
Volvo (automobiles)	2.36
Svenska Cellulosa (paper and packaging)	2.30
Electrolux (consumer goods)	2.33
Assa Abloy (security products)	2.13
Tele2 (telecoms operator)	1.68
Skanska (construction)	1.67
Pharmacia (pharmaceuticals)	1.45
Atlas Copco A (engineering)	1.44
Europolitan (telecoms operator)	1.29
Stora Enso (paper and packaging)	1.25
ABB (engineering)	0.89
Autoliv (automotive components)	0.73
Atlas Copco B	0.67
Holmen (forest products)	0.64
Eniro (publishing)	0.62
SKF (engineering)	0.55
Wm-Data (IT consulting)	0.32

Note: * Weightings are approximate

Table 7.1 The OMX index

Trading in Norway takes place on the Oslo Børs, which was merged with its rivals in Bergen and Trondheim in 1991, and demutualized and floated a decade later. Bonds and derivatives are also traded on the exchange. Listing prospectuses need to be approved by Oslo Børs' board of directors, and for large-cap stocks and market value of at least NoK300 million, a three-year trading history and a 25-percent free float is mandatory. The exchange is in turn regulated by the Banking Insurance and Securities Commission. Trades are cleared and settled through VPS, the central securities depository. Settlement is via book entry and the normal settlement period is the third business day following the trade.

The benchmark index for Norway is the OBX, comprising the 25 biggest stocks and dominated by banks and formerly state-owned companies like Statoil and Telenor (see Table 7.2). Major shareholders must disclose their interests upon reaching thresholds of 10 percent, 20 percent, one-third, half, two-thirds and 90 percent of the voting rights. The obligation to make a general offer is triggered with 40 percent of the rights, and the price must be equivalent to the highest price paid within the past six months. A squeeze-out rule applies above 90 percent, although the compulsory acquisition of minorities must be sanctioned by the Ministry of Justice.

Securities trading in Denmark takes place on the Copenhagen stock exchange, which remains unlisted but is a limited liability company owned by its members and the issuers of shares and bonds. Until very recently, it was considered illiquid because much of the share trading was done over the counter between banks. However, Copenhagen has done well out of the creation of Norex, with on-exchange volumes growing as a result.

Listings must be approved by a committee of the exchange, and the share capital must be at least DKr8.5 million. The framework legislation governing the trading of listed companies is the Danish Securities Trading Act, which is policed by the Danish Securities Council. Trading is on the SAXESS system, while clearing and settlement is handled via book entry at Vaerdipapircentralen, the Danish securities depository. This is a

Company (sector)	Weighting
Norsk Hydro (diversified resources)	25.00
Orkla (holding company)	11.61
Statoil (oil and gas)	9.70
Storebrand (financial services)	6.00
Den Norske Bank (financial services)	5.91
Tomra Systems (engineering)	5.46
Norske Skogindus (forestry, paper)	5.12
Telenor (telecoms operator)	4.79
Amersham (pharmaceuticals)	3.66
Royal Caribbean (leisure)	3.20
Tandberg (electronics)	2.83
Petroleum Geo-Services (oilfield services)	2.79
Bergesen DY (marine transport)	1.94
Frontline ltd (marine transport)	1.66
Schibsted (newspaper publisher)	1.46
Kvaerner (engineering)	1.42
PAN Fish (fish farming)	1.26
TGS Nopec Geophysics (oilfield services)	1.11
Nera (telecoms equipment)	0.94
InFocus (consumer electronics)	0.89
EDB Business (IT services)	0.86
Tandberg Televis (broadcast engineering)	0.84
Merkantildata (software, IT consulting)	0.76
Opticom (IT hardware)	0.49
Eltek (safety engineering)	0.10

Table 7.2 The OBX index

sophisticated operation; it pioneered paperless settlement of bond trades way back in 1983, and can settle equity trades in real time or in blocks.

The benchmark index is the KFX, comprising the 20 biggest and most liquid companies (*see* Table 7.3). It is dominated by Novo Nordisk, Tele Danmark (TDC) and the banks. Market-sensitive information is disclosed via the internet or fax-based StockWise system. Major shareholders must disclose their holdings starting at 5 percent and make repeat disclosures as the stake increases or decreases in 5-percent increments. The obligation to make a general offer is triggered once majority control is attained, and there is a squeeze-out rule above 90 percent.

Company (sector)	Weighting
Novo-Nordisk (pharmaceuticals)	18.86
Danske Bank (financial services)	17.50
TeleDanmark (telecoms operator)	10.87
H Lundbeck (pharmaceuticals)	8.23
D/S 1912 (shipping)	5.57
D/S Svendborg (shipping, oil services)	5.17
Nordea (bank)	4.73
Vestas Wind Systems (wind turbine)	4.04
Group 4 Falck (security services)	3.74
ISS (support services)	3.39
Danisco A/S (foodstuffs)	3.20
William Demant (medical equipment)	2.97
Novozymes (pharmaceuticals)	2.21
Coloplast (healthcare)	2.12
Carlsberg A/S (brewer)	2.00
GN Store Nord (telecoms equipment)	1.34
Jyske Bank (financial services)	1.26
NavisionDamgaard (software)	1.02
NEG Micon (wind turbines)	0.94
Kobenhavns Lufth (airport operator)	0.83

Table 7.3 The KFX index

THE NOREX ALLIANCE

Long before Euronext and iX were dreamed up, the Scandinavian exchanges were pooling their resources in a bid to lure back turnover in their biggest stocks from overseas financial centres. Norex is the vehicle for this campaign.

The central problem facing the exchanges is that they are simply too small on their own to compete. Even though more trades in companies like Nokia and Ericsson are executed in New York than Helsinki or Stockholm, those stocks still dominate trading volume and capitalization of their home markets.

Norex began in 1998 as an alliance between Stockholm and Copenhagen. It then spread to include Oslo, Iceland and the three Baltic states of Latvia, Lithuania and Estonia, although they have since fallen by the wayside. It remains an alliance, not a full merger. Companies from each country still see their shares traded in the currency of that country on the national stock exchange. Yet Poul-Erik Skaaning-Jørgensen, president of the Norex holding company Nordic Exchanges AS, is quick to point out that in many ways Norex is more integrated than markets like Euronext. It has a common rule book for member firms, and a common trading system, OM Group's SAXESS.

SAXESS is a totally order-driven system, matching buy and sell orders according to volume and price. Most trading takes place within the 'trading lot' market, where blocks of shares of a pre-determined size are traded. However, there is also an 'odd-lot' market where smaller orders can be matched. Retail investors can plug almost directly into this via a broker's system. Similarly, very large deals can be agreed between brokers over the telephone, but they must still be notified to SAXESS.

Company	Weighting
Nordea	10.10
Ericsson	8.49
Nokia	7.93
Novo-Nordisk	6.11
Svenska Handelsbanken	5.64
Hennes & Mauritz B	5.46
Norsk Hydro	4.89
UPM-Kymmene	4.04
Stora Enso	3.37
Securitas	3.30
Skand Enskilda Banken	3.21
TeleDanmark	3.13
Skandia Foraskring	3.09
Sandvik	2.82
Investor B	2.67
ForeningsSparbanken Ser A	2.59
Electrolux Ser B'	2.56
Volvo B	2.52
SCA B	2.30
Orkla	2.27
Telia	2.21
Statoil	1.85
Skanska B	1.72
Tele2	1.71
Vestas Wind Systems	1.70
Telenor	1.14
Atlas Copco	1.10
Group4 Falck	1.06
Sonera	0.64
Europolitan	0.38

Table 7.4 The FTSE Norex 30 index

The individual exchanges still have their own indices, typically dominated by one or two big companies, although pan-Nordic products are under development and FTSE International has already devised a Norex 30 index (see Table 7.4). The exchanges have also, in conjunction with Morgan Stanley Capital International, devised common industry classifications that work across the four markets.

Norex firmly believes there will be more consolidation. Poul-Erik Skaaning-Jørgensen says: 'We have definitely made no secret of the fact that we see ourselves as part of consolidation. We don't think there will ever be a single European equity market, but increasing convergence around platforms like SAXESS, Xetra and SETS.' But perhaps the most obvious next move for Norex is to get the Finns on board. 'Many people expected that once the derivatives were listed on Eurex, there would be a broader link-up with Frankfurt,' says Skaaning-Jørgensen. 'But that hasn't happened ... we would certainly prefer to have Helsinki as a full member of the Norex alliance.' With Finland in the fold, Norex would be the world's seventh-largest stock exchange.

HELSINKI – THE ODD MAN OUT

Finland's stock exchange is owned by the HEX Group, one of whose shareholders is OM. The relationship is not a totally harmonious one, however; one particular sore point between them is the proportion of turnover in Nokia shares that takes place in Stockholm as opposed to Helsinki.

This is one reason why HEX is not part of the Norex alliance; another is that Finland sees itself as much more closely aligned with the rest of Europe than do the other Scandinavian countries. Finland's derivatives trading now takes place on Eurex, the derivatives exchange operated jointly by the German and Swiss stock exchanges, and has a cross-membership agreement with Euronext (see Chapter 3). HEX is also looking east and has already acquired the Tallinn exchange in Estonia.

Listings in Helsinki must be approved by the board of HEX in the case of blue chips, while in the case of mid-cap companies (the I list) and new market (NM) stocks, the assent of the chief executive officer of HEX is all that is required. Blue chips must have a free float of at least 25 percent, and must also have a three-year trading record and sufficient distributable reserves to pay dividends. Their market value must be at least FMk200 million. For smaller stocks the free-float threshold is 15 percent, and the trading record requirement drops to two years for I-list companies and one year for NM companies. The market value requirements are FMk20 million and FMk10 million respectively. There is also a pre-list, designed to stimulate investor interest and allow companies to evaluate whether a listing is appropriate to their development. Companies are usually on the pre-list for up to a year before graduating to the main markets.

The framework legislation for share trading is the Securities Market Act, which is supervised by the Financial Supervision Agency (FSA), which is in turn allied to the Bank of Finland. All shares are supposed to carry equal weight, but in practice a company's articles of association can overrule this. However, the difference in voting rights may not be more than 20-fold. Trading is executed via HEX's Heti system, a PC-based order-driven trading platform. The central securities depository is also owned by HEX Group, and since 1992 has been paperless.

The benchmark index is the HEX 20, which comprises the 20 most liquid companies. The HEX all-share covers all the stocks on the main list, but not those on the mid-cap market or the NM, both of which have their own benchmarks. Even after the collapse of the technology bubble, Nokia still accounts for around half the capitalization of the entire market. Another benchmark, the HEX portfolio index, aims to reduce the influence of Nokia by imposing a 10 percent ceiling on index weightings.

Major shareholders must disclose their ownership starting at 5 percent and at 10, 15, 20, 25, 33, 50 and 66 percent. However, a general offer is not usually triggered until the stake reaches 66.67 percent, unless a company's articles of association specify otherwise. Not surprisingly, most do – 33.33 percent and 50 percent are the most common thresholds. There is a squeeze-out rule at 90 percent.

STATE-OWNED COMPANIES THAT WORK

Despite its increasingly popular appeal, shareholder capitalism in Scandinavia still has clear distinctions. The most obvious of these is a high level of residual state ownership, in some cases in companies and industries that would not be deemed strategic elsewhere. There are various reasons for this. One practical one is that for many years governments simply did not need the money. Scandinavian countries have small populations and are generally rich in natural resources. Only when governments began to look at the consequences of providing generous retirement incomes for increasingly grey populations did that start to change. In addition, because Scandinavian countries had always invested heavily in public services and industries, there was not a backlog of costly investment that needed to be spread among shareholders as well as taxpayers.

There was also no big ideological push for privatization. One pattern of thinking that underlay privatizations in the UK in particular was that nationalized, public-owned institutions were useless – over-manned, bureaucratic, inefficient producers of goods nobody wanted. But Scandinavian countries attempted to run their publicly-owned corporations as efficiently as their peers in the private sector – and by and large succeeded. They were helped by early adoption of competition – telecommunications and energy were deregulated in Scandinavia long ago, and companies part-owned by the government of one country compete in neighbouring lands, often with other partly state-owned firms.

> Scandinavian countries attempted to run their publicly-owned corporations as efficiently as their peers in the private sector

State ownership is most widespread in Finland, where the Government owns significant stakes in 11 major listed companies (*see* Table 7.5). Although it accepts that state ownership is in many cases no longer necessary, it appears in no hurry to sell off its silverware. This has ramifications for the way companies do business. All companies part-owned by the Government have a two-tier board structure, with a supervisory board overseeing the management. Then there's the issue of mergers and acquisitions. The Finnish Government could block a takeover of any of 'its' companies, because it has yet to reduce its stake in any of them to below 10 percent. Sonera, the Finnish telecoms company, has come to symbolize the difficulties in reconciling partial state ownership with the demands of the marketplace. Its former chief executive, Kaj-Erik Relander, was a sharp critic of government meddling in the company.

Company	Shares	Votes	Minimum
Finnair	58.4	58.4	50.1
Fortum	70.7	70.7	50.1
Kemira	56.2	56.2	15.0
Metso	11.6	11.6	0.0
Outokumpu	40.0	40.0	10.0
Partek	30.2	30.2	0.0
Rautaruukki	40.1	40.1	20.0
Sampo	40.3	40.3	0.0
Sonera	52.8	52.8	0.0
Sponda	47.2	47.2	0.0
Stora Enso	15.1	24.1	0.0

Source: Finnish Foundation for Share Promotion

Table 7.5 Major Finnish state holdings

Norway, which like Finland was ruled by Sweden for decades, is also protective of its smattering of blue-chip companies. When Elf Aquitaine tried to take over Saga Petroleum, state-controlled Norsk Hydro stepped in with a higher bid to see off the French. It was a similar story when Sampo, the Finnish bank, attempted to take over Storebrand, the Norwegian insurer. It dropped its $2 billion bid after failing to secure the necessary 90-percent acceptance levels. The crucial 10 percent was held by Den Norske Bank (DnB), in turn 47-percent owned by the state. The rhetoric of politicians was clear – they wanted the insurer to remain in Norwegian hands. The finance minister, Carl Eirik Schjøtt-Pedersen, said it was 'of vital Norwegian interest that Storebrand remains a Norwegian company that is owned and run from Norway'. He was quite happy for DnB shareholders to face a dilutive offer and for Storebrand shareholders to realize lower value, in order for this to happen.

Box 7.1 Equity investment in Scandinavia

The exchanges
Stockholmsborsen (www.stockholmsborsen.se), Oslo Børs (www.oslobors.no) and København Fondbors (www.xcse.dk/uk/index.asp) are all part of the Norex alliance (www.norex.com). Helsinki (www.hexgroup.com) is not. All the Norex exchanges are switching to OM Group's (www.om.com) Saxess trading system.

Clearing and settlement
This is still done under national jurisdictions. In Norway, this is Verdipapiersentralen (www.vps.no), in Denmark Vaerdipapiercentralen (www.vp.dk), in Sweden VPC (www.vpc.se/english/index.html). In Finland, clearing and settlement (www.apk.fi) is owned by Hex Group.

Indices
Sweden's benchmark is the OMX, Norway's the OBX, Denmark's the KFX, and Finland's the HEX 20. There are several pan-Scandinavian indices, including the FT Norex 30 and the Stoxx Nordic Index.

Regulation
Norex members have a common rule book, but companies are regulated according to national company law. Fortunately, legal structures are similar in the Scandinavian countries. The regulator in Sweden is Finansinspektionen (www.fi.se), in Denmark it is the Danish Financial Supervisory Authority (www.ftnet.dk), and in Norway the Banking and Insurance Commission (www.kredittilsynet.no). In Finland, securities market supervision is via the Financial Supervision Agency, which reports to the Bank of Finland (www.bof.fi).

Shareholder associations
These are very active, especially in Sweden and Finland. In Sweden, smaller shareholders are represented by Aktiespararna (www.aktiespararna.se) – a very good English-language website, while Finland has a Foundation for Share Promotion (www.porssisaatio.fi/english/main.asp). In Denmark, there is the Danish Shareholders Association (www.shareholders.dk) and in Norway Aksjesparerforeningen (www.aksjesparerforeningen.no).

Dealer associations
Danish Securities Dealers Association (www.dbmf.dk), Norwegian Association of Stockbrokers (www.nfmf.no), Swedish Securities Dealers Assocation (www.fondhandlarna.se) and Finnish Securities Dealers Association (www.apvy.fi).

More information
For a very useful, up-to-date table of links to news providers in English, see www.finanssiden.com/News/fnewsnorden.htm.

His dilemma is understandable. A total release of state ownership could result in some of Scandinavia's best companies being 'cherry picked' by vastly bigger international concerns. Yet preventing mergers and other corporate activity could result in companies becoming inward-looking and too small to compete effectively. It will be interesting to see how far Finland and Norway in particular are prepared to go down this route, although the idea of 'Nordic champions' is at least a lesser evil. For Sweden, state ownership is less of an issue. Several of its companies have already merged with overseas concerns – Astra AB with Zeneca of the UK, Asea with Switzerland's Brown Boveri to form ABB. The two bastions of its engineering industry have both passed into partial foreign control, with General Motors buying Saab Automobile, and Ford buying the car-making division of Volvo.

TOP LISTINGS IN SCANDINAVIA

NOKIA AND ERICSSON – POWERING THE TECHNOLOGY REVOLUTION

Scandinavia's two biggest and best known companies are associated in most people's minds with mobile phones (see Fig. 7.1). But Nokia (www.nokia.com) only started dabbling in telephony in the 1980s. It was originally a pulp and paper manufacturer, named after the river on which its mill was sited. During the 1960s it became a mini-conglomerate, before moving into more glamorous sectors like fibre-optics in the 1970s. Its telephones business really took off in 1981 when it bought 51 percent of the state-owned Finnish telephone company, renaming it Telenokia. In 1988 it bought Ericsson's data division. But the move into consumer electronics was ill-timed, and the Nokia Data business was sold to ICL in 1991, with the proceeds helping pay for the acquisition of UK mobile-phone maker Technophone. New chief executive Jorma Ollila decided this was the future, and set about selling everything else. By 1998 Nokia was the world's biggest seller of handsets. The next big thing was to be the mobile internet, and Nokia has invested heavily in developing wireless internet technology.

By contrast, Ericsson (www.ericsson.com) has always been involved in telephony. Established as a telegraph repair shop by Lars Magnus

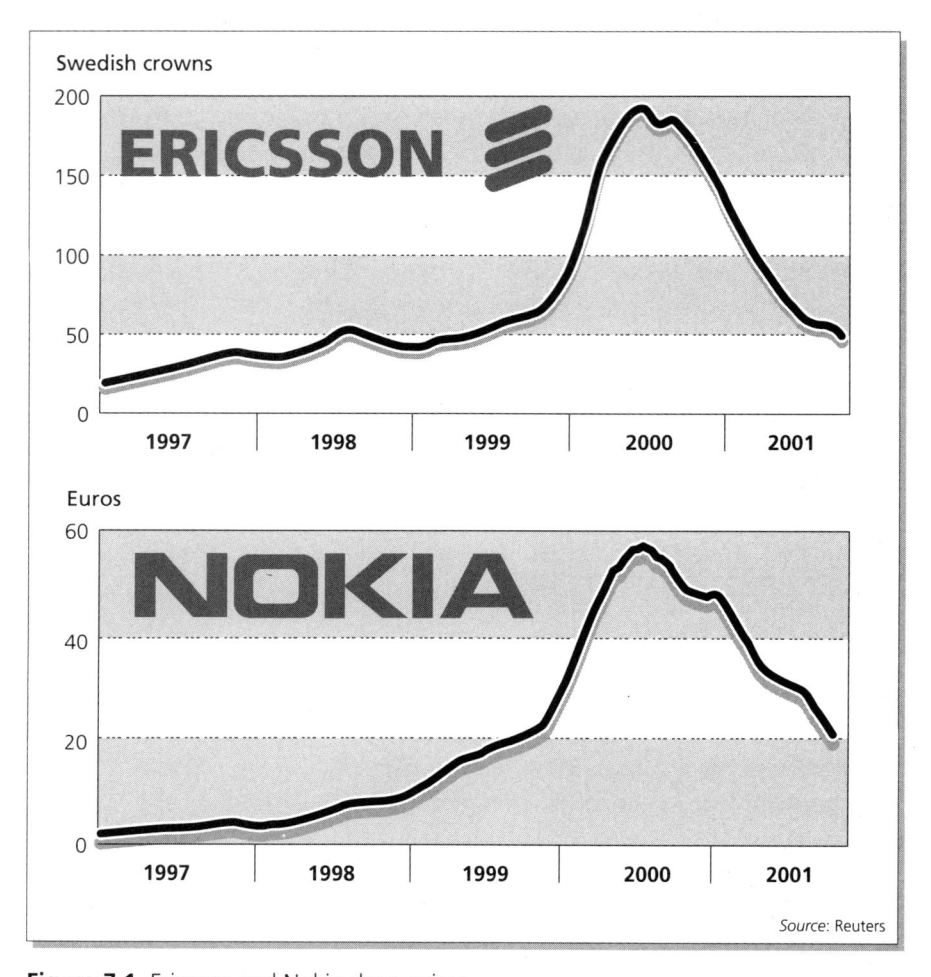

Figure 7.1 Ericsson and Nokia share prices

Ericsson in 1876, within two years the firm was making telephones. Control of Ericsson passed to the Wallenberg family in 1960. For many years during the 1970s and 1980s its key product was AXE, a computer-controlled exchange. That set the stage for its world-leading position in the field of wireless infrastructure – the behind-the-scenes equipment that powers mobile phone networks – although it trails Nokia and others in handset sales. Like Nokia, its future remains inextricably linked with the success or otherwise of third-generation mobile networks, and also its Bluetooth system that allows short-range wireless communication between electronic devices.

Both companies are vitally important to their respective countries. Ericsson accounts for 15 percent of Sweden's exports, and Nokia an even greater share of Finland's. Heavy overseas selling of Ericsson shares tends to weaken the Swedish krona and some analysts think the downturn in mobile phone markets will materially affect growth in gross domestic product (GDP). Economists at ETLA, the Research Institution of the Finnish Economy, calculated that of Finland's 3.5 percent GDP growth in 1999, 1 percent was directly attributable to Nokia.

But there are also important differences. Nokia products are widely perceived as cool, young and fashionable, whereas Ericsson's handsets lost market share because, despite being well-engineered, they were not funky enough. The management styles are also very different. Ericsson was hopelessly overmanned, with hordes of middle managers contributing to the decision-making paralysis that resulted in the company losing its way in the handset market. Its board is dominated by two spheres: the Wallenbergs on one hand, and Industrivarden on the other. Between them, they control over 80 percent of the votees, because their A shares carry 1,000 votes apiece against one vote per B share. There has been management upheaval, too – chairman Lars Ramqvist picked Sven-Christer Nilsson as chief executive in 1998, only to dispense with his services just over a year later.

By contrast, Nokia's top management team is well entrenched, and although non-Finns sit on its board, it remains a very Finnish company. Discussion is direct and action decisive, compared to the consensus-driven approach at Ericsson. It unified its shares into a single class carrying one vote apiece in 1999, and no major shareholder has more than around 0.5 percent of the company

TOWARDS A NORDIC TELECOM

Each of the main Scandinavian countries has privatized its telecoms operator, although state holdings remain. Sweden's Telia (www.telia.com) was privatized in June 2000, with the Government selling 20 percent to investors. It was followed in September of the same year by Norway's Telenor (www.telenor.com), which was valued at around half the level of its Swedish counterpart.

Now the question is when the four, or some of their number, will combine to form a single Nordic telecoms unit. Most of the companies seem to acknowledge that they are too small to challenge the likes of British Telecommunications, Deutsche Telekom and France Telecom for investors' attention. But a 'Nordic Telecom', operating across a region with high levels of internet and mobile phone penetration, would be a different matter.

The practicalities are what makes such a tie-up difficult. The pantomime of the Telia/Telenor merger illustrated this perfectly. Talks between the Swedes and the Norwegians began before either company was floated, but the two sides seemed to have different agendas. Although Telia was the bigger company, the Norwegians wanted a merger of equals to preserve national pride. After much wrangling, the deal went ahead. Then there was a row over which country should be home to the combined group's mobile phone operations. Sweden's industry minister called Norway 'the last Soviet state'. The (Norwegian) chief executive of the combined group punched a reporter. Eventually, the whole thing was called off.

Ownership is the obvious sticking point. Out of the four operators, only Tele Danmark has no state ownership left, although it does have a major shareholder – SBC Communications of the US. SBC's opposition blocked a planned merger with Telenor. While Telia, the main player in the countless rounds of merger talks, has a relatively clean Scandinavian focus, the others have significant interests that would not sit easily within a 'Nordic Telecom'. Sonera owns a 43-percent stake in a German third-generation mobile phone business with Spain's Telefonica. Such interests would drain investment away from the home market.

BANKS – CONSOLIDATION PACESETTERS

Scandinavia's banks have had more success in marrying themselves off to their neighbours. The bandwagon started rolling back in 1996 when Merita of Finland and Nordbanken of Sweden merged to form Nordea (www.nordea.com). The enlarged company went on to acquire others, including Norway's Christiania Bank and Unidanmark.

However, the bandwagon seems to have juddered to a halt of late. The European Union blocked the merger of SEB (www.seb.se) with ForeningsSparbanken (www.foreningsparbanken.se), while the proposed combination of Finland's Sampo (www.sampo.fi) and Norway's Storebrand (www.storebrand.no) was broken up by Den Norske Bank, with a little help from the Norwegian Government.

NATURAL RESOURCES – THE TRADITIONAL STALWARTS

Investors today fret that Finland's stock market, and even its whole economy, is too dependent on the fortunes of Nokia. Yet the Finns are fond of pointing out that ten years ago the same investors complained that it was too dependent on forestry and mining. Forestry was Finland's biggest industry before mobile phones came along.

The two big players are Stora Enso and UPM-Kymmene (www.upm-kymmene.com), which between them have comprehensively restructured the world industry after a wave of acquisitions in North America and Asia. Stora-Enso (www.storaenso.com), formed by the merger of Sweden's STORA and Finland's Enso, is particularly interesting – STORA's roots go back to 1288, when King Magnus granted a charter to mine copper from the Kopparberg Mountain. It acquired its first sawmill in 1885 and launched newsprint production in 1900. The company decided to focus on forestry in the 1970s, and in the early 1990s the Falun copper mine finally closed. Enso was a more recent creation, set up by Norwegian Hans Gutzeit and his family in 1872. It was reincorporated in Finland in 1896, but the First World War and the Russian Revolution decimated its markets, and it was sold to the state of Finland in 1919. The Second World War saw many of its facilities destroyed, but it recovered strongly after the war. The merger with STORA was sealed in 1998, 710 years after King Magnus' granted the mining rights.

Norway also has a heavy contingent of natural resources companies; indeed, the heaviest weighting in the index is held by a natural resources conglomerate. Norsk Hydro (www. hydro.com) has major oil operations offshore Norway as well as in North America and West Africa. It is also a major producer of fertilizers and chemicals and light metals like magnesium. The 'Hydro' bit of the name came from its origins using hydro-electric power to extract nitrogen from the air to produce fertilizer, something it started doing in 1905. The Norwegian Government became a major (but not controlling) shareholder after the Second World War, and Norsk Hydro-Elektrisk Kvaelstofaktieselskap was before long the largest chemicals producer not only in Norway but the whole of Scandinavia.

The move into oil began in the late 1960s, and the Government took its stake to 51 percent in 1971. Oil remained the focus of its attention, but the company also used acquisitions to extend its interests in fertilizer production and move into light metals; Norway's abundant supplies of hydro power make it an ideal location for aluminium production. Government control was relinquished in 1999, partly to balance the takeover of listed Saga Petroleum by the then-unquoted and state-owned Statoil.

SAAB AND VOLVO – RIVALLING THE GERMANS

Sweden's industrial scene was always less biased towards natural resources because of its substantial engineering sector. However, as in the UK, there are no longer any quoted car manufacturers. Saab, which started life as an aerospace company (Svenska Aeroplan AB) in 1937 was brought under the full control of General Motors in 2000. The American giant had bought a 50-percent stake in 1990, seeking an upmarket European marque to go with its mass-market Vauxhalls and Opels. The aerospace division of Saab (www.saab.se) is owned by the Wallenberg's Investor group.

It is a similar story at Volvo. The company started life as a subsidiary of ball-bearing maker SKF in 1915, and began building cars in 1926 and trucks in 1928. In 1935, it became an independent company, although most of its sales were into the domestic market. It embraced the 1980s mania for conglomerates, buying into food, drugs, energy and investment companies in a bid to reduce dependence on cars. But it was becoming clear that, like Saab, Volvo was too small to carry the ballooning costs of developing and marketing new models. It looked for ways to acquire scale, pursuing a merger with France's Renault that was shot down by a public outcry in Sweden. Six years later, however, the public mood had changed and Volvo sold its car division to Ford for $6.5 billion. The Volvo that remains quoted today (www.volvo.com) is one of the world's biggest manufacturers of trucks and buses.

FRAMFAB – CASHING IN ON THE START-UP CULTURE

The phenomenal rise of Nokia and Ericsson, and the enthusiastic adoption of all things technology-related, has resulted in a proliferation of smaller, more entrepreneurial companies, which for a while attained almost cult status. Many were headed by bright young things from Sweden's best universities and seemed to embody much that was holistic and wholesome about Scandinavia. Perhaps none epitomized this quite like FramFab (www.framfab.com), headed by 28-year-old Jonas Birgersson. Birgersson had little technical background, having studied military history at university (he would pepper his presentations to investors with quotes from Napoleon). He wore fleecy jumpers and combat boots, shaved relatively infrequently and continued to live like a student, in a modest one-bedroom flat, even when FramFab's value was at its giddy peak.

Unfortunately for investors, Birgersson had little commercial experience either. He founded Framtidsfabriken (The Future Factory) in Lund in 1995 after failing to convince Telia, the state telecoms group, with his vision of a network revolution. As the technology bug took hold, he soon became a household name, and FramFab was busy advising the nation's blue-chips on their e-business strategies. Revenues soared and the share price increased 14-fold between the company's flotation in June 1999 and the end of the technology boom in March 2000. But FramFab was on a growth binge that was ultimately too difficult to control. Staff numbers shot up as the FramFab merged with one company after another, often in unrelated sectors. When corporate spending on all things internet-related began to slow down, FramFab was pole-axed. Revenues plunged, losses ballooned and the share price fell 99 percent. By the time FramFab launched a rescue rights issue in May 2001, Birgersson had resigned. The issue was successful, although as the *Financial Times'* influential Lex column noted: 'Why anyone would want to save Framfab, other than to exhibit in a museum of internet excess, is mystifying.'

INVESTOR AB – WALLENBERGS UNDER SIEGE

The concept of an industrial holding company, with a hotch-potch of stakes in seemingly unrelated businesses, may well be dead in many other countries. In most markets, diversity is out and focus is prized. But it is difficult to do much investing in Sweden without running into Investor (www.investorab.com). Its core holdings comprise stakes in some of Scandinavia's biggest companies, including ABB, Astra Zeneca, Atlas Copco, Electrolux, Ericsson, Gambro, OM, Saab AB, Scania, SEB and WM-data.

The company started life in 1916 as an offshoot of Enskilda Bank. It was rushed into being to circumvent a new law that would have prevented the bank owning shares. It was listed in 1919. Since that time, it has been a pivotal player in Swedish corporate history, acting as kingmaker in many a deal. It rescued Astra and L. M. Ericsson from near-insolvency. It picked up the pieces of Kreuger's matchstick empire. It brokered the merger of Asea with Brown Boveri to form ABB, and the combination of Astra and Zeneca of the UK. It sold Saab Automobile to the US.

Throughout its life, Investor has been dominated by the Wallenberg family; there are currently three members of the clan on its board of directors, and each of them also sits on a number of investee company boards. Two family foundations have control, along with the current directors, of around 42 percent of the votes, thanks to Investor's dual-share system.

As one of the most powerful companies in Scandinavia, Investor certainly gets plenty of public attention. The Swedish shareholders society, Aktiespararna, was highly critical of its decision to assent to the merger of Astra with Zeneca of the UK, and later of the management problems at Ericsson. It has also attracted attention from overseas: Swiss activist Martin Ebner has clashed with the Wallenbergs, saying they should sell more of the group's assets. The family's reputation suffered a grievous blow in 2002, when it was revealed that Percy Barnevik, one of Sweden's most respected businessmen, had pocketed over €60m of pension benefits from his tenure at ABB, the engineering company. The sum caused uproar in egalitarian Sweden. Barnevik subsequently resigned as chairman of Investor, and the group also took the unusual step of revealing the pension and bonus payments made to all its senior executives.

CARLSBERG – PROBABLY THE BEST-KNOWN COMPANY IN DENMARK

Alongside children's toy Lego (which remains in private hands), Carlsberg (www.carlsberg.com) is Denmark's most famous and successful export. Although it has around 70 percent of Denmark's beer consumption stitched up, it sells 85 percent of its output outside the country. It was founded by J.C. Jacobsen in 1847, and named after his son Carl. But the two fell out, and Carl started a rival operation practically next door to his father. The breweries were re-amalgamated after the death of both men.

Since 1873 there has also been competition from Tuborg, not just in terms of beer production, but in the race to endow Copenhagen with the most philanthropic arts venues, statues and museums. Eventually, in 1969, the two companies merged, and Carlsberg went on and make major acquisitions in the UK (Tetley) and sign distribution deals in North America with Anheuser Busch and Labatts, and with India's United Breweries in 1995. Carlsberg is still controlled by the charitable Carlsberg Foundation, whose charter states it must hold at least 51 percent of the operation.

NOVO NORDISK – HORMONAL IMBALANCE

Denmark's leading pharmaceutical company produces remedies for depression, epilepsy and haemophilia. But it remains the world's biggest producer of the hormone that it was created in order to produce – insulin. One half of the enterprise, Nordisk, was founded by Nobel prize winner August Krogh and his wife in the 1920s. The other, Novo, was created by Harald and Thorvald Pedersen, two Nordisk employees who left to set up their own rival insulin producer in 1924. They also devised a syringe that diabetics could use to inject their own insulin. By 1989 Novo was the world's second-biggest producer behind the US's Eli Lilley, while Nordisk was number three. The merger of the two created a world leader. In addition to insulin, Novo Nordisk (www.novonordisk.com) is also a significant producer of human growth hormones and HRT products for menopausal women. The Novo Nordisk Foundation owns around a quarter of the company.

8

ITALY, SPAIN AND PORTUGAL

ITALY – *SALÒTTO BUONO* STILL IN BUSINESS

Our mission is to try to transform the concept of the Borsa from a black box ... to a glass house.

Massimo Capuano, CEO Borsa Italiana

ITALIANS USED TO SHUN SHARES, scooping up instead large returns on buying government bonds that offered high, largely risk-free interest, whilst the State tried to service its huge debt. What there was of an equity culture in the 1970s and 1980s was enjoyed by the super rich, who dabbled on the Milan stock exchange, a pastime known as *giocàre in Borsa*, while the bulk of investor money went into bonds. The few brave individuals who ventured on to the Borsa in those days were referred to as the *parco buoi* or cattle market. Small investors found it difficult to know why some stocks moved, with many brokers left out of the picture too.

Poor public knowledge of what went on in the elite world of Italian equities made the Borsa look like an opaque, black box to outsiders. Inside this *salòtto buono*, or refined dining room, powerful corporate families like Fiat, the Agnellis or the De Benedettis went about their business, largely free of too much public scrutiny. According to Giuliano Gregorio, an exchanges industry consultant:

> The small shareholders usually had little power and could not influence what was going on. Companies generally did not go to the stock exchange to raise capital. Banks were more than happy to lend money to companies, and the bosses of big firms preferred to run everything without the bureaucracy of the Borsa, or the demands of public disclosure.

Raising money on the stock exchange was also not an easy task at the time, leaving companies to take the easier option of turning to banks for cash.

Italian shares, like those in many of the euro zone countries, became more attractive when the convergence of debt markets ahead of the single currency's launch pushed down yields on Italian bonds from about 15 percent to 5 percent. When the existing bonds expired, investors saw how paltry returns would be on new issues and began looking elsewhere for better returns. Initially, small investors bought into mutual funds, but as new economy companies began to list on the Milan exchange to raise cash, people began buying shares directly. The arrival of the internet and online trading also broke down entry barriers for small investors in stocks, and shares became fashionable, amid huge marketing campaigns. Big privatizations of state-owned companies brought in international investment banks as advisers who offered chunks of newly available Italian shares to fund managers outside Italy, triggering an increase in information about Italian equities. The Italians themselves also bought shares in part-privatized companies, like industrial holding company IRI, banks, Telecom Italia and energy companies.

> "Shares became fashionable, amid huge marketing campaigns"

However, tax advantages favoured covered warrants, or securities notes – which could be promoted effectively by the dense sales networks of Italian banks – and these hindered the drive to equities. The lack of pension funds in Italy also robs the market of a major money source that listings in the Netherlands or the UK enjoy. Thus individual investors in Italy still lack long-term goals, and prefer shorter-term tactics in the market. Today's Italian stock market is dominated by mostly defensive-type shares, like the traditional safe havens of banks and utilities, with telecoms acting as a proxy for technology shares that are largely absent. Banks account for around half of the market's capitalization (*see* Figure 8.1).

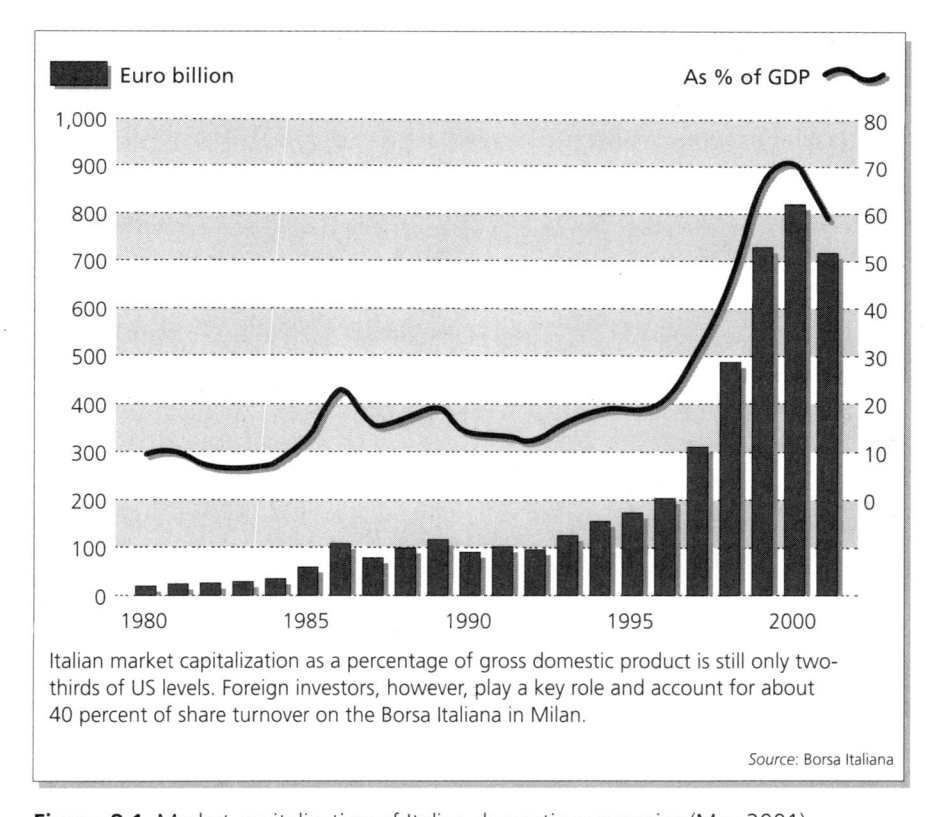

Italian market capitalization as a percentage of gross domestic product is still only two-thirds of US levels. Foreign investors, however, play a key role and account for about 40 percent of share turnover on the Borsa Italiana in Milan.

Source: Borsa Italiana

Figure 8.1 Market capitalization of Italian domestic companies (May 2001)

PENSIONS AND OTHER PROBLEMS

By 2001 Italy was frantically looking for ways such as tax breaks to stimulate the country's poorly developed private pensions industry in order to cut down the huge amounts of money the State was spending on pensions for the country's ageing population. If the current demographic trend continues, a fifth of Italy's 59 million population will be aged over 65 by 2015, compared to 17 percent in 1999. The Governor of the Bank of Italy Antonio Fazio has said the country faces a pensions crisis by 2005 unless there is reform. Italy is one of the European Union members that spends most on pensions – around 15 percent of gross domestic product.

If Italy is able to encourage its population to turn to private pensions, then equities are likely to be one of the long-term winners, helping to underpin the Italian stock market. However, the whole issue of pension reform will be difficult to resolve because of heated labour union opposition – during the 1994 attempt to scale back state pensions, over a million people took to the streets, triggering a fall of the government.

Cross-holdings between companies are also a bone of contention in Italy where they are more pervasive than in other European countries. This makes the market less of a takeover play for investors than it would otherwise appear. The percentage of a company's share that is freely floated – available for investors to trade – is much lower in Italy than in many other European countries because of the grip cross-holdings have on large chunks of shares. 'When buying stocks in Italy, investors always need to think about who controls the company,' advises Jason James, a European equities strategist at HSBC Securities.

Investment bank Mediobanca, for example, is seen as a classic example of an Italian stock that is allowed to be an Italian blue chip, but is closely held and with little known about how it operates. Not surprisingly, 'secretive' is the usual description for the company whose discrete fingers are to be found in a wide range of Italy's corporate pies.

There is also still the reluctance among Italian companies to list publicly. Market experts estimate there are a thousand firms that would be eligible to list, and the exchange is encouraging many, especially the traditional, family-owned operations, to float. The exchange promotes going public as a way for family-owned companies to avoid inheritance problems by making the firm shareholder owned. Better standards of corporate governance have certainly shed more light on Italian companies but some dark corners remain. As Massimo Capuano, Milan exchange's chief executive has said: 'The change in terms of mindset in less than ten years has been rapid. Our mission is to try to transform the concept of the Borsa from a black box, something people did not know very well, to a glass house.'

CORPORATE GOVERNANCE – THE DRAGHI–PREDA DOUBLE ACT

Italy's corporate governance rules are based on two separate provisions: the 1998 new companies law Testo Unico della Finanza, also called the Riforma Draghi, which strengthened the protection of investors, especially minority investors, and the so-called Codice di Autodisciplina, also known as the Codice Preda, which was adopted by the Italian stock exchange in October 1999.

The Draghi law, named after a top Italian Treasury official Mario Draghi, put into effect the European Union's Investment Services Directive (ISD) on a national basis. It applies to takeovers, corporate governance and the handling of share-price sensitive information. Five years ago few Italian companies had investor relations staff, but now – as a result of the Draghi Law – they are common. Unlike Draghi, the Codice Preda corporate governance rules, named after former Milan exchange chairman Stefano Preda who headed a 1998 report into corporate governance, are voluntary. The exchange, however, forces companies who choose not to observe any of the 13-point Preda code to say why publicly.

The aim of the two rafts of measures is to encourage wider ownership of Italian companies, but Professor Antonio Salvi, a lecturer in corporate finance at Milan's Bocconi University and at the University of Venice, said the opposite has been happening. Instead, he claims that over a period of three to four years the big, institutional shareholders in Italy have increased their holdings from 45 percent to just over half of the country's market capitalization, as stiffer corporate governance rules took effect. He explains:

> These provisions have triggered some sort of entrenchment of control. As minor shareholders have greater protection, the reaction of the big shareholders seem to have bolstered their positions. We have the corporate governance laws, but the problem is that companies should change their mentality. Entrepreneurs must decide if they wish to list their companies or not.

Luigi Spaventa, the head of stocks regulator Consob, agrees, asserting that by 2000 the strong shift in investment from debt to equity had not been accompanied by a change in corporate governance. Instead, companies often ignore the Preda self-governing code that recommends that minority shareholders have the right to vote by proxy at shareholder meetings. Unfortunately Consob has fairly limited powers to act on behalf of small investors. Any misbehaviour it spots must be reported to a local judge, triggering what is often a slow and bureaucratic process.

SALÒTTO BUONO STILL IN BUSINESS

Despite all the corporate governance changes, deals among financial barons pay scant heed to small investors, ensuring that the days of *salòtto buono*, or gentleman's club, are not over yet for Italy.

For example, in 2001 carmaker Fiat took control of Montedison by offering minority shareholders only the minimum price required by Italian law – and did so only after the deal had already been effectively signed, sealed and delivered, giving little time for shareholder consultation. Even more brazen was tyremaker Pirelli which in 2001 took control of one of the country's biggest companies, Telecom Italia, all in the space of a weekend, and without making an offer to minority shareholders at all. Pirelli chairman Marco Tronchetti Provera, through a complicated set of so-called Chinese boxes or pyramid of holdings, controls the €55-billion Telecom Italia after taking a stake worth a fraction of that in the telephone company's parent, Olivetti. No takeover process was triggered by Pirelli's move because the stake in Olivetti that changed hands was only 27 percent, just short of the 30-percent trigger point for having to launch an official takeover bid. The whole off-market transaction – which did not allow the market to offer an opinion – simply underlined how much progress Italy still needed to make to reach a transparent system of corporate governance that does not trample on minority shareholder rights. Deals such as Pirelli taking control of Telecom Italia present a poor image of corporate Italy. Consob intervened to rule that the big losses at Olivetti, the holding company for Telecom Italia, should be consolidated into Pirelli's own accounts. But late February 2002, a court backed an appeal by Pirelli against Consob's ruling.

Analysts believe that since Italy is ruled by a right-wing government headed by business magnate Silvio Berlusconi, further progress in corporate governance is likely to be slow. Elected in 2001, Berlusconi's financial empire spans shops to television networks. The Italians coined the term *Berlusconismo* to describe the extent of his interests in their everyday lives, while the man himself is described in the newspapers as simply *Il Cavaliere*, The Knight.

KEEPING IT IN THE FAMILY

The upside of a country having a less developed equity culture is often the existence of colourful families, and Italy has its fair share of them. Undisputedly, the Agnellis of carmaking dynasty Fiat are at the top of a corporate tree that is laden with world famous family names like Benetton, Gucci, Versace, Pirelli and others. Giovanni Agnelli, known in the Italian press as *l'Avvocato*, has cut a glamorous figure in Italian finance for decades and even in his ninth decade showed no sign of letting up. In 2001, by controversially teaming up with Electricité de France, Fiat took control of Montedison, an industrial holding that used to be owned by Mediobanca, the secretive investment bank.

Critics said the cheeky takeover of Olivetti by two of Italy's financial clans, Pirelli and Benetton, which took control of Telecom Italia, was a clear signal that family-style capitalism in Italy is alive and kicking, despite the introduction of Anglo-Saxon-style corporate governance laws. Benetton's move to back Pirelli's bid surprised Italy. The company was founded by Luciano Benetton, his brothers and sister in 1965 and is now one of the world's best-known clothing brands, which is backed by controversial advertising campaigns.

But it's not always easy to keep the family name going. Giovanni Agnelli's son Edoardo committed suicide, and his nephew and chosen heir, Giovanni Alberto Agnelli, died from cancer, making it likely that the heir will not have the Agnelli name tag. The Benetton clothing empire has also recently been forced to deny there are rifts in the family. According to Fausto Bongiorni of Italian shareholder lobby group Assorisparmio: 'There are no big families anymore, but some prominent persons. We don't just have one *salótto buono* but three or four, with some links between them. It's less of a family phenomenon and more to do with entrepreneurs.'

SHAREHOLDER ACTIVISM – THE *DISTURBATORI* GETTING IT TOGETHER?

Disgruntled small shareholders cut a lone figure in Italian corporate life until recently, acting out their frustrations at annual meetings, which were the only chance they had to speak directly to officials. If everyone is due their 15 minutes of fame as the cliché goes, Italy's small investors would go one step further and harangue company bosses at annual meetings for hours, earning themselves the nickname *disturbatori* or 'pain in the neck'.

> **Disgruntled small shareholders cut a lone figure in Italian corporate life until recently**

That disparaging attitude towards small investors in Italy has slowly changed, helped by lobby groups like Assorisparmio, which was set up a decade ago. However, Assorisparmio is to some extent shackled by Italian law, which lacks a class action provision. Class actions have been used by shareholders in the US as a vehicle for many people to band together to take a company to court – a cheaper and more effective alternative to each individual shareholder filing their own lawsuit. Usually there are agreed criteria that people have to comply with in order to be included in a class action lawsuit. A typical condition would be holding a company's shares between certain dates. Instead, in Italy each individual investor has to file their own lawsuit against a company or intermediary – an expensive and long process. Whilst small investors welcomed the Draghi and Preda corporate governance rules, Assorisparmio's Fausto Bongiorni has said it is too soon to say how effective the changes will be in improving respect to minority shareholders:

> There are limits to the new laws. The right of the shareholder is protected less than the right of intermediaries such as banks. We need a class action law, but there is no realistic hope of getting this. We also want the market regulator Consob to function better, with stronger and more precise intervention, and be

deeper in its examination of problems. To make the market more sound, we also need more pension funds.

Small investors were also burnt after the high-profile float of the internet-via-TV company Freedomland, which made its debut at €105 per share on the Milan exchange in April 2000. The stock crashed to around €3 a year later as founder Vigilio Degiovanni stepped down following a police investigation into false accounting. Degiovanni denied wrongdoing, but police sequestered his controlling stake in the company.

Assorisparmio is worried that at times Italy's stock market is too isolated from the rest of Europe. To counteract this, the association has joined the pan-European shareholder lobby association in Brussels – Euroshareholders (*see* Chapter 9).

BORSA ITALIANA – EUROPE'S FOURTH BIGGEST STOCK EXCHANGE

The Borsa Italiana in Milan traces its roots to 1808 and is the result of the merger of ten regional exchanges by the early 1990s. The exchange is housed in a stunning marble palace in the country's financial capital – a building constructed under fascist Mussolini's regime at the start of the 1930s. Like other old bourse buildings across Europe, the main trading hall is empty, now that Italy has switched to fully electronic trading of shares.

The MIB 30 blue-chip share index of top 30 companies was launched in October 1994. Compiled by the exchange itself, the index is reviewed twice a year in March and September. In early 2002, the Borsa Italiana teamed up with the US ratings agency and stock index compiler Standard & Poor's to create a new Italian market index, the S&P Mib45, for launch in April 2002. The new index was expected to become the main reference for the Italian stock market, comprising 45 quoted ordinary shares, including foreign stocks and some from the Nuovo Mercato growth market segment. The S&P Mib45 is managed by a committee of five, with S&P having three members and the Borsa two.

The new index is based on free-float in an attempt to attract a greater number of foreign investors and encourage Italian companies to free up chunks of closely held stock as a large number of Italian companies are controlled by a single shareholder or a group of shareholders that vote as a bloc. The Borsa's MTA or main market segment, handles trading in blue chips (those listings defined with a market capitalization of above €800 million). The MTA also trades the STAR companies whose market cap is below €800 million, but adhere to equally strict regulations. The Ristretto trading segment was created in the 1970s and caters for companies that do not want to meet all the rules of the main stock market. Most of the listings are co-operative banks. Finally, the Nuovo Mercato segment is for budding new economy companies.

Italian stock market regulation is divided between the exchange, which oversees everything between itself and the intermediaries or market professionals (such as banks and brokers) who trade on the exchange. Italy's independent market regulator Consob oversees all relations between the intermediaries and the investor. A company that wants to list on the exchange is approved by the Borsa itself, but Consob has the powers to approve initial public offering prospectuses. From 2002, market-sensitive news from companies has to be distributed via the Borsa's NIS or network information system. The exchange and Consob have 15 minutes before the information is made public to decide whether share trading in the company's stock should be suspended to give investors more time to digest particularly sensitive news like a takeover bid.

Ordinary shares, each with a vote at shareholder meetings, make up 90 percent of Italian traded shares, but two regional banks have only preference shares that have no voting rights. Carmaker Fiat has ordinary, savings and preference shares.

In response to pressure from Italy's online brokers and banks, the Borsa introduced an unofficial evening session in 2000 to capture small investors who want to buy and sell shares, especially online, after they return home from work. The Borsa also trades covered warrants and derivatives.

> **Box 8.1 Equity investment in Italy**
>
> **Stock exchange**
> Based in Milan Borsa Italiana (www.borsaitaliana.it).
>
> **Clearing**
> Cassa di Compensazione e Garanzia, 60-percent owned by Borsa Italiana.
>
> **Settlement**
> Monte Titoli: Borsa Italiana has a very small stake. All clearing and settlement is done electronically, free of paper.
>
> **Regulation**
> The Commissione Nazionale Per Le Societa E La Borsa (Consob) (www.consob.it) regulates relations between market intermediaries, like banks and brokers, and their clients, the investor. Consob can intervene on behalf of Italian investors who have filed a complaint against an intermediary, but foreign investors are advised to take their complaints to their own national stocks watchdog. There have been attempts to increase Consob's powers to stem insider trading and conflicts of interest on company boards, and discourage shareholder pacts.

TOP LISTINGS IN ITALY

ENI
www.eni.it

Rome-based ENI is an integrated energy company, operating natural gas networks, refineries, electric power plants, service stations and engineering operations. Officially created as Ente Nazionale Idrocarburi in 1953, it has oil reserves in Italy and Africa. The Italian Government still owns just short of a third of the company.

TELECOM ITALIA GROUP
www.telecomitalia.it

A former state-owned telephone monopoly and still Italy's biggest fixed line telephone company. It holds just over half of the country's leading wireless company Telecom Italia Mobile (TIM) (www.tim.it), which is also one of Italy's blue chip shares. It is combining with Telecom Italia's internet Service Provider Tin.it, and web-gateway company, and yellow pages publisher Seat Pagine Gialle (www.seat.it), itself an Italian blue chip stock controlled by publisher De Agostini, are being combined.

ENEL
www.enel.it

Electricity supplier Enel accounts for about two-thirds of Italy's generating capacity, serving nearly 30 million customers. The Italian Government still holds about 70 percent of the company but has indicated it wants to cut its ownership stake to below half. Enel has also moved into telecoms and owns Infostrada, the fixed-line operator, and controls Wind, which operates fixed-line and wireless services.

GENERALI
www.generali.com

Founded in 1831 in Trieste, Assicurazioni Generali is Italy's top insurance company, but also operates across the world in a group of more than 500 companies. Germany accounts for almost a third of income. Shareholders include the discrete and influential Mediobanca investment bank and Germany's Commerzbank.

SANPAOLO IMI
www.sanpaolo.it

Turin-based SanPaolo IMI was created by a merger in 1998 of Istituto Bancario San Paolo di Torino, a large retail bank, and Istituto Mobiliare Italiano. The San Paolo name dates back to the sixteenth century when citizens of Turin set up a foundation to help orphaned girls and nobility that had fallen on hard times. SanPaolo IMI has branches in Italy, Europe, North America, Asia and South America.

INTESABCI
www.bancaintesa.it

Based in Milan, it is Italy's largest banking company. It offers a broad range of services from high-street banking to investment banking, fund and asset management. It has over 4,000 branches in Italy and elsewhere in the world. It is about 40-percent owned by a collection of stakeholders led by French bank Crédit Agricole.

OLIVETTI
www.olivetti.it

From typewriting fame to telecoms, Olivetti has been in a hurry to forge a more dynamic image, culminating with its audacious 1999 hostile takeover of much bigger Telecom Italia for $33 billion. Olivetti owned 55 percent of Telecom Italia, but in 2001 tyremaker Pirelli and the Benetton family teamed up to buy out Olivetti's biggest stakeholder, giving control of Telecom Italia and Olivetti to Pirelli.

BANCA FIDEURAM
www.bancafideuram.it

A provider to rich Italians of services like mutual funds, life insurance and other private banking services. SanPaolo IMI owns a controlling stake in the company.

SPAIN – THE LATIN AMERICAN CONNECTION

When something goes wrong in Latin America, the Spanish index responds.
Javier Lazaro, Goldman Sachs, Madrid

Over the past 20 years Spain has made the jump from being an emerging market to a developed economy, but its stock market is still affected by emerging market forces from its colonial past – Latin America. It is also a market where two large banks, Banco Bilbao Vizcaya Argentaria (BBVA) and Santander Central Hispano (SCH) have their long fingers in most of Spain's corporate pies, making them central to the economy and financial system.

Utilities also play an important role in the Spanish share market, but they form a sector that is always at the whim of the Government's public service regulator. In the Madrid exchange's IBEX blue-chip index of top 35 Spanish companies, just six listings – BBVA, SCH, telephone firm Telefonica, oil company Repsol, and the two biggest utilities, Endesa and Iberdrola – account for 70 percent of the benchmark's capitalization (*see* Fig. 8.2). Enrique Perez Pla of securities house Schroder Salomon Smith Barney's Madrid operation, explains: 'The only issue for the foreign investor is that an important part of revenues in the biggest stocks depend a lot on regulatory framework by the Government, and this is particularly true for utilities. The IBEX 35 represents 90 percent of Spanish market capitalization, with foreign investors accounting for 60 percent of share trading.'

It is the same top six or so companies that have invested heavily in Latin America. For example, BBVA and SCH have about a third of their assets in Latin America. Latin American operations account for around a third of net income for Spanish listed firms. The top blue chips like SCH, BBVA, Repsol and Telefonica have invested about $60 billion in Latin America. Telefonica has big chunks of telephone companies in Peru, Argentina, Brazil and Chile, which together represent more than half of the company's income. Many of the utilities have also been diversifying into telecom services. The end result is a

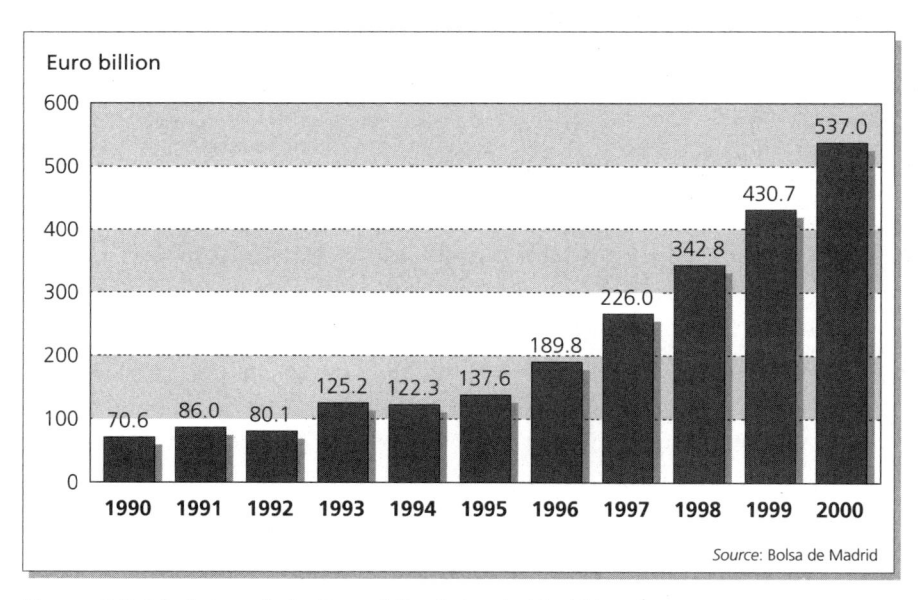

Figure 8.2 Market capitalization of the Bolsa de Madrid

market that focuses on banks, utilities and telecoms, with a strong Latin-American emphasis. This can have its dangers: since 2000, Argentina has been facing a big crisis over its debts and the pullback in technology, media and telecom shares was continuing apace in Europe and the US, the Madrid stock market faced a particularly rocky time. 'When something goes wrong in Latin America like in Argentina, the Spanish index responds,' claims Javier Lazaro of investment bank Goldman Sachs in Madrid. He adds: 'The Spanish index is not a proxy for Latin America or an emerging market, but the latter do have an impact on the margin. The European-based business of these companies counterbalances the Latin American risk.'

RISING EQUITY CULTURE

Spain's equity culture has only developed in the last decade and still lags behind many other European countries, let alone the US. However, strong economic growth and the need to step up individual retirement provision mean that Spain is catching up fast. As elsewhere in continental Europe, small investors acquired a taste for stocks as the Government began privatizing state-run companies like Telefonica. Spain's mutual funds now hold about €50.2 billion, with a quarter in the form of equities. The pension fund industry, weak by US and UK standards, is beginning to grow as individuals, rather than companies, put aside money for retirement, helped by tax incentives. However, many pension funds and individual pension plans have the bulk of their cash not in stocks but in bonds and cash, although the level of equities in these funds is expected to grow.

❝Small investors acquired a taste for stocks as the Government began privatizing state-run companies❞

Goldman Sachs has estimated there are about half a million small investors in Spain. The record number of participants in a new public offering was 1.5 million people in Telefonica's Telefonica Moviles wireless unit. Figures from the Madrid stock exchange show that, directly and indirectly, small investors accounted for 33.6 percent of total market capitalization by 1999, up from 24.44 percent in 1992 (*see* Fig. 8.3). The value of shares held by Spanish families also rose fourfold from €98 billion in 1994, or 17 percent of their total assets, to €403 billion by 1999, or 36 percent of total assets, as stocks became the main financial asset in households.

Percentage of total capitalization of listed Spanish companies

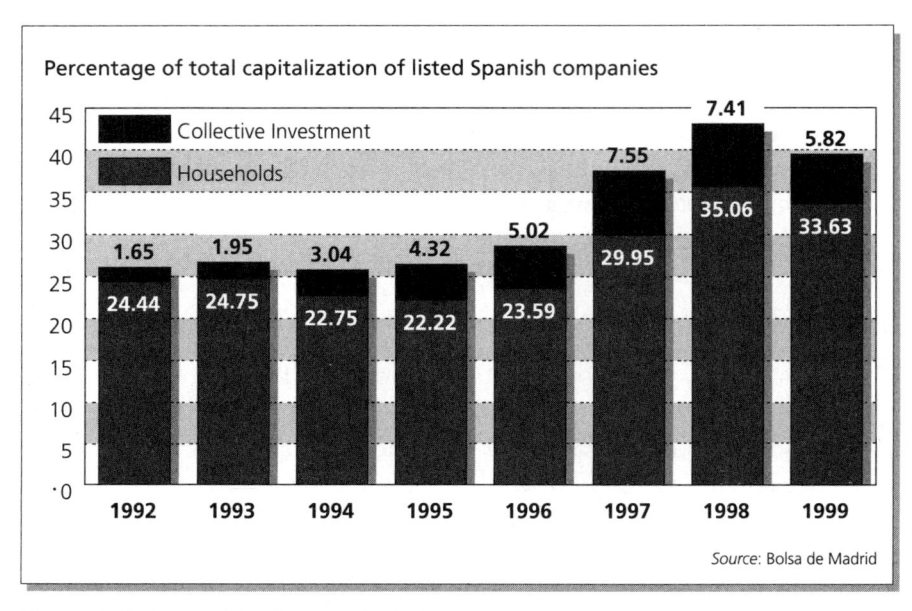

Year	Households	Collective Investment
1992	24.44	1.65
1993	24.75	1.95
1994	22.75	3.04
1995	22.22	4.32
1996	23.59	5.02
1997	29.95	7.55
1998	35.06	7.41
1999	33.63	5.82

Source: Bolsa de Madrid

Figure 8.3 Ownership of shares in Spain

Foreign investors hold about 35 percent of the country's equity base, but the Madrid exchange does not expect it to climb much above this level in percentage terms. By 2000 more than one in every two euros traded on the Spanish stock market came from a non-resident investor (*see* Fig. 8.4). Between January and September of that year, European Union countries accounted for about 85 percent of the cash poured into Spanish stocks. Nearly 60 percent of total foreign investment came from the UK, though this reflects London's role as a leading financial centre, rather than any huge appetite among UK investors for Spanish equities. The US represented some 11 percent of total non-Spanish investment in shares in 2000.

The State's stake in Spanish stock-market capitalization fell from 16.6 percent in 1992 to almost zero by 1999, as the equity culture grew and the public bought more shares. In 2001 small investors lined up

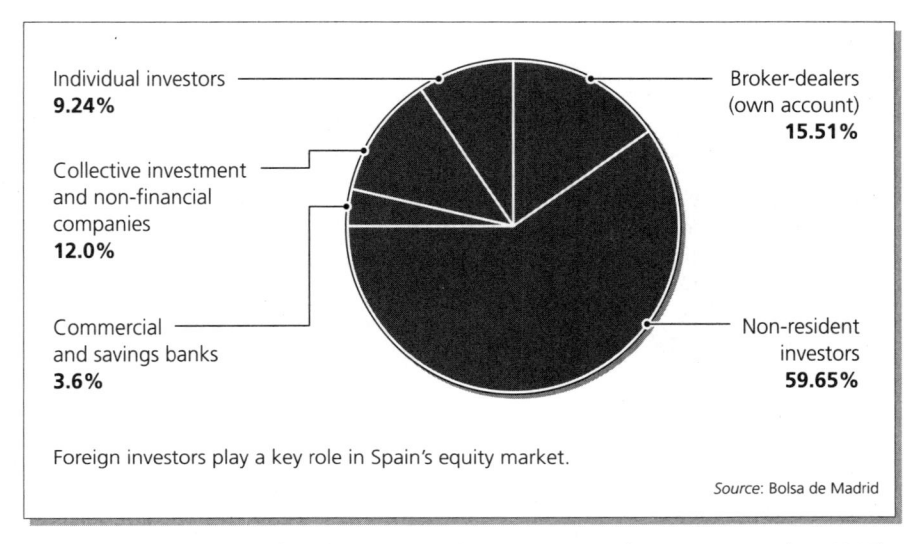

Investor type	Percentage
Individual investors	9.24%
Collective investment and non-financial companies	12.0%
Commercial and savings banks	3.6%
Broker-dealers (own account)	15.51%
Non-resident investors	59.65%

Foreign investors play a key role in Spain's equity market.

Source: Bolsa de Madrid

Figure 8.4 Distribution of trading in Spain by investor type (January–December 2000)

in droves to take part in the float of Inditex, a clothing company. The offering benefited from the public's familiarity with the firm, and the fact that it was not a technology company, since this was a time when new economy shares were being shunned.

Spain's company float rules differ from elsewhere in Europe in that it is necessary to wait a day and a half between the pricing of an initial public offering and the start of trading in the stock. Usually, trading begins in the morning, straight after the evening the issue was priced.

BANCARIZACION

Spain's two biggest banks, BBVA and SCH, reach into every corner of the country's economic and financial foundations – a set-up sometimes called *bancarizacion*. Both banks hold stakes in industry, with BBVA, for example, holding about 8 percent in Repsol and Iberdrola, and about 5 percent in Telefonica.

BBVA (*see* Figure 8.5) and SCH account for about half of the country's asset management sector and pension funds, and they also operate the largest stockbrokers in Spain. As Javier Lazaro of investment bank Goldman Sachs explains: 'We have an economic arena concentrated

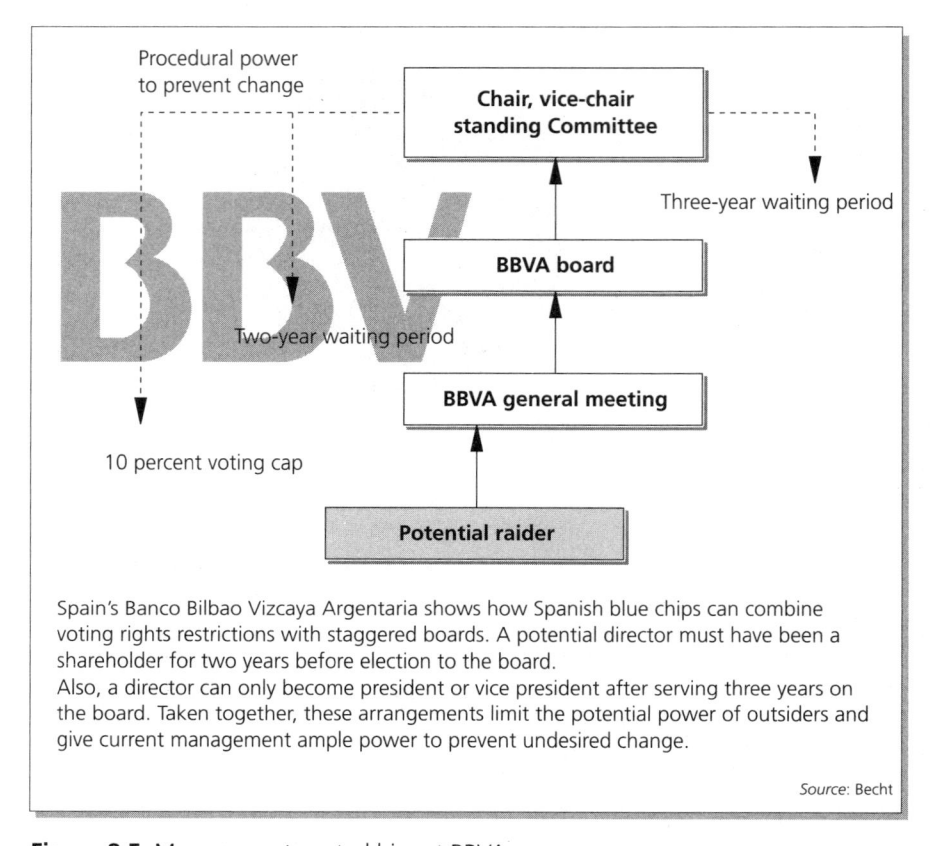

```
                    Procedural power
                    to prevent change         ┌──────────────────┐
                    ┌ ─ ─ ─ ─ ─ ─ ─ ─ ─ ─ ─ ─ │  Chair, vice-chair  │ ─ ─ ─ ─ ─ ┐
                    │                         │ standing Committee  │           │
                    │                         └──────────────────┘           │
                    │                                  ▲                      │
                    │                                  │                      ▼
                    │                                  │              Three-year waiting period
                    │                         ┌──────────────────┐
                    │                         │    BBVA board    │
                    │                         └──────────────────┘
                    │                                  ▲
                    │   Two-year waiting period        │
                    │                         ┌──────────────────┐
                    ▼                         │ BBVA general meeting │
             10 percent voting cap            └──────────────────┘
                                                       ▲
                                              ┌──────────────────┐
                                              │  Potential raider  │
                                              └──────────────────┘
```

Spain's Banco Bilbao Vizcaya Argentaria shows how Spanish blue chips can combine voting rights restrictions with staggered boards. A potential director must have been a shareholder for two years before election to the board.
Also, a director can only become president or vice president after serving three years on the board. Taken together, these arrangements limit the potential power of outsiders and give current management ample power to prevent undesired change.

Source: Becht

Figure 8.5 Management control bias at BBVA

around two big poles. This is not the norm in every country in Europe, but it's very much part of Spain and very unlikely to change in the near future.'

But both banks carefully eye each other's portfolio and try to avoid abusing their clout in the economy. For instance, if BBVA wanted to buy a stake in another telecom company, it would have to exit Telefonica, or if it wanted to acquire a utility, it is doubtful if it could also hang on to its share of Iberdrola.

BANESTO CASE STILL LEAVES BITTER TASTE

The 'Banesto case' in 1993 was Spain's biggest financial scandal and still leaves a bitter taste in the mouths of small investors. It forced the country's central bank to step in with a rescue package. Banco Espagnol de Credito-Banesto ran up a deficit of $4 billion that year, tipping the bank into crisis and putting Spain's banking hero Mario Conde behind bars. Conde was accused of syphoning off millions of pesetas from Banesto accounts for his personal use. The bank's collapse cost the State 192 billion pesetas to bail it out, and a parliamentary committee said the huge level of bad debts had been concealed from shareholders and auditors. Banesto was taken over by Banco Santander in 1994.

Spain's shareholder lobby group, Asociacion para la Defensa del Accionista (ADA) based in Barcelona, is still angry with the way market regulator Comision Nacional del Mercado de Valores (CNMV) failed to protect small investors. Banesto was allowed to issue shares totalling 40 billion pesetas just four months before the Bank of Spain had to intervene. In 2001 Banesto finally paid compensation to US investment fund Carlisle Ventures for the 2 million shares it bought in the Banesto's share issue. Spain's small investors, however, were still battling to get similar compensation when Carlisle won its case. 'The judicial system is Spain is expensive and sluggish, making the small investors practically defenceless in their disputes with big corporations,' said ADA's Ignacio de Caralt.

ADA also questions the independence of the investor protector or ombudsmen at the Madrid and Barcelona stock exchanges, which the association said both are nominated with the market regulator CNMV's approval. CNMV president Pilar Valiente was forced to resign amid public outcry in September 2000 during a probe into Gescartera, a brokerage with $100 million in missing funds. CNMV had taken over management of Gescartera three months earlier, though Valiente denied that she may have acted to prevent a government takeover of the brokerage in 1999. Some 2,000 investors were affected by the shortfall in funds at Gescartera which had run a pyramid investment scheme.

The Madrid exchange created its investor protector in 1991, to examine complaints by individuals about transactions on the bourse. The exchange insists that confidence in the exchange has risen over the years as seen in the big rise in the number of complaints, up from 162 in 1991

> **Complaints about public offerings have increased as more investors take part in company floats**

to 341 in 2000, the increase in line with the growth in trading volumes over the years. Complaints about public offerings have increased as more investors take part in company floats.

ALL FOR ONE AND ONE FOR ALL

For a country with a relatively modest population, Spain has many exchanges. This is partly the result of the continued clout held by the regions, although Madrid dominates in equity trading. In February 2002, Spain grouped all its financial, equity, fixed income and other markets under a single holding company, a process driven by Antonio Zoido, chairman of the Madrid stock exchange (Bolsa Madrid). The new holding company comprises the fixed-income exchanges AIAF and SENAF, the stock markets in Madrid, Valencia, Bilbao and Barcelona, the MEFF futures exchange, the citrus futures exchange, and the clearing system Iberclear. The moves come against a backdrop of consolidation among Europe's exchanges in response to the huge single market created by the euro.

Although Spain has four stock exchanges, trading turnover is concentrated in Madrid. For trading in the IBEX 35 shares, all four bourses are interconnected by the SIBE systems. Volumes on SIBE in 2000 were worth a record 81.3 trillion pesetas, up 71 percent from the prior year, and 10 times higher than in 1995. The top-traded stock was telephone company Telefonica, followed by the two main banks BBVA and SCH.

Madrid's growth market Nuevo Mercado segment was launched in April 2000, unfortunately timed to coincide with the start of the global pullback in shares led by the very type of technology companies the Bolsa's new segment was trying to attract.

Madrid's Latibex is an international market for Latin American securities, launched in December 1999, hoping to become the focus for South American shares during European trading hours. By the first quarter of 2001 Latibex was trading in 14 companies with a market capitalization of €90 billion. The Madrid stock exchange wants to expand Latibex, hoping it will enable the bourse to offer something different to European investors.

Box 8.2 Equity investment in Spain

Stock exchange
Bolsa Madrid (www.bolsamadrid.es). Over 1,100 companies are listed. The Nuevo Mercado growth stock segment had 12 listings in 2001.

Clearing and settlement
Servicio del Compensacion y Liquidacion de Valores (SCLV). All registration of share ownership is done electronically by SCLV.

Regulation
Comision Nacional del Mercado de Valores (CNMV).

Shareholder protection
Investor Protector, employed by the Madrid stock exchange (email: protector@bolsamadrid.es).

Shareholders' group
Asociacion para la Defensa del Accionista (ADA) (e-mail: asociacion.ada@teleline.es).

TOP LISTINGS IN SPAIN

TERRA LYCOS
www.terralycos.com

Barcelona-based Terra Lycos was formerly known as Terra Network before its takeover of US web portal Lycos. It operates more than 140 websites in 19 languages across more than 40 countries. Spanish telecom group Telefonica owns 36 percent of Terra Lycos.

AMADEUS
www.global.amadeus.net

Amadeus Global Travel Distribution, based in Madrid, runs one of the world's largest travel reservation and ticketing systems. It handles flights on about 500 airlines and hundreds of hotel chains. Two-thirds of sales are from Europe. It was set up in 1987 by Air France, Iberia, Lufthansa and SAS as an alternative to a global distribution system dominated by US airlines.

UNION ELECTRICA FENOSA
www.uef.es

> Spain's third largest utility after Endesa and Iberdrola, serving especially the Madrid region. To diversify from its core generating operations, it has stakes in broadcast carrier Retevision, various cable companies and mobile phone operator Amena. BSCH owns 10 percent of Fenosa.

BANCO POPULAR ESPANOL
www.bancopopular.es

> One of Spain's biggest banks after the two giants BSCH and BBVA. Banco Popular has a history of delivering on profits.

IBERDROLA
www.iberdrola.es

> Based in Bilbao, Iberdrola is Spain's second largest utility after Endesa. It has expanded into Latin America with companies in Brazil, Bolivia, Chile, Guatemala and Mexico. In 2000 it agreed to be taken over by rival Endesa but the marriage was abandoned the following year.

ENDESA
www.endesa.es

> Spain's biggest utility is now fully privatized. It has combined its telecom holdings with those of Fenosa and Telecom Italia to form Auna, which may itself become listed. Privatization of Endesa began in 1988 two years after Spain joined the European Community. It was fully privatized ten years later. Endesa has stakes in Enersis, Chile's largest power company, and in Spanish broadcast company Retevision. Endesa also has holdings in French and Italian generating companies.

REPSOL
www.repsol-ypf.com

> Spain's biggest oil and gas company. In 1999 it bought YPF, Argentina's leading oil company. Repsol has service stations in Spain, Portugal and the UK. It has a 47-percent stake in Gas Natural, giving it control of Spain's natural gas supplier Enagas.

TELEFONICA
www.telefonica.es

Spain's leading telephone company also owns a majority stake in the country's top mobile-phone operator Telefonica Moviles. The company has extensive operations in Latin America. It has stakes in Compania de Telefonos de Chile and in ENTEL, Argentina's former state-owned telephone company. Telefonica bought a controlling stake in Peru's main telephone company in 1994, and also has a share in Brazil's Companhia Riograndense de Telecommunicacoes.

BANCO BILBAO VIZCAYA ARGENTARIA
www.bbva.es

One of Spain's two main banks, Bilbao-based BBVA also has extensive operations in Latin America following the creation of BBVA from the merger of Banco Bilbao Vizcaya and Argentaria, Caja Postal y Banco Hipotecario. BBVA also has operations in European countries like France, Italy and Portugal.

SANTANDER CENTRAL HISPANO
www.bsch.es

SCH was created by the merger in 1999 of Banco Santander and Banco Central Hispanoamericano. Banco Santander was set up in 1857 to finance trade in Latin America. A member of the Botin family held a top job at the bank for decades. SCH has operations in Brazil and Mexico, and, like arch-rival BBVA, plays a key role in Spain's economy and financial market, with extensive industrial holdings.

PORTUGAL – IN SPAIN'S SHADOW

Portugal's stock market is a story of fits and starts, but one that is ultimately overshadowed by Portugal's long-standing rival, neighbouring Spain.

The 1974 revolution that overthrew Portugal's long dictatorship triggered a wave of nationalizations, stopping any onward march in equities in its tracks. The global stocks crash in the mid-1980s was another setback, which lasted longer – about a decade – and badly damaged the infant equity culture. Privatizations in the 1990s helped rekindle a stock market, as small investors bought shares of former state-owned companies. For example, about 10 percent of the country's population of 10 million bought shares in the EDP electricity utility. Another sign of change was the merger between Bolsa de Valores de Lisboa (the Lisbon stock exchange) and Bolsa de Derivados do Porto (the Oporto derivatives exchange) into one single market, which improved trading efficiency, cut operating costs and helped to improve volumes. But Portuguese market capitalization remains small – about €100 billion, or less than a handful of decent-sized western blue-chip shares.

Portugal's stock market underwent a seismic change when global stock index compiler Morgan Stanley Capital International (MSCI) reclassified Portugal from emerging market to developed market status. This change meant that favourable comparisons with other more risky emerging markets like Russia or Latin America ended, and global fund managers now had to compare Portuguese companies with rival blue chips in advanced economies. Many managers simply shunned the former as still too risky: 'The transfer from emerging market to developed market was very bad. We were the top emerging market and now we are a small developed market,' said Bernardina Ribeiro, marketing director of the Lisbon and Oporto stock exchange (BVLP). In 2001 the stock market was also unnerved by the Government constantly changing cabinet members.

Just like Spain, Portugal's historical links with South America, particularly its former colony Brazil, are to be felt on the stock market. Portugal Telecom, Electricidad de Portugal and SONAE all have stakes in Brazilian companies. Portugal Telecom has more revenues coming from Brazil than from its domestic market. Other listed companies have been playing increasing roles in Eastern Europe. These include banks such as Banco Comercial Portugues, distribution groups like SONAE and Jeronimo Martins, as well as manufacturing companies such as Corticeira Amorim, a top global cork-products maker.

Portuguese industry was traditionally the fiefdom of a select number of families, although they have now been replaced by a small number of financial groups. However, issues like corporate governance and shareholder rights are not developed. 'The idea of shareholder value does not exist yet,' claims Joao Paulo Peixoto, founder of FUTOP, which specializes in futures and options management, and president of IESF, the Portuguese business school. 'We have the rules, but we don't have the culture.'

BLINDAGEM RULES

Full-blooded corporate activity is also stifled by so-called *blindagem* or Portugal's home-grown version of the anti-takeover poison pill. As Peixoto said: 'Some company rules are drawn up in such a way that it's very difficult for anyone even with the biggest chunk of a company to actually govern it.'

Equity culture was also given a knock in 2000 when the Government imposed a tax on profits from small-investor share dealing. Investors who bought shares after 1 January 2001 and held them for more than 12 months would have to pay 20-percent tax, compared to zero tax before. The change immediately sent investors scurrying over the border to buy Spanish shares because of more favourable tax treatment.

EURONEXT HOPE

Investment houses in Portugal have been putting their cash into stock markets elsewhere in the euro zone because the range of companies in Portugal is too narrow, making an industry-sector-based strategy impossible. Mindful of its location on Europe's Atlantic periphery, in 2000 the Lisbon and Oporto stock exchange decided to throw in its lot with Euronext, the Franco-Benelux bourse (*see* Chapter 4). Centuries-old rivalry still ruled out a tie-up between Portugal and its Iberian neighbour Spain, despite its glaring logic.

The Portuguese exchange hopes that merging with Euronext will attract investors from outside the country in a bid to bolster flagging share liquidity. Bernardino Ribeiro of the BVLP explains: 'We think things will change with the merger with Euronext. It will give us access to other markets and listed companies in Portugal will have better visibility.'

> **Box 8.3 Equity investment in Portugal**
>
> **Stock exchange**
> Bolsa de Valores de Lisboa e Porto (www.bvlp.pt) – created by the merger of the Lisbon and Oporto exchanges in February 2000 and headed by Alves Monteiro.
>
> The BVLP had 108 companies listed in 2001. It compiles the PSI 20 and PSI 30 blue chip indices, reviewed half yearly. From April 2002 it will be fully merged with Euronext.
>
> **Clearing**
> The clearing house is part of the exchange.
>
> **Settlement**
> Interbolsa, dealing in paper and electronically held shares: both have equal voting and other rights. Interbolsa is expected to merge with Euroclear, Euronext's settlement house of choice.
>
> **Regulation**
> Comissao de Mercados de Valores Mobiliarios – Portuguese Securities Market Commission (www.cmvm.pt).
>
> **Shareholders' group**
> Associacao dos investidores e Analistas Tecnicos do Mercado de Capitais (e-mail atm@atm-associacao.pt).

TOP LISTINGS IN PORTUGAL

PORTUGAL TELECOM
www.telecom.pt

PT is the country's largest telephone service provider in the wireless and fixed-line areas. In September 2001 the company gave up its attempt to acquire the 59 percent in Brazil's top mobile carrier Telesp Celular that it does not own. PT's investment in Telesp is part of a venture with Spain's Telefonica. PT has half of its assets and generates some 18 percent of core earnings in Brazil.

ELECTRICIDADE DE PORTUGAL
www.edp.pt

> EDP is a holding group for utilities that generate and distribute electricity in Portugal. The company has stakes in Brazilian electricity distributors. It also owns nearly all of Onitelecom, Portugal's second largest fixed-line telephone company. The Portuguese Government hold slightly more than half of EDP in the form of a golden share.

BANCO COMERCIAL PORTUGUES
www.bcp.pt

> BCP is the country's largest bank, based in Oporto. It serves retail, corporate and financial clients.

SONAE
www.sonae.pt

> A conglomerate with activities ranging from retail distribution in Portugal and Brazil, to wood panel production, shopping centres, media, and fixed and mobile telecommunications.

9

PAN-EUROPEAN INVESTING

The message for traditional stock exchanges is all too clear: shape up or shut down.
Werner Seifert, Deutsche Börse CEO

THE PUSH TOWARDS A PAN-EUROPEAN stock market has been driven above all by the euro. In one fell swoop, the switch by 11 countries in January 1999 to trading shares in the single currency created a huge, currency-risk-free stock market, but one still distorted by differing national regulations, tax laws, corporate governance and level of equity culture. Not only does the single currency make it easier to trade in shares from many countries in Europe, the creation of a euro zone has also spurred restructuring by companies, takeovers, lower interest rates and deregulation – all factors which help stock markets flourish.

Citizens in many large countries, like Germany, Italy and France, will also have to take more direct responsibility for their retirement in future, and investing in equities is expected to become a key generator of money for old age provision. Global investment bank Morgan Stanley believes that between 2001 and 2010 the gross demand for European equities will top $10 trillion.

This chapter looks at some of the building blocks that are key to constructing a truly pan-European stock market, rather than just a rag bag of national exchanges and jurisdictions. It considers developments in corporate governance, stock exchange and post-trade consolidation, regulation, pan-European share indices, and the rise of online trading as an equity culture gathers pace.

IMPROVING CORPORATE GOVERNANCE – SHAREHOLDERS UNITE!

Housed down a side street near the former Belgian stock exchange is an organization that reflects the equity culture taking root in Europe. Euroshareholders (www.wfic.org) is a 12-year-old umbrella organization for 13 national shareholders' associations from across Europe, helping individual investors present their arguments to pan-European lawmakers who will have increasing influence over takeovers, regulation and other aspects of a wider European stock market. Like other shareholder-focused groups in Europe, Euroshareholders' key aim is to improve corporate governance standards across the region. It also lobbies for better small-investor access to company initial public offerings (IPOs). As its secretary-general Jean-Pierre Paelinck explains: 'We consider that investors are not so well respected and protected as they deserve to be. After all, without shareholders, there would be no market.' Sweden's SARF (www.aktiespararna.se), the Dutch VEB (www.veb.net), Germany's DSW (www.dsw-info.de) and ADAM (e-mail adam.bp.208.chartres@wannado.fr) in France are Europe's most active and hard-hitting national shareholder lobby groups, and the driving force behind Euroshareholders.

Corporate governance, or how a company is managed and controlled, is usually based on transparency and accountability, concepts that were largely alien to many managers in continental Europe just a few years ago. The level of corporate governance is an indicator of how seriously a company takes the long-term interests of its shareholders. In Anglo-Saxon countries, where share ownership is much more dispersed, corporate governance is most often concerned with possible conflicts of interest between executive and non-executive directors and shareholders. In contrast, continental European countries have traditionally had reference or dominant shareholdings, and problems have arisen between shareholders and shareholder representatives on the board.

> **The level of corporate governance is an indicator of how seriously a company takes the long-term interests of its shareholders**

As the Anglo-Saxon model of running companies becomes the norm in continental Europe, small investors are beginning to use tried and tested Anglo-Saxon tactics, such as taking errant firms to court. France's ADAM went to court in 2000 and successfully forced electrical-components maker Schneider to improve its takeover offer to preference shareholders in Legrand. In 1999 VEB in the Netherlands won compensation for shareholders in electronics company Philips.

Corporate governance also affects how companies come to the market for the first time, and how the new shares are distributed. As Paelinck of Euroshareholders has said: 'The allotment system in IPOs is not even serious – they give to retail investors what the others don't want.' But Euroshareholders is also trying to strike the right balance as to how much influence individual investors should have on a company. 'We don't want the boards of companies to only look after the interests of the shareholders,' Paelinck said. Euroshareholders is also looking at the effects of consolidation among exchanges; for example the merger of bourses in Brussels, Amsterdam and Paris to create Euronext raises cross-border concerns for individual investors.

Deminor (www.deminor.com), a private consultancy company, is another European corporate governance monitoring company referred to by institutional investors. Deminor claims that studies in the US have shown that good corporate governance is beneficial to a company's share price, and that investors are willing to pay a premium on shares of a company that is well-governed. The consultancy publishes a survey each year rating each of the 300 companies in the Eurotop 300 index, indicating how they rate in terms of rights and duties of shareholders, range of takeover defences, disclosure on corporate governance, and board structure and functioning. As Fig. 9.1 shows, there are still widespread differences between European countries.

European corporate governance: a mixed picture				
Major countries	Rights and duties shareholders	Takeover defences	Disclosure	Board structure
UK	4	4	5	5
Germany	4	3	2	1
France	3	1	3	3
Switzerland	2	1	1	1
The Netherlands	1	1	3	2
Italy	4	1	3	2
Spain	2	1	2	3
Sweden	2	3	2	2
Belgium	3	1	3	3

Country ratings are defined as the median of company ratings on each country level. 5 = best practice, 1 = questionable standards.

How companies behave towards their shareholders and other companies varies across Europe. The UK is close to US levels of corporate governance, while countries like Belgium lag significantly. Poorer corporate governance has not stopped foreign investors buying French, Swiss or Dutch blue chips, however.

Source: Deminor

Figure 9.1 Deminor ratings

A company's style of corporate governance is becoming ever more important to investors, who are increasingly aware of the need for minority shareholder rights. A useful source of information is the European Corporate Governance Institute (ECGI), which was set up in 1996. Its website (www.ecgi.com) has been put together by business school academics and allows investors to read national corporate governance codes and rules from all the European Union countries and other parts of the world. One of ECGI's compilers is Marco Becht, an academic at ECARES and Solvay Business School, Université Libre de

Bruxelles. Writing with Colin Mayer (2001) of the University of Oxford, he argues that continental European companies still have high levels of concentration of control, with single blockholders often controlling more than 50 percent of corporate votes:

> In contrast, a majority of UK listed companies have no blockholder owning more than 10 percent of shares and the majority of US-listed companies have no blockholder with more than 6 percent of shares. The evidence of a free market in corporate control emerging in continental Europe is limited to date. There is a marked variation within Europe, ranging from a 'private control bias' in Germany, to a modest management control bias of the Anglo-American variety in the Netherlands and Spain.

In the UK, financial institutions, pension funds and life insurance companies are the dominant class of shareholders, but in continental Europe it is other companies, families and individuals who are the key shareholders. Thus in Germany and Austria, families, individuals and other companies have the largest blockholdings. For example, in the German carmaker Porsche, the Porsche family holds half of the voting stock, and an estimated further 10 percent of non-voting stock.

OUT OF COURT

Even for a shareholder lobby group, let alone individual shareholders, to take a company to court is a daunting, costly and time-consuming task, especially in cross-border cases. In 2000 the European Commission launched FIN-NET, an out-of-court complaints network for financial services. FIN-NET (http://europa.eu.int/comm/internal_market/en/finances/consumer/adr.htm) has been designed to publicize the different national schemes, such as banking and insurance ombudsmen, to which investors can turn in an attempt to resolve disputes and avoid costly legal cases. The website lists all the national organizations to which investors can take their complaints, with many of them offering a service in English as well as their national language. The scheme is designed particularly to help speedy resolution of consumer disputes when the service provider is located in a European Union member state other than where the consumer lives. (For national ombudsmen or complaints handling authorities, *see* the relevant country chapters.)

PAN-EUROPEAN STOCK INDICES – THE BATTLE OF THE BENCHMARKS

As the boundaries between national markets and a broader, pan-European arena became blurred by the euro, it became clear that national benchmarks on their own, like the DAX in Germany or Italy's MIB 30, could not reflect the new, bigger market. Into the breach stepped a clutch of rival stock-index compilers, each vying to become the pan-European equivalent of the FTSE 100 or Dow Jones industrial average, to which commentators would refer when talking about the region's share market.

On a national level, supremacy in indices was relatively easy. For example, the DAX and the MIB 30 are compiled by the Frankfurt and Milan stock exchanges, while the FTSE is a joint venture between the London Stock Exchange and the *Financial Times* newspaper. Little surprise, therefore, that the same exchanges crop up behind the new stables of competing indices, vying to become the main benchmark for Europe.

FTSE International (www.ftse.com) launched a series of Eurotop indices. Among the best known is the Eurotop 300 index of Europe's top 300 companies by market capitalization. There is also the Eurotop 100 of the top 100 companies.

The Stoxx Ltd (www.stoxx.com) stable of European indices is a joint venture between the American Dow Jones & Co. (which compiles the Dow Jones industrial average and owns *The Wall Street Journal*), and three continental European stock exchanges: Euronext Paris, the Deutsche Börse in Frankfurt and the Swiss exchange in Zürich. The two best-known Stoxx indices are the Euro Stoxx 50, which comprises the top 50 companies in the 12-nation single currency euro zone, and the Stoxx index, which includes the top 600 companies from across

Europe. Derivatives exchanges like Eurex, jointly owned by the Deutsche Börse and the Swiss exchange, introduced futures contract linked to some of the Stoxx cash equity market indices. The Euro Stoxx 50 derivatives contracts have been the most successful so far of any stock futures contract in Europe.

Morgan Stanley Capital International (MSCI) (www.msci.com) is the world's foremost share-index compiler, with trillions of dollars benchmarked against its global indices by funds from across the world. MSCI is still the leader in Europe as a benchmark for the professional investors. Standard & Poor's (www.standardandpoors.com), whose S&P 500 US market index is one of the most heavily tracked by US investors, is also trying to build up a presence in Europe with its own European indices.

> Banks and funds have created investment products that track some of the European indices, allowing investors to have exposure to all of Europe

Increasingly, banks and funds have created investment products that track some of the European indices, allowing investors to have exposure to all of Europe. With the shift in Europe – and globally – to buying and selling shares along industry group or sector lines – such as technology companies or energy firms – FTSE, Stoxx and others have also introduced European industry sector indices. All have two series of sector indices, one for euro-zone-only sectors, the other for pan-European sectors.

Reviews of pan-European indices affect investments. Just as the anticipation of changes in a national index like the DAX triggers moves in the shares of companies expected to enter or exit the index, the same is true ahead of reviews of some pan-European indices, particularly those such as the Euro Stoxx 50. Dates of index reviews are given on index providers' websites.

Since 1999, index compilers have changed how much weighting or influence they give a particular company in a share index. The shift to so-called free-float was made in order to reflect more accurately how much of a company's share base is actually freely available for investors to buy and sell, rather than being tightly held in the hands of a family or state. For example, a sizeable chunk of Germany's Deutsche Telekom telephone company, one of Europe's largest, is still majority-owned by the German Government, but its weighting in the DAX had been disproportionately larger than the actual availability of shares on the market. FTSE, Stoxx, MSCI, the DAX and others have now largely completed their shift to free-float-based calculations for inclusion in indices.

SUPERBOURSE – A SLOW TRAIN COMING?

The impending arrival of the euro and lure of a huge, single market in shares stoked dreams that Europe too would have a superbourse to rival the two US titans, the New York Stock Exchange and Nasdaq. Europe has 32 stock exchanges, 16 of which are in the European Union. The US has just seven, though trading in the US can be fragmented in a different way, for instance because of the many alternative trading systems that handle Nasdaq shares. The big banks and brokers in Europe who handle orders for shares want a one-stop shop where they can buy stocks of companies listed across Europe more cheaply and efficiently than going to each exchange separately. The desire has become more urgent as funds and other big investors increasingly want to buy shares on an industry group basis – an exercise that can mean having to be a member of many exchanges, which is an expensive and complicated process. Indeed, the Global Straight-through-processing Association, an industry body, has estimated that between 2002 and 2007 cross-border trading volumes in Europe will grow a compound 45 percent a year to a million trades a day from 200,000.

To cope with this increased trade, in 1997 the Deutsche Börse and the Paris Bourse announced they were talking about co-operating with each other, bringing together Europe's second and third largest stock exchanges. But a year later the Franco-German courtship was off after Frankfurt said it was looking to form an alliance with the London Stock Exchange (LSE). Angered, Paris, and the other small exchanges like Madrid and Milan, insisted on joining the Anglo-German link-up too. Not surprisingly, the eight-bourse alliance proved too unwieldy to

PAN-EUROPEAN INVESTING

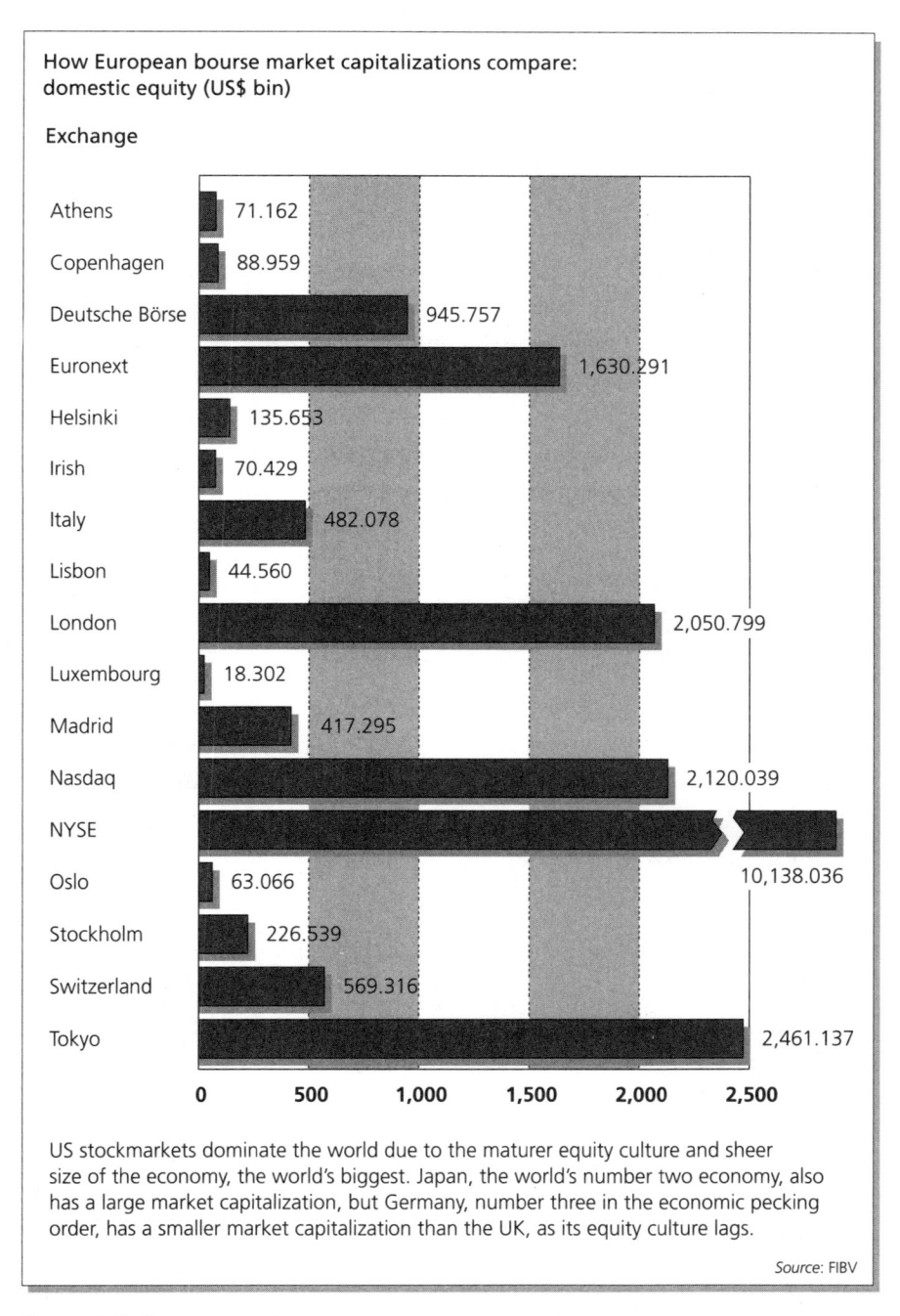

How European bourse market capitalizations compare:
domestic equity (US$ bln)

Exchange	US$ bln
Athens	71.162
Copenhagen	88.959
Deutsche Börse	945.757
Euronext	1,630.291
Helsinki	135.653
Irish	70.429
Italy	482.078
Lisbon	44.560
London	2,050.799
Luxembourg	18.302
Madrid	417.295
Nasdaq	2,120.039
NYSE	10,138.036
Oslo	63.066
Stockholm	226.539
Switzerland	569.316
Tokyo	2,461.137

US stockmarkets dominate the world due to the maturer equity culture and sheer size of the economy, the world's biggest. Japan, the world's number two economy, also has a large market capitalization, but Germany, number three in the economic pecking order, has a smaller market capitalization than the UK, as its equity culture lags.

Source: FIBV

Figure 9.2 European exchanges

survive much beyond creating a blueprint for common trading rules – though this alone was a major step forward in bringing consistency to share trading in the region.

Instead, in 2000 Frankfurt and London decided they would merge to form a cross-border exchange called iX, with Milan and Madrid promising they would join later. But opposition to iX was evident from the day it was unveiled. The UK's smaller brokers felt they were presented with a fait accompli that would only benefit the big investment banks like Merrill Lynch, who were the driving force behind iX. Instead of replacing two national markets with a single international platform, iX created five segments – an Anglo-German blue chip market, UK and German smaller companies markets, the UK alternative investment market, and an Anglo-German growth stock market in Frankfurt, half owned by Nasdaq. Regulation was also complex.

Not to be outdone, Paris announced it was merging with exchanges in Amsterdam and Brussels to form Euronext, which was officially launched in September 2000. The Lisbon and Oporto stock exchange joined Euronext in 2002.

iX was laid to rest after the Stockholm stock exchange, a minnow compared to London and Frankfurt, made an audacious hostile bid for the LSE, which in turn called off the iX plan, leaving Frankfurt fuming. Stockholm's bid for London also failed amid lack of support from the British market users.

Euronext does represent considerable consolidation among Europe's plethora of national exchanges, but is still too small to dominate the euro zone, let alone the region overall. Many commentators believe a key opportunity was missed when Frankfurt and Paris failed to push ahead with their initial co-operation plans.

After the bruising iX debacle, London, Frankfurt, Milan, Madrid and others were left licking their wounds and looking to build up their businesses – and therefore their negotiating clout – before any more rounds of consolidation. For example, the LSE began courting London's futures and options exchange LIFFE in a bid to build an equity to derivatives powerhouse in Europe's top financial centre.

But Euronext joined the bidding battle for LIFFE and in late 2001 won, after paying handsomely. This left the London Stock Exchange's strategy in tatters once again.

Deutsche Börse chief executive Werner Seifert, writing in 2000, concluded that market participants are losing patience with fragmentation in shares and derivative trading in Europe, and the lack of regulatory and supervisory oversight. Stock-market participants, like the funds, are now exploring ways of cutting costs, like E-Crossnet, which matches shares that a group of funds want to buy and sell, so enabling the group to by-pass stock exchanges altogether. 'The message for traditional stock exchanges is all too clear: shape up or shut down,' says Seifert.

Some exchange officials blame the differing regulatory regimes in Europe for making bourse mergers difficult, but watchdogs have shown themselves willing to accommodate new set-ups. For example, regulators in Paris, Amsterdam and Brussels regularly meet to harmonize their work now that Euronext is up and running. Watchdogs in London and Frankfurt also worked on devising a common approach to regulating iX before the merger plan bit the dust.

Differences in trading technology, governance, company law, language and culture are also hurdles in the race to consolidate. In addition, industry consultants blame top exchange officials, who stand in the way of mergers that would relegate exchanges to a junior role in some way. It was relatively easy for Paris to merge with three much smaller exchanges in Amsterdam, Brussels and Lisbon, but bringing together two large stock markets like London and Frankfurt or Frankfurt and Euronext is more difficult. Still, a merger of two of the big three may just be a matter of time.

MODEST PROGRESS TOWARDS A
PAN-EUROPEAN HOLY GRAIL

After the 'big bang' merger ideas blew up, exchanges retreated to launch more modest pan-European trading initiatives that, so far, have lacked the clout a merger among the big three would have. In 2000 the Swiss exchange merged its blue-chip segment with a UK electronic stock exchange, Tradepoint, to form a new pan-European exchange called virt-x or virtual exchange, which launched in June 2001. Virt-x was the first exchange offering the ability to trade in all major European stocks using one rulebook within one single, regulatory environment. Regulated by Britain's Financial Services Authority, virt-x is the main platform for Swiss blue chips like Nestlé, Novartis and Roche. This makes it a 'must' in most global portfolios, but it has been less easy for virt-x to generate turnover in shares that are listed on rival bourses, which is where the bulk of the trading volumes remain.

The Stockholm stock exchange and Morgan Stanley investment bank launched Jiway electronic stock exchange in November 2000 to handle cross-border share orders from online brokers. The volumes it attracted were tiny, because many small investors turned their backs on trading shares, thereby hitting online brokers – who were Jiway's clients. The venture's future was even more in doubt when Morgan Stanley pulled out within less than a year of its launch. The project was effectively put on ice by the end of 2001.

After the failure of iX, Nasdaq decided to buy a controlling stake in ailing pan-European growth market Easdaq to form a foothold in Europe. Nasdaq-Europe launched in June 2001 with ambitious plans to become the European IPO market of choice. Nasdaq-Europe faces an uphill task until it hooks up with one of the established European bourses and obtains critical mass and real local roots. Meanwhile, in 2000 the Deutsche Börse teamed up with Dow Jones Indexes, the stock index compiler, to trade US shares so that the calculation of the Dow Jones industrial average index of top US blue chips can start earlier in the day before handing over to New York.

> **Alliances and partnerships came back in fashion as big-bang merger attempts failed**

Alliances and partnerships came back in fashion as big-bang merger attempts failed. In September 2001 Euronext signed a cross-membership agreement with the Helsinki bourse in Finland, and a similar tie-up with the Luxembourg bourse. Such links offer members access to listings on each other's platforms, while leaving the door open to closer co-operation in future.

Euronext signed a cross-membership agreement with the Warsaw stock exchange in early 2002. Warsaw, eastern Europe's biggest exchange, was already using Euronext's NSC trading technology and looking to deepen ties with Western exchanges to tap wealthier investors.

Exchanges are also becoming more willing to move on each other's turf. The LSE has launched its International Retail Service, which offers cross-border trading in European shares for the UK's small-investor focused brokers. The Deutsche Börse signalled its intent to take on Euronext by launching a segment to trade Dutch and French blue chips.

Whilst few of the cross-border ventures launched in 2001 made much initial progress, it is not clear whether this is simply because of the pullback in global equity markets that sent investors racing for the exits, or because of a poor business model. No bourse has yet been successful in grabbing the lion's share of trading in a stock that is listed on a rival exchange, since liquidity in a share has so far remained in its home market.

There are fears that the failure of exchanges to trade successfully in each other's shares, coupled with growing competition from alternative trading systems, could unduly scatter or fragment the core pool of liquidity in a share that has hitherto remained within its home market. Regulators are concerned that this fragmentation will make so-called 'price discovery', or the creation of a price in the share by bringing buyers and sellers together, less reliable. Traders are duty bound to offer 'best execution', or the best available price in the market, and if in future there will be many pools of trading in the same share, market watchdogs fear it will be more difficult for traders to guarantee investors the best deal. However, industry experts argue that technology is making rapid strides all the time and can help traders scan prices for the same share across many markets in order to find the best one for the investor.

FLOATING

In 2001 the Deutsche Börse, Euronext and the LSE became public companies listed on their own markets. The Stockholm stock exchange was the world's first bourse to list, followed by the Australian exchange in Sydney. Bourse officials have said that going public forces exchanges to act like commercial, for-profit companies, be less beholden to a narrow group of members, and offer a transparent valuation when clinching deals with other exchanges.

Elsewhere in Europe, change is more slow. Milan has said it wants to avoid mergers for now until it becomes clear which is the winning combination or grouping that emerges in Europe. In Spain, Madrid is focusing on moves to bring all the country's exchanges under one grouping to improve efficiency before floating.

With exchange consolidation initially put on the back burner after the iX disaster, and while bourses went public and polished their corporate strategies, market users turned their attention to the post-trade service providers for possible cost-saving rationalization.

The investment banks, who are the most active users of stock markets in Europe, complain that trading across borders in Europe is vastly more expensive than, for example, dealing in their home market or in the US, which has a stock market of comparable size to Europe. Banks say higher costs for cross-border trades are partly due to Europe's numerous back-office or post-trade clearing and settlement systems that handle the exchange of shares and their ownership for the investors' money. (Clearing takes place between trading and settlement – when buy and sell positions in shares are cancelled out or netted – between the different parties before establishing the final positions for settlement. Settlement completes the transaction as the seller transfers the shares to the buyer and the buyer pays the seller.) A single European clearing and settlement system would slash trading costs, the banks argue. To press their case, they formed a lobby group, the European Securities Forum.

Some post-trade mergers have taken place. The Deutsche Börse's clearing unit merged with Cedel, a Luxembourg bank that handles cross-border securities settlement, to form Clearstream. In early 2002, Deutsche Börse was negotiating to buy the half of Clearstream it did not already own in order to create a huge, one-stop trading to settlement shop which Frankfurt insists is the best business model to offer investors cheaper trading and a wider range of products. French settlement house Sicovam merged with Clearstream's arch-rival, international settler Euroclear, to become the settlement house for Euronext. The Dutch and Belgian settlement houses are also teaming up with Euroclear, as will the Portuguese equivalent.

But post-trade consolidation ground to a halt for much of 2001 because Euronext, which owns clearer Clearnet and Deutsche Börse, which then owned half of Clearstream, both floated. The Deutsche Börse is also reluctant to dismantle the 'vertical silo' or the one-stop trading-to-settlement set-up it owns. Many market users would prefer 'horizontal' integration whereby clearing and settlement services from different countries integrate and stand alone from exchanges. However, clearing and settlement generate a lot of income for the exchanges, who understandably do not want to jeopardize these cash cows – especially now that they are listed, for-profit companies who must make money for their shareholders.

Europe envies the efficiency and cost savings that Americans enjoy by having just one clearing and settlement system – the Depository Trust & Clearing Corp – although it is often forgotten that it took years of arm twisting and Congressional agreement before such a monopoly could be created in the land of free competition.

As the big investment banks and institutional investors look to trade shares on a more global basis, exchanges in Europe have been forced to look at markets beyond the region. Euronext signed up in 2000 for a ten-exchange Global Equity Market (GEM) project that included the New York Stock Exchange and the Tokyo stock exchange. The plan was to create a share-trading order book in global blue chips listed from the ten exchanges with trading that would move between time zones to 'follow the sun'. As the market headed south and small investors began hibernating throughout 2001, there was little obvious progress with the GEM plan. Other exchanges like the Deutsche Börse and the LSE preferred a go-it-alone approach of offering investors the opportunity to trade in shares whose main listing was elsewhere, for example in the US.

REGULATION – WATCHDOGS BARK
TO BRUSSELS TUNE

If death and taxes are two certain things in life, then regulators and rules are two certainties for stock markets.

Stock market regulation in Europe is often quite similar but enforced in different ways (*see* Fig. 9.3), with over 50 bodies across the region involved in regulation. First-line supervision of markets, including control of insider trading and market manipulation, is in the hands of the stock exchange in Belgium and Ireland. In Germany, the states (*Länder*) are in charge of supervising the markets and brokers, while the securities commission (BAWe) controls insider trading and company news disclosure. In Austria, Germany, Luxembourg, the Netherlands and Switzerland, the exchange alone authorizes share issues. France has two organizations, the Commission des Opérations de Bourse and the Conseil des Marches Financiers, although they are being merged.

In the European Union (EU), attempts are underway to harmonize how new market rules are made and enforced in the 15 member states, whose national regulators increasingly look to Brussels to set the tone for future share market rulemaking. In the EU the Investment Services Directive (ISD) sets the conditions for the single licence for investment firms and exchanges to provide services across borders. A financial services action plan, published in 1999, also called for a single market in financial services by 2005.

Acknowledging that the ISD badly needed updating to handle the arrival of the euro, the EU turned to a 'committee of wise men', chaired by Alexandre Lamfalussy, former president of the European Monetary Institute, the forerunner to the European Central Bank. The committee's recommendations were given the green light by the European Council in Stockholm in March 2001. The Lamfalussy report outlined four levels of EU securities market regulation:

- An agreed broad framework of principles, including allowing fast track procedures.

PAN-EUROPEAN INVESTING

Europe's regulatory maze: distribution of competences in securities market regulation and supervision

	Approval of IPO prospectus	Control and surveillance of markets	Control of intermediaries	Control of clearing and settlement systems (CSDs)	Surveillance of takeovers
Bel	SC	SE/SC	SC	CB/SC	SC
Den	Securities Council/SE	Securities Council/SE	FSA	FSA	Securities Council
Ger	SE	Länder/SE/SC	SC/BS	BS	
Gre	SE/SC	SC	SC	CB	
Spa	SC	SC	SC	CB/SC	SC
Fra	SC	CMF/SC	BS/SC	CB/CMF/MoF	CMF/SC
Ita	SC/SE	SC/SE	SC/CB	CB/SC	SC
Ire	Gov	SE/CB	CB	CB/MoF	
Lux	SE	SC	SC	CB	
Ned	SE	SC/SE	SC	CB/SC	
Aus	SE	SC	SC/MoF	MoF	Take-over commission
Por	SC	SC	SC	CB/SC	SC
Fin	FSA	FSA	FSA	FSA/CB	FSA
Swe	FSA/SE	FSA/SE	FSA	FSA	SE/Take-over Council
UK	FSA	FSA	FSA	CB/FSA	Take-over Panel
Swi	SE	SE/SC	SC	CB	Swiss Take-over Board/SC
US	SC/CFTC/SE	SC/CFTC/SE	SC/CFTC	CB	States/SEC

Notes: SC = securities commision; SE = stock exchange; FSA = integrated financial sector supervisor; CB = central bank; BS = banking supervisor; MoF = Ministry of finance. In case two boodies are mentioned for a certain function, they are given in order of importance. In Germany, the states (Länder) are in charge of supervising the stock exchanges and intermediaries. The French Conseil des Marchés Financiers (CMF) is a self-regulatory body. In the US, the derivatives markets are supervised by the CFTC (Commodities and Futures Trade Commission).

Europe's regulatory maze is a key hurdle to creating a truly seamless and unified financial market in Europe. Many politicians don't want a single European watchdog like the Securities and Exchange Commission in the US, while sceptics say creating such an animal would take years anyway. Ironing out regulatory differences, as well as differences in accounting laws, will take time.

Source: Centre for European Policy Study (CEPS), Brussels

Figure 9.3 CEPS regulatory set-ups

- A new European Securities Committee (ESC) to decide on how the broad principles are put into practice. The committee would be advised by a committee of member-state market regulators (CESR). The European Parliament would also be kept informed.
- A framework of enhanced co-operation and networking between member-state watchdogs.
- Stronger enforcement of EU laws.

From the start, the Lamfalussy proposals were bogged down in a power struggle inside the EU, with the European Parliament wanting to have power of veto over the ESC. Some politicians fear the ESC is simply a first step towards a European equivalent of the Securities and Exchange Commission, the powerful US stocks watchdog.

However, the ESC was finally set up, along with its adviser, the Committee of European Securities Regulators (CESR). But the first two proposed new directives to come out of the process – one on creating a pan-European listing prospectus for companies, the other on handling market abuse – were badly received, with the EU accused of failing to consult market users. Unless these two new directives, the updating of the Investment Services Directive and other new laws are adopted by 2003, it will be difficult to have everything in place at state level by the 2005 deadline for a truly single market.

Stock exchanges in Europe that still have responsibility over approving IPO prospectuses have been against the proposed prospectus directive because they could lose these powers to an independent watchdog. The stock exchanges argue that having key regulatory powers makes them stand out as a 'brand' in an industry where electronic trading rivals are muscling in on traditional bourse turf. But regulation experts argue that with exchanges publicly listed on their own markets, the bourses must avoid conflicts of interest by handing over their regulatory powers to an independent watchdog. According to Karel Lannoo, chief executive and senior research fellow at the Centre for European Policy Studies: 'In some cases like IPO prospectuses, it

❝Bourses must avoid conflicts of interest by handing over their regulatory powers to an independent watchdog❞

does not make much sense to leave it to the stock exchange. The most striking example of the conflict of interest inherent in maintaining both functions under the same roof is Deutsche Börse, which supervised its own listing.'

It is not only within the EU institutions that there is tension over who should regulate what – there are also battles within countries. For example, there is tension between the German Government and the Länder states over regulatory roles. So whilst Europe tries to devise a regulatory system for the region as a whole, it is still trying to retain an important role for national regulators, in order to keep domestic politicians and others happy. It is a tricky balancing act that may end up pleasing nobody. Markets are certainly changing at a faster rate than the rules governing them, but watchdogs don't want to bark too soon in case they devise new rules for situations that fail to materialize – like the iX exchange merger plan that collapsed.

LOGGING ON – THE ONLINE SHARE REVOLUTION PAUSES

Europe's online brokers enjoyed a golden if brief era between 1998 and early 2000 when small investors logged on to buy the latest fashionable internet stock debut, or a Nasdaq darling. Trading via the web was evidence of a growing equity culture, especially in continental Europe. However, the bulk of trading was within national markets because this is still cheaper than buying shares from another country – a result of the complex and more costly settlement process.

Investment bank JP Morgan Chase reported that the number of online broker accounts in Europe rose from 400,000 at the end of 1997 to 3.7 million at the end of 2000 (*see* Fig. 9.4). The bank's financial services analyst Huw van Steenis said: 'We have seen an explosion of interest in online brokerage driven by the blossoming of an equity culture across Europe, and given a kicker by the bull market from 1998 to 2000 in technology, media and telecom shares.'

Little wonder that some bourses moved quickly to extend their trading hours to entice people to go online after work to trade stocks.

Germany's Deutsche Börse, the Milan exchange, and Stockholm all introduced evening trade as they sought to become more retail-friendly, though volumes remained thin, leaving disgruntled brokers killing time towards the end of the longer trading day. By late 2001, Stockholm had abandoned its evening trade because of scant dealings. Helsinki was also due to scale back its extended trading hours by mid-2002.

Growth in European Online Accounts

	1999 Q4	2000 Q1	2000 Q2	2000 Q3	2000 Q4	2001 Q1	2001 Q2
France	140	215	310	355	415	465	478
Germany	780	1,200	1,550	1,710	1,880	2,000	2,090
Italy	40	100	150	185	230	280	328
United Kingdom	70	150	215	250	280	305	320

The rapid rise in online accounts tracked the run-up in stock markets, especially the technology shares. By the second half of 2001 the number of new accounts opened had dwindled amid the global stocks pullback, triggering consolidation and restructuring among Europe's online brokers.

Source: J P Morgan

Figure 9.4 Online trading accounts

Online brokers have opened up a whole new world for European investors, giving them access to near-instant company information, stock prices and charts that were once just the preserve of banks and big institutional investors. To find out the latest research on a company, investors can also click on sites such as www.multex.com, while others such as www.europeaninvestor.com has links to many European and US markets, as well as links to companies. The www.onvista.co.uk site has a database covering more than 30,000 companies worldwide. For investors unsure of some market terms, there is help from www.investorwords.com. Financial information from Reuters is available on www.reuters.co.uk as well as on gateways like www.yahoo.com. The *Financial Times* operates the www.ft.com site.

Companies themselves have become much better at maintaining their own sites, where they post their press releases, results and other news. Stock exchanges have also improved the breadth of information on their websites, with the LSE (www.londonstockexchange.com) offering real-time quotes on international shares through its International Retail Service. In addition, BlueSky Research (www.blueskyinc.com) gives ratings for the different online brokers to help investors chose which one they want to use.

Online accounts are still only represent 1 percent of the total population in Europe – well behind the US where the equivalent figure is six times higher. But when the Nasdaq's record-breaking run-up into the record books began turning sour in March 2000, small investors were left nursing losses and their appetite for trading online dwindled. Continued losses at online brokers during 2001 exposed too many websites chasing too few punters. In the 12 months to mid-2001, trades per account at online brokers fell 55 percent in Germany, 63 percent in Italy, 64 percent in France and 44 percent in the UK.

Brokers suffered a double blow because commissions also shrink when volumes tumble. Furthermore, with many of the online brokers themselves publicly listed, their own share prices also tumbled as the market – and their trading volumes and sales – retreated. Some of the big German online brokers, like Consors and comdirect, were among those hardest hit. The brokers were so closely tied to the tech-sector bubble that they, too, became tarnished on the way down. Not surprisingly, in early 2002 two German online brokers, DAB and comdirect, decided to close their units in Italy. Many of the online brokers were giving up on their pan-European dreams that proved costly during the bear market.

Online broking has not taken off to the same extent in the UK as it has in the rest of the Europe. The UK online sector growth was largely driven by existing investors switching from telephone-based trading to the web, while in the rest of Europe those who were opening online accounts were largely new to the stock market. Half of all new German shareholders chose to open an online trading account.

Although the UK accounts for one-third of all European shareholders it has less than 10 percent of European online accounts. One reason for this is that the UK's antiquated market structure is hindering the development of a bigger pool of online investors. Unlike the rest of Europe, the UK has stamp duty on share trades, and exchanging money for shares still means taking possession of paper certificates rather than an electronic transaction elsewhere. Investors in the UK have been turning to spread betting on the stock market as an alternative to online trading in order to avoid the stamp duty. This also allows them to sell short a stock or index – an attractive facility when markets are falling and very volatile.

Exchanges are also introducing investors to new products like exchange traded funds (ETFs) and single stock futures. EFTs are traded like shares but usually track an industry sector like technology or pharmaceuticals, or stock indices like the German DAX or the Euro Stoxx 50. The market began in the US. ETFs make it easier and cheaper for an investor to get exposure to a sector or region without having to buy a wide range of different shares. By early 2002, there was $106 billion invested globally in ETFs, the bulk in the US, with only about $5 billion in Europe where the market is barely two years old.

London derivatives exchange LIFFE and others have also been trying to persuade investors to buy single stock futures, which also gives a cheap way of getting exposure to the underlying share price without having to pay the UK stamp duty that is levied on share trading. But the take-up of single stock futures in Europe has been slow because, unlike ETFs, there is no US single stock futures market to serve as a model to give investors confidence to use them. However, the US is expected to allow trading in these products sometime in 2002.

Box 9.1 Equity investment in Europe

Exchanges

Federation of European Securities Exchanges (www.fese.be).

FIBV – World Federation of Stock Exchanges (www.fibv.com).

Both websites give statistics, background information, links to all stock exchanges.

Watchdogs

Committee of European Securities Regulators (CESR) (www.europefesco.org) for the latest up-to-date information of pan-European stock market regulatory moves.

European Shadow Financial Regulatory Committee (www.aei.org), academics which comment on regulatory developments.

FIN-NET (http://europea.eu.int/comm/internal_market/en/finances/consumer/adr.htm) is an out-of-court complaints network for financial services, launched by the European Commission.

Lobby groups

Euroshareholders (www.wfic.org/esh) is an umbrella organization for national shareholders lobby groups in Europe.

European Securities Forum (www.eurosf.com) is the lobby group of the big investment banks in Europe.

Apcims (www.apcims.co.uk), UK smaller broker association, merging with European Association of Securities Dealers to create a new pan-European lobby group that represents smaller brokers and dealers acting on behalf of retail investors.

European Financial Services Round Table (www.efsrt.org), a grouping of banks and other financial services providers.

Corporate governance

European Corporate Governance Institute (www.ecgi.org).

Deminor (www.deminor.com).

Stock index compilers

FTSE International compiles UK FTSE and Eurotop indices (www.ftse.com).

STOXX Ltd compiles pan-European Stoxx and Euro Stoxx indices (www.stoxx.com).

MSCI compiles MSCI global stock indices (www.msci.com).

Standard & Poor's compiles US S&P500 benchmark (www.standardand poors.com).

10

CONCLUSION – A STEEP LEARNING CURVE

We cannot take everything which is US as the unquestionable benchmark. I do not think that with what happened to Enron we can simply continue with that train of thought.
Baron Alexandre Lamfalussy

OVER THE PREVIOUS CHAPTERS, we have seen how despite talk of a pan-European equity market, there remains fundamental structural differences between Europe's bourses and between companies from different jurisdictions. Corporate governance is still a dog's dinner.

In markets like the UK and the Netherlands, huge institutional shareholders own the majority of shares, and wield heavy influence in matters such as corporate governance or even company strategy. In others, like Switzerland and Italy, families dominate even the biggest blue chips, with the result that decision-making is often biased towards preserving control or serving a family agenda rather than enriching shareholders. In other jurisidictions, particularly Scandinavia, the state still controls substantial stakes in important listed companies, with the result that mergers and acquisitions take on a heavy political and nationalistic significance. Rules and regulations relating to listing, trading, disclosure and takeovers vary surprisingly widely from one area to the next. In the UK, ownership of a company above 30 percent triggers the obligation to make an offer to all shareholders. In Finland, the legal threshold is over 60 percent.

There are also differing views on how the back office should be run. Exchanges like London think the user should be free to choose, and that clearing and settlement should be horizontally integrated and independent from the exchange. Others, like Deutsche Börse, think big clearing houses owned by stock exchanges themselves are the best way to lower dealing charges.

The European Union has the ambitious aim of turning Europe into the world's most competitive economy by 2010. An industry forum, the European Financial Service Round Table, has said that closer integration of the European financial market would raise economic growth in the region by at least 0.5 percent a year or €43 billion annually.

Attempts to harmonize often divergent rules and customs have met with decidedly mixed success. The scale of ambitions relating to the combination of stock markets has been trimmed. The unsuccessful bid by OM of Sweden for the London Stock Exchange (LSE), the LSE's failed combination with Frankfurt, and the refusal of the Finns to sign up to the Norex project have underlined how national pride, bruised egos and entrenched interests can combine to scupper the most grandiose projects. The two combinations so far have shown the limitations of combining market operations in the face of contradictory national rulebooks.

In one instance, Euronext mounted a price stabilization exercise. While perfectly legal on the Paris Bourse, where Euronext is listed, the operation would have been illegal in Amsterdam – which is part of Euronext. It was to avoid such contradictions that Norex chose to establish itself as an alliance of markets rather than a merger.

Similar factors have prevented the adoption of harmonized rules across the EU. Nowhere was this more evident than with the collapse of the Takeover Directive, which was 12 years in the making. The arguments over a proposed pan-European Prospectus Directive have only really just begun.

But both pieces of legislation show that while governments are fond of talking about creating a pan-European market, they find it less easy to agree on the vital details of how it should operate and whose version of company law should prevail. Trading operations and back-office functions remain highly fragmented. The inability of governments, stock exchanges, administrators and regulators to create anything resembling a pan-European equity market has been, so far at least, an enormous missed opportunity to capitalize on the introduction of the single European currency. Exchanges in euroland quote share prices in euros, but the currency has brought few of the cost benefits that might be expected, other than the elimination of currency risk. The extent of this failure becomes evident when compared to the impact the euro has had on the bond markets, which have become much deeper and more liquid since the currency was introduced. It also means that Europe, a market of 380 million people, continues to play a secondary role to the US when it comes to equities. This is more than a matter of national pride. Europe has created some great global companies, like Vodafone, Nokia, Unilever and Royal Dutch/Shell, but a significant proportion of the turnover in their shares happens in the US. It's no surprise that far more European company shares are traded in the US than American shares in Europe (*see* Figs 10.1, 10.2).

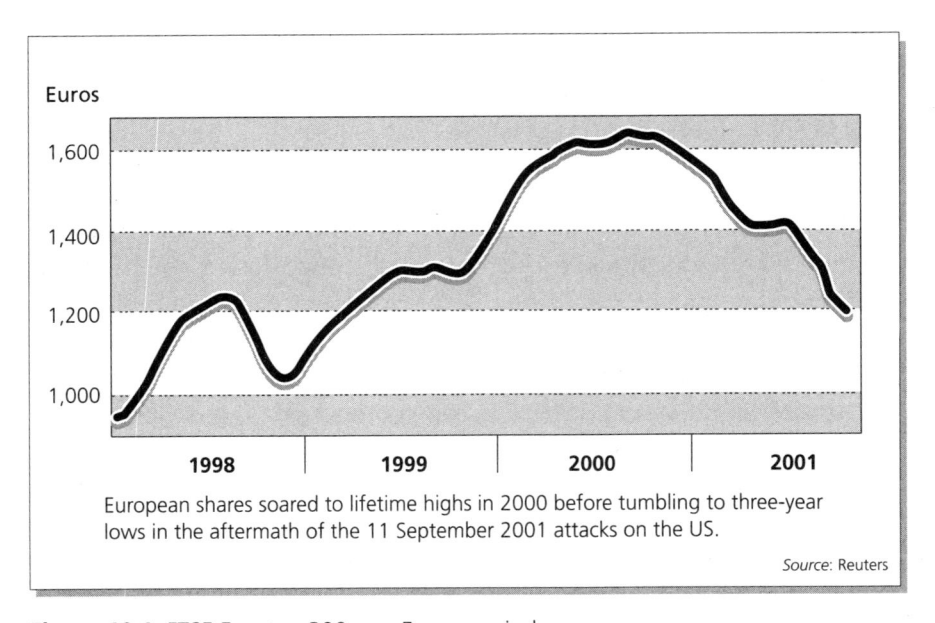

European shares soared to lifetime highs in 2000 before tumbling to three-year lows in the aftermath of the 11 September 2001 attacks on the US.

Source: Reuters

Figure 10.1 FTSE Eurotop 300 pan-European index

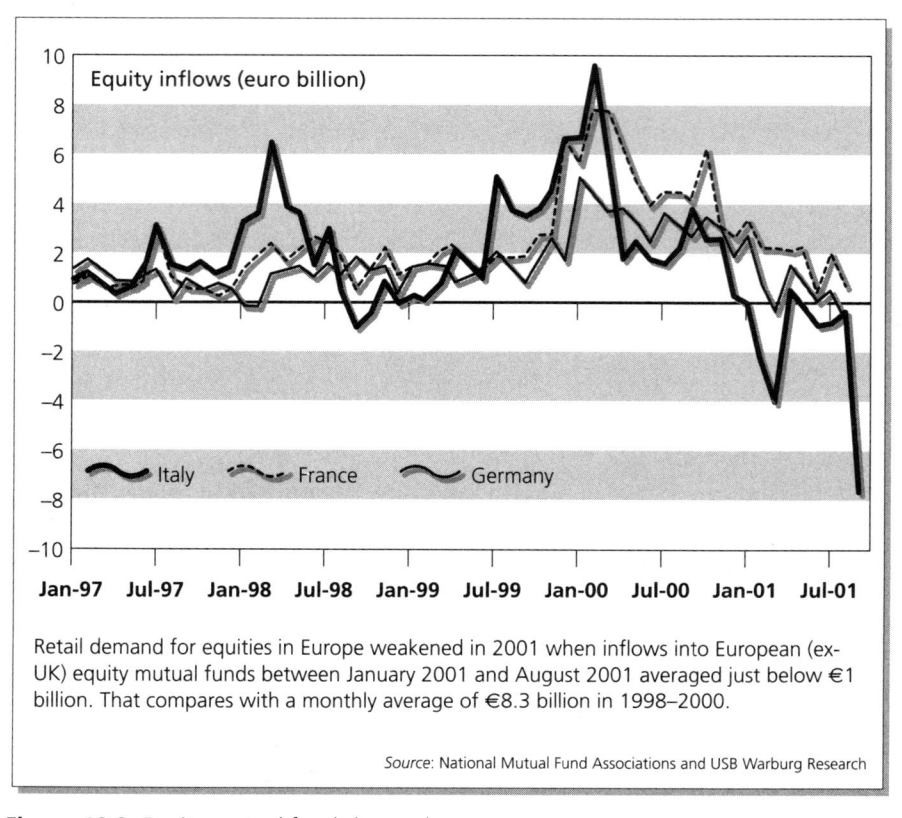

Figure 10.2 Equity mutual funds by market

EVOLUTION NOT REVOLUTION

The difficulties of agreeing pan-European rulebooks, of improving disclosure, of harmonizing trading platforms and settlement arrangements, are unlikely to be resolved quickly. But most players remain firmly committed to the ideals. 'Delivering lower costs and deeper liquidity across European markets is an essential component of the economic restructuring of Europe. On that basis we can take on America in rather more effective competition,' said Don Cruickshank, chairman of the London Stock Exchange. In the meantime, investors are likely to see more gradual processes of convergence – and in theory at least, the biggest, most liquid, best-regulated bourses with the most transparent companies, should start to take market share from the less liquid, more opaque markets.

Outright mergers between stock exchanges, with all the technical and managerial problems they entail, are likely to be less favoured than looser alliances or convergence around a common trading system or a common back office. All the Norex members, for instance, trade using OM's SAXESS system, although their clearing and settlement is still run through national securities depositories. Frankfurt's Xetra system has been successfully exported to the Wiener Börse in Vienna and the Dublin Stock Exchange. The Paris Bourse NSC system was adopted by the Euronext exchanges. 'A number of country-specific issues will delay further mergers between exchanges, but I think within maybe more than ten years, we will have a number of small, local exchanges and one or two major exchanges,' said Jelle Mensonides, investment director at Dutch ABP, one of the world's biggest pension funds.

BANKS SPEAK WITH FORKED TONGUES

One major problem on the route to that goal is the divergent priorities of the banks and other financial institutions, which all agree on the need for cheaper dealing but have different blueprints for how it might be achieved. Not only are such institutions the end users of stock markets, they are in many case also their owners. This was certainly true in the days of member-owned institutions, and it's arguably even more true in the era of for-profit exchanges. Some of the big bulge bracket banks made healthy profits by exploiting current market inefficiencies, offering cross-border trading and post-trade services. They would see this income stream reduced if exchanges and clearing houses were more efficient. But other institutions, or sometimes different departments within the same firms, argue that a more efficient stock market in Europe would generate much larger trading volumes, thus what the banks would gain in greater commissions would more than offset reduced revenues in other services. It will be interesting to see what effect the bear market, with the inevitable squeeze on costs, will have on investment bank attitudes to exchange consolidation. Then there are the smaller players, who trade the mid-market and penny stocks the big boys aren't interested in. They point out that national markets will always be needed for those stocks that aren't liquid enough or international enough to trade on the pan-European mega-markets of the future. This was one of the big problems with the iX merger – many of the UK's mid-market players thought the whole project was very much the agenda of the integrated US investment banks, who would have most to gain from consolidation (*see* Fig 10.3).

(total assets in euro billion and as percentage of respective GDP)

	Bond market	Equity market	Bank assets
EU11	114%	87%	231%
EU15	111%	109%	205%
US	182%	187%	62%

Bonds and banks dominate Europe's financial make-up outside the UK.

Source: Centre for European Policy Study

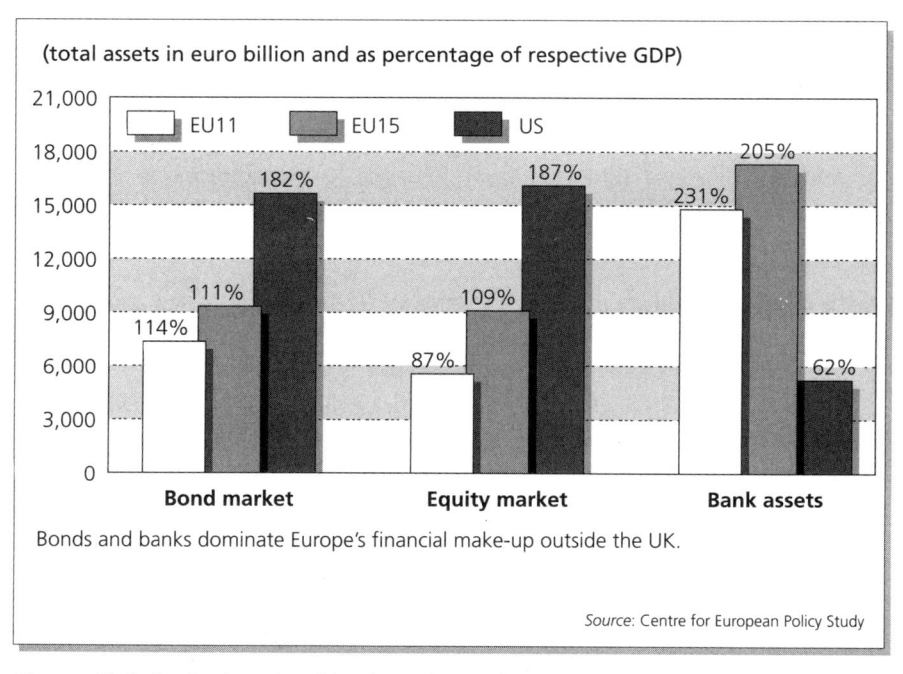

Figure 10.3 Equity, bond and bank markets in the EU and US (1999)

HARMONIZING CORPORATE GOVERNANCE

Even if markets are harmonized, there are still the questions of accounting, company law and corporate governance to be sorted out. The importance of the accounting issue was highlighted by the crash in late 2001 of US energy trading giant Enron. It was revealed that off-balance sheet shenanigans had created the biggest company failure in US history. The European Commission partly blamed US accounting standards, known as Generally Accepted Accounting Principles (GAAP), for allowing questionable balance sheet moves at

Enron. The EU believed such dubious practices could not have happened under its own International Accounting Standards (IAS), which Europe hopes will become the global norm. The growing awareness of how these differ from one jurisdiction to the next has also tempered expectations of how far and how fast market integration can be expected to run.

'Europe cannot expect to replicate all the favourable conditions that have nurtured dynamic equity markets in the United States,' said Alasdair Murray in *The Future of European Stock Markets*, published by the Centre for European Reform. 'Equities are a legal construct, intimately bound up with the legal and political culture of a country. This means that some inconsistencies between national markets will inevitably persist. But this need not and should not undermine the basic case for a single market in European equities.'

While differing accounting systems and national versions of company law will take years to converge, improvements in corporate governance are likely to be quicker as they do not require delicate negotiations between governments and regulators. Investors can force change by voting with their wallets, and there are many signs of this happening.

At one end of the scale, the emergence of big pension funds and institutional investors in countries where historically they have not been present is starting to force change. Leading American proponents of transparency and good governance like CalPERS, the state of California employee pension fund that publishes corporate governance rankings on its website, are turning their fire on Europe's most opaque companies.

Hermes is another fund manager that's decided to do something about poor corporate behaviour in Europe. There is plenty of academic evidence to show that companies that are transparent and treat all their shareholders equally and fairly generate better returns over the long term compared with those run in a more devil-may-care fashion.

Individual crusaders like Switzerland's Martin Ebner are waging wars of attrition against secrecy, management complacency and two-tier share structures that promote the interests of a select few over those of the many. And at the other end of the scale, associations championing the rights of small investors have sprung up across Europe. Some of the better organized ones, such as those in Germany and Sweden, have been surprisingly successful in forcing change.

Scales are also falling from investors' eyes when it comes to some of the more outlandish claims made about listed companies and their ability to generate wealth. Newspapers have gleefully reported stories of over-mighty Swiss banks firing analysts who dared to criticize companies that were corporate clients. Orange, part of France Telecom, scored a very public own-goal when it insisted all analysts rating the company before flotation submit their research to the company for before publishing it. Failure to comply would lead to key financial data being withheld. Only a handful of analysts dared, or could afford, to resist. In Germany, shareholder groups are hounding investment banks through the courts over some of the claims made in Neuer Markt listing prospectuses. Governments are also feeling the heat. Recognizing the inadequacy of regulation in its own suddenly burgeoning equity market, the German government has introduced several key pieces of legislation, revamping the takeover code and pushing for much better corporate governance at companies that traditionally answered to creditors, not shareholders. Ministers constantly stress the importance of improving the competitiveness of Finanzplatz Deutschland.

SHAREHOLDERS MAN THE BARRICADES

Over the longer term, however, the most important factors in creating a pan-European equity market won't be the things done by governments or agreed between stock markets. It is the greater acceptance of and understanding of equity markets among members of the public that will shape the kind of US equity culture that bourse chiefs yearn for. The US had a massive head start over Europe in equities, having long encouraged pension and mutual funds to flourish at a time when continental Europeans preferred to put their money in bonds or bank accounts, while the state often picked up much of the pension bill (*see* Fig. 10.4). According to the European Union, if all EU member states beefed up their private pension provision to the fully funded levels in the Netherlands, the UK, Switzerland and Ireland, some €5 trillion would have to flow into the financial markets during the coming decade, with equities in Europe and elsewhere a major beneficiary.

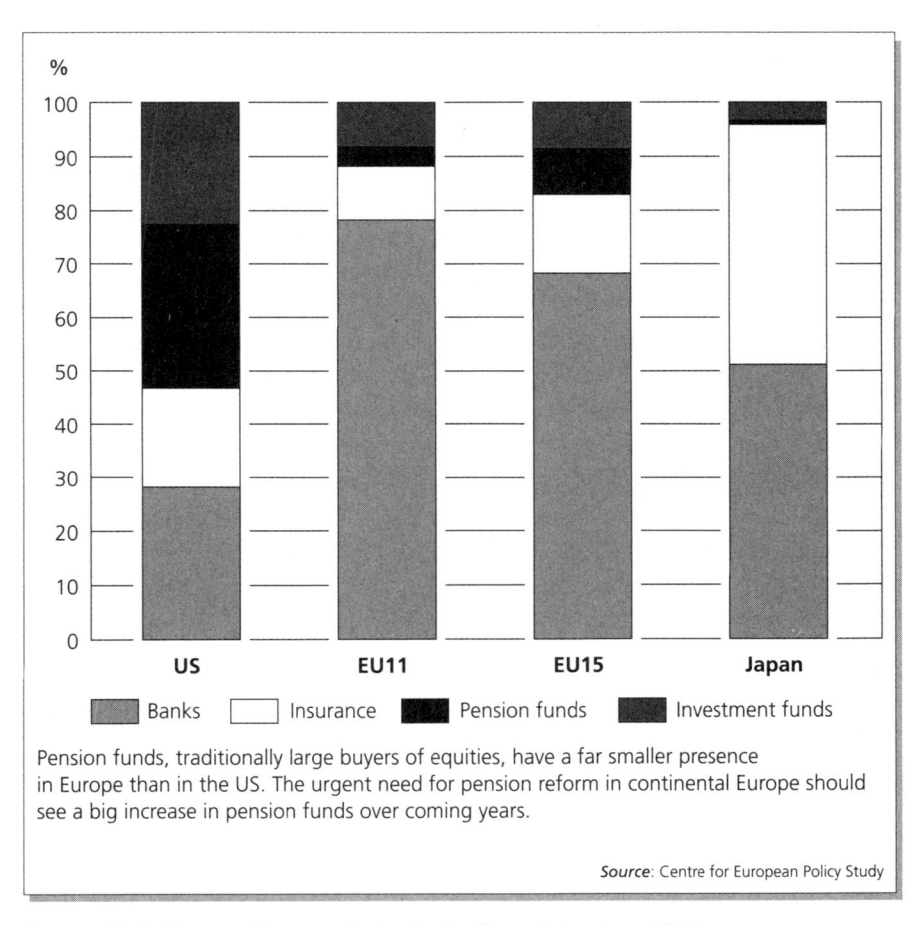

Pension funds, traditionally large buyers of equities, have a far smaller presence in Europe than in the US. The urgent need for pension reform in continental Europe should see a big increase in pension funds over coming years.

Source: Centre for European Policy Study

Figure 10.4 Shares of intermediaries in the financial system 1999

As Reto Francioni, Swiss Exchange chairman, pointed out in the Foreword to this book, the pullback in stock markets in reaction to the ending of the technology bubble and the ructions arising from the destruction of the World Trade Center don't alter one iota Europe's demographics or its rickety pension provision. Europe's people are having fewer children and living longer – and half a century of relative prosperity has raised their expectations of what retirement should be about. The shrinking working population cannot support pay-as-you-go schemes indefinitely. Self-financing personal and occupational pension schemes, which are at least partly reliant on equities, remain the preferred way out of this looming crisis. Furthermore, the older generations that have run Europe's family-controlled companies since the post-war era are gradually bowing out. Their offspring are less wedded to cautious expansion and conservative levels of bank finance, and more likely to turn to the equity markets for finance. They are often educated overseas, speak English, the language of international business, and have fewer hang-ups about being transparent with investors.

But it would be a mistake to think that Europe will one day be just like the US. Many of the corporate traditions that so frustrate US fund managers are deeply ingrained in the social fabric of European countries. Swiss families such as the Schmidheinys or the Hoffmans will not countenance relaxing their hold on the companies they have controlled for decades.

It would require a seismic shift in attitudes for the French to abandon the 35-hour week. And the German system of co-determination, whereby unions and other stakeholders have a say in appointing the managers of a listed company, is sacrosanct even to the country's shareholder action groups. 'I am quite glad Europe does not just copy what's happening elsewhere but steals the best elements,' said Paul Arlman, secretary general of the Federation of European Securities Exchanges. Such opinions are reinforced by the emergence of concrete evidence that shareholder value is not the elixir of life.

Some academic studies have demonstrated that companies that are endlessly restructuring, constantly relocating factories to the cheapest labour markets, ruthlessly playing suppliers off against each other and cynically exploiting customers in the interest of ever-growing earnings per share, do not actually outperform in the longer term.

It is the paragons of stability and gradual progression that generate the most consistent overall returns. There is plenty of evidence also to suggest that many mergers and acquisitions, which generate fortunes for the investment banks, end up destroying value for shareholders. The acquisition binges of Marconi and Swissair brought those companies to their knees. The merger of Daimler Benz and Chrysler turned into a nightmare.

Maybe Europe's recent experience with systems other than pure shareholder capitalism, be they bank-based finance systems or fixed-income investments, will combine with the recent sharp downturn in markets to generate a more balanced view of the strengths and weaknesses of equity investing. The continent's investors will learn that if something looks too good to be true, it often is. Companies should inform investors when things are going badly as well as when they are going well and they should treat all shareholders equally. The Holy Grail of a mature, balanced market full of sophisticated and realistic investors is what will create a true pan-European capital market. There is much yet to be done, as this book has vividly demonstrated. But we have made a start.

BIBLIOGRAPHY

Augar, Philip (2001) *The Death of Gentlemanly Capitalism*, London: Penguin Books.

Becher, Jörg (1998) *Das schnelle Geld: Martin Ebners Weg zur Macht*, ABC Verlag.

Becht, Marco and Mayer, Colin (2001) *The Control of Corporate Europe*, Oxford: Oxford University Press.

De la Vega, Joseph (1688) *Confusion de Confusiones*, New York: John Wiley & Sons.

Edwards, Jeremy and Fischer, Klaus (1994) *Banks, Finance and Investment in Germany*, Cambridge: Cambridge University Press.

Gros, Daniel and Lannoo, Karel (2000) *The Euro Capital Market*, Chichester: John Wiley & Sons.

Kennedy, Allan (2000) *The End of Shareholder Value*, Texere Publishing.

Mackay, Charles and Tobias, Andrew (1841) *Extraordinary Popular Delusions and the Madness of Crowds*, New York: John Wiley & Sons.

Murray, Alasdair (2001) *The Future of European Stock Markets*, London: The Centre for European Reform.

Seifert, W.G., Achleitner, A.-K., Mattern, F., Streit, C.C. and Voth, H.-J. (2000) *European Capital Markets*, London: Macmillan.

GLOSSARY OF TERMS

A and B shares: Different classes of equity shares. The difference between the two is usually in terms of voting rights, and one class is often much more liquid than the other.

After-hours dealing: Dealing taking place after the official close of business on a stock exchange.

AGM: Annual General Meeting. Called some time after the financial year-end, inviting shareholders to vote acceptance of the company's annual report, balance sheet and final dividend. Companies often use the meeting to tell shareholders about corporate business prospects in the early months of the new financial year. An EGM or extraordinary general meeting is often held to discuss and vote on a specific issue such as a merger.

AIM: Alternative Investment Market. A UK market for smaller or high-risk companies that do not qualify for a full listing on the London Stock Exchange.

AMEX: American Stock Exchange.

Amortization: The reduction of principal or debt at regular intervals. This can be achieved via a purchase or sinking fund. The term is also used by companies to describe the depreciation of fixed assets; the opposite of accretion.

Annual report: A status report on the current condition of a company. Issued once a year for shareholders to examine before the AGM.

Apcims: Abbreviation for Association of Private Client Investment Managers and Stockbrokers, a UK body representing the interests of smaller brokers and investment managers who represent individual, rather than institutional, clients. In January 2002 it announced it was planning to merge with the European Association of Securities Dealers to create a new pan-European lobby group.

Ask: A market maker's price to sell a security, currency or any financial instrument. Also know as offer, a two-way price comprises the bid and ask. The difference between the two quotations is the spread.

Back office: The department in a financial institution that processes deals and handles delivery, settlement and regulatory procedures.

BaWe: Bundesaufsichtsamt für Wertpapierhandel. The German federal market regulator.

Bear: A market player who believes stock prices will fall and would, therefore sell a stock with a view to repurchasing it at a lower price. The opposite of a Bull.

Bear market: A market in which prices have been falling for a prolonged period, often defined as falling more than 20 percent from the market's high.

Big bang: A term for the liberalization of the stock market that occurred in the UK in the late 1980s. It involved the ending of demarcation between merchant banks, brokers and jobbers, and the abolition of fixed commissions.

Big Board: Colloquial name for the New York Stock Exchange.

Blue-chip stock: A generic term for the stocks of major companies with sound earnings and dividend records and above-average share performance.

Bolsa: Spanish term for stock exchange.

Bottom fishing: Buying of a company's shares by an investor who believes they are not likely to fall much further.

Bourse: French term for stock exchange.

Broker: Brokers act as agents for buyers and sellers of stocks, for which they charge a commission or brokerage. There are two main categories of brokers: inter-dealer brokers who only work with specialist market makers, and client or agency brokers who deal on behalf of institutional or retail clients.

Bull market: Market in which prices have been rising for a prolonged period. Opposite of bear market.

CAC 40: The CAC 40 is the principal French stock index covering 40 French equities.

Central counterparty (CCP): This guarantees a trade is performed and that credit risk is limited. It ensures there is a buyer for every seller and a seller for every buyer, and that trades are conducted anonymously to avoid the investor's hand being shown.

CESR: Committee of European Securities Regulators. A European Union committee made up of watchdog representatives from EU member states to advise the European Securities Committee in formulating and carrying out changes to securities regulations.

Clearing-house: A clearing-house is the administrative centre of the market through which all transactions are cleared after being traded on the stock exchange or alternative trading system. In addition to administering trades, the clearing-house guarantees the performance of contracts. It becomes the counterparty to both the buyer and seller of a contract when a trade has been matched, greatly reducing counterparty risk.

Clearstream: The Luxembourg based international stock and bond settlement house. Half owned by the Deutsche Börse, the other held by Cedel, a group of banks and brokers. In January 2002, the Deutsche Börse was buying the half of Clearstream it did not already own.

CMF: Conseil des Marches Financiers, the French financial market supervisor.

COB: Commission des Operations de Bourse (COB). French regulator which has broad powers to probe, fine and verify information published by listed companies.

Common stock: Common stock or ordinary shares represent ownership in a limited liability company. These are companies in which the owners' liabilities are limited to the shareholders' funds and the shareholders usually appoint directors to manage the company on their behalf. Holders of common stock are entitled to dividends when they are declared. They have the last claim on the assets and income of a company.

CONSOB: Commissione Nazionale per le Societa e la Borsa. Italy's official body for regulating and supervising companies and the Milan stock exchange.

Corporate governance: A catch-all term for issues surrounding the way companies are structured and run. It embraces subjects as diverse as treatment of employees, treatment of shareholders, internal controls and financial planning.

Correction: A correction in technical analysis refers to a price movement in the opposite direction of the trend. Stock markets that move sharply in one direction can often correct part of that move.

Crest: The UK settlement organization that is owned by market users like banks and brokers.

Custody: Traditionally, this term means the storing and safekeeping of stocks together with maintaining accurate record of their ownership. As a result of an increase in cross-border trading, there is a growing need for custody services in several countries. Rather than have several custody services in several countries, investors may prefer to use an international custody service.

DAX 30: This is the most widely followed German stock index which consists of 30 blue-chip equities. Based on market capitalization.

Day traders: Traders who buy and sell assets on their own account but always close out or liquidate their positions at the end of the day.

Dual listing: A company which is listed on more than one stock exchange.

Easdaq: The pan-European stock market modelled on the US Nasdaq. It failed to make much headway and was later taken over by Nasdaq to create Nasdaq Europe.

EBITDA: Earnings Before Interest, Taxes, Depreciation and Amortization.

ECB: European Central Bank, which sets interest rates in the euro zone.

ECN: Electronic Communications Network. Many ECNs are used for creating electronic stock markets.

EPS: Earnings per share. Net profit divided by the number of ordinary shares outstanding.

Eurex: The European derivatives exchange owned by the Deutsche Börse in Frankfurt and the Swiss Exchange (SWX) in Zurich. Trades futures and options.

Euroclear: The international stocks and bonds settlement house based in Brussels. Incorporates Sicovam, the French settlement house and is also merging with CIK and Necigef, the Belgian and Dutch settlement houses.

Euronext: The cross-border exchange created by the merger in September 2000 of stock exchanges in Brussels, Amsterdam and Paris. The Lisbon and Oporto exchange joined in 2002.

Eurotop: A series of pan-European stock indices compiled by FTSE International. The most widely known are the Eurotop 300 of the leading 300 companies in Europe.

Fixed income: The fixed income market comprises cash markets and credit markets like corporate and government bonds that pay a determined rate of return or interest.

Flotation: The process whereby a company raises new capital. The term is most commonly used to describe when a private company is making its first public issue. This is also known as 'going public' or issuing an IPO or initial public offering.

Free float: This term refers to the proportion of a company's shares deemed to be available to the market at any one time. Blocks of shares that are unlikely to be sold, such as those held by founding families, parent companies or governments, are not part of the free float. Most stock indices now base the weightings of constituents on free float.

FSA: Financial Services Authority. The UK securities market regulator.

FTSE 100: The FTSE 100 is the benchmark index for equity prices on the London Stock Exchange. Known as Footsie, it includes 100 of the largest UK stocks, by market capitalization.

IBEX: The index of top 35 Spanish blue-chip shares traded on the Madrid stock exchange.

Insider trading: Exploitation of inside or privileged information for profit in market transactions. This is illegal in many countries.

Institutional investors: Financial institutions like pension funds and investment trusts, which invest large amounts of capital in financial markets on behalf of their clients.

Investment bank: A US term used to describe banks that specialize in financial market activities rather than lending and money transactions.

IOSCO International: Organization of Securities Commissions. An organization comprising the securities administrations or market watchdogs from more than 50 countries.

IPO: Initial public offering, whereby a company's shares are offered to the public for the first time.

LCH: The London Clearing House. Provides risk management and central counterparty services to numerous exchanges, for example the London Stock Exchange, virt-x, London Metal Exchange. Owned by a wide range of market users. Euronext has an indirect stake through its ownership of London derivatives exchange LIFFE.

LIFFE: The London International Financial Futures and Options Exchange. Trades futures, options and single stock futures. Acquired by Euronext at the end of 2001.

Liquidity: The volume of shares in the market necessary for orderly trade to take place. The more 'liquid' a stock is, the easier it is to buy and sell. It can be difficult to deal in less liquid stocks.

Long: Investors are described as 'long' when they have bought assets in the hope that prices will rise and that they can sell them when prices have peaked. The opposite of short.

Market capitalization: The value arrived at when a company's share price is multiplied by the number of shares issued. Most indices now base weighting in an index on free-float market capitalization or multiplying the share price with the number of shares that are available for all investors to buy.

Market maker: A specialist broker who is willing to act as counterparty to a trade.

Mibtel: The Mibtel index is the benchmark all-share index for the Italian stock market. The MIB 30 is the Milan blue chip index.

Mittelstand: The term applied to the hundreds of thousands of small or medium-sized, often family-run and usually privately owned businesses in Germany. They are a central pillar of the German economy.

MSCI Indices: The Morgan Stanley Capital International stock indices. A group of regional, national and industry performance benchmarks designed to help compare world equity markets. More international equity fund money is benchmarked against MSCI indices than any other rival index.

Nasdaq: The National Association of Securities Dealers' Automated Quotations System. An electronic stock market in New York listing many leading high-tech companies. The exchange's index, the Nasdaq Composite, has became an alternative benchmark to the Dow Jones Industrial Average on the New York Stock Exchange.

Netting: A system whereby outstanding share contracts can be settled at a net figure, i.e. receivables are offset against payables to reduce credit exposure to a counterparty and minimize the number of trades that need settling.

Neuer Markt: The German market for growth stocks, set up in 1997 to rival Easdaq. The Neuer Markt is part of the Deutsche Börse in Frankfurt.

Norex: An alliance of Nordic stock exchanges, founded by Stockholm and Copenhagen, using Stockholm's SAXESS electronic trading system. Oslo also intends joining, but a key player in the region, Helsinki, has declined to take part so far.

Official list: The main market of the London Stock Exchange.

OMX: The Swedish blue chip index, which tracks 30 of the largest stocks in the country traded on the Stockholm Stock Exchange.

P/E ratio: The price earnings ratio. Calculated by dividing the share price by a company's earnings per share. This ratio is one of the most important ratios to determine investment value and is widely used by the media as an indicator of whether a stock is expensive or cheap relative to its peers.

Penny stocks: A type of ordinary share, which is of negligible value but which may prove to be a good speculative investment. In the US, a share priced at less than one dollar, in the UK at less than one pound, and in the euro zone at less than one euro.

Poison pill: A defence mechanism put in place by a company to outwit a predator in a potential hostile takeover. Examples are the issue of high yielding bonds, conditional rights to shareholders to buy shares at a large discount if the takeover succeeds or making massive long-term commitments to the company's pension funds.

Preference shares: Preference or preferred shares entitle a holder to a prior claim on any dividend paid by the company on ordinary shares, or to its assets in the event of a liquidation. Typically these shares do no carry voting or pre-emptive rights.

Privatization: Has two possible meanings. The first is when a state-owned company is sold to investors, either via an IPO or a sale. The second is where an investor or a company buys back all the shares of a company quoted on a stock market, thus returning to private ownership.

Prospectus: Document provided by the issuing company giving detailed terms and conditions of a new stock or debt offering.

Quote driven: A market is described as being quote driven when registered market makers are required to display bid and offer prices, and in some cases the maximum bargain size to which these prices relate. The London SEAQ system and Nasdaq are examples of quote driven markets. The opposite is order driven, where buyers and sellers are automatically matched.

Rating agency: An agency which forms an opinion on the quality of a company's fixed income securities and its ability to pay back investors what it has borrowed. The two main agencies are both American: Moody's and Standard & Poor's.

Rights issue: A form of fundraising where existing shareholders are offered the right to buy more shares, often at a discount. The rights themselves can be traded, unlike in an open offer.

RNS: Regulatory News Service. The UK mechanism for disseminating price-sensitive company information. RNS is owned by the London Stock Exchange. From April 2002, several companies, such as Businesswire and PR Newswire and the LSE's RNS service, will have the right to distribute company information as competition is introduced.

S&P500: A major barometer of the US stock market. The S&P500 represents some 80 percent of the market value of all issues traded on the New York Stock Exchange. It comprises 500, mainly NYSE listed firms. It is compiled by Standard & Poor's.

SEC: The Securities and Exchange Commission. The US stock market regulator.

SETS: The London Stock Exchange's order driven trading system, generally used for the larger and more liquid stocks.

Settlement: The conclusion of a stock, bond or other security trade. The buyer receives ownership of a stock in return for money, or the seller delivers securities and receives cash. This can be carried out by a national Central Securities Depository like Crest in the UK or an international depository like Clearstream and Euroclear or a central counterparty in some cases.

Share: A share represents ownership in a company and the right to receive a share in the profits of that company. Also called a stock.

Shareholder value: Describes the ability of a company to deliver value to shareholders in terms of both dividends and growth in the company's share price.

Share split: The process by which a company's share capital is further sub-divided, often to make shares less expensive in absolute terms. The opposite is a share consolidation.

Short: Investors are described as being 'short' when they have sold assets in the hope that they can buy them back when prices have fallen. The opposite of long.

SMI: Swiss Market Index. The SMI consists of securities (bearers shares and participation certificates) from major Swiss companies.

STE: Stichting Toezicht Effectenverkeer, the Dutch securities watchdog.

STOXX: Shorthand for the series of stock market indices covering stock markets in Europe. The most popular is the Euro STOXX 50 which comprises the top 50 companies in the euro zone. The index compiler is owned by the Dow Jones Company, the Euronext Paris, the Deutsche Börse and the Swiss Exchange.

Takeover panel: The body that regulates takeover activity in the UK. Unlike most of its European equivalents, its rulings have little force in law.

techMARK: A family of indices established by the London Stock Exchange in late 1999 to provide a benchmark for high-growth technology stocks.

Underwriting: The process by which an investment bank supports a company's fundraising. The bank will often buy the shares itself if investors do not buy enough of them.

Virt-x: A pan-European stock exchange, created by the merger of UK electronic exchange Tradepoint and the blue-chip segment of the Swiss Stock Exchange to trade pan-European blue chips.

Xetra: The name for the order-driven electronic trading system used by the Deutsche Börse in Frankfurt. The system is also used for trading Irish and Austrian shares.

Yield: The return on a share relative to its price, expressed as a percentage and calculated by dividing the total dividend over a year by the share price.

Incisive, informative, impartial news and stories from the best of Reuters photographers and journalists

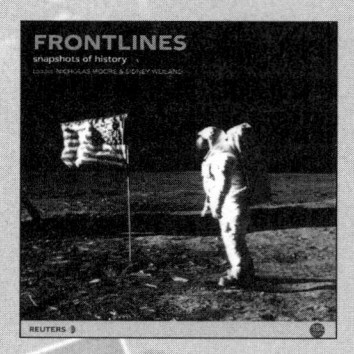

FRONTLINES
Ed. Nicholas Moore

ISBN 1903 68401 3

Think of the major news stories of the post-war era, the places where they unfolded and the personalities involved…

"C19? That's the execution cell. You're lucky, mate, to come out of there alive."
– Sandy Gall, on being held in a Ugandan death cell.

THE ART OF SEEING
Ed. Ulli Michel

ISBN 0 273 65011 4

"Pictures marking most of the world's great events over the past 15 years, mostly of conflict, but also of great beauty, the work of masters of their art."
– The Star, South Africa

The Art of Seeing offers a fascinating selection of news pictures taken by Reuters photographers who have had the vision and ability to see and capture extraordinary incidents. This collection comprises a story with many threads: celebration, adversity, conflict, diplomacy, triumph and disaster – and offers some of the most spectacular, disturbing and significant images you will ever see.

BRANDS IN THE BALANCE
Kevin Drawbaugh

ISBN 0 273 65035 1

"An intelligent, informative and highly readable book about any organisation's most important assets – their brands. This book is a great contribution to the history and future possibilities of branding. It is recommended for anyone with an interest in brands, whether brand lovers, or brand sceptics."
– Rita Clifton, CEO, Interbrand

Find out more about the books featured here at
www.business-minds.com